LITERARY
Mama

LITERARY Mama

Reading for the Maternally Inclined

Edited by
Andrea J. Buchanan and Amy Hudock

SEAL PRESS

Published by Seal Press
An Imprint of Avalon Publishing Group, Incorporated
1400 65th Street, Suite 250
Emeryville, CA 94608

AVALON
publishing group incorporated

ISBN-10: 1-58005-158-8
ISBN-13: 978-1-58005-158-3

Library of Congress Cataloging-in-Publication Data
Literary mama : reading for the maternally inclined / edited by Andrea J. Buchanan and Amy Hudock.
p. cm.
ISBN-13: 978-1-58005-158-3 (pbk.)
ISBN-10: 1-58005-158-8 (pbk.)
1. Mothers--Literary collections. 2. Motherhood--Literary collections. 3. Mother and child--Literary collections.
4. American literature. I. Buchanan, Andrea J. II. Hudock, Amy E.
PS509.M6L58 2006
810.8'092052--dc22
2005023857

Interior design by Elise Winter
Cover design by Gerilyn Attebery
Cover Illustration by Justin Marler

Printed in the United States of America by Worzalla
Distributed by Publishers Group West

9 8 7 6 5 4 3 2 1

Contents

III. *M*others Raising Men, Exploring Mothering

IV. *S*ex, Fertility, and the Body

V. *M*others, Fathers, Parents

VI. Surviving Illness and Loss

VII. Healing the Past to Live in the Present

Introduction

A woman who is a mother and a professional writer sits down to write, rushing to meet a deadline. She takes a moment to reflect on where she left off and then quickly jumps back into the story. As she writes, creating an alternate world, her real world intervenes: The children demand food, the husband wonders where his good pants are, the baby swallows a button, a delivery arrives, the husband wants her attention and insists that she stop her "scribbling," one of the kids destroys the first page of her manuscript. She perseveres, writing through the distractions for as long as she can, and then finally surrenders to the domestic chaos, telling her husband to just hand her the baby already and wondering aloud why she bothers trying to balance a writing career and motherhood.

Another woman who is a mother and a professional writer tries to convince a bookstore to host a reading for her new book on motherhood. The manager is unenthusiastic, predicting that even in the unlikely event the writer draws an audience, book sales will be minimal, because mothers don't buy books. The woman writer suspects the manager believes that mothers don't *write* books. The woman writer eventually convinces the bookstore to schedule a reading. Despite the inconvenient time chosen, the event draws a good crowd and many books are sold. The bookstore manager later apologizes to the woman writer for having given her such a difficult time. "I'm sorry," the manager says. "I didn't realize you were a *writer.*"

The first woman is a fictional character in a story written by Fanny Fern and published in 1853. The second woman is a writer whose book was published in 2003.

Separated by 150 years, these two writers share many of the same dilemmas: how to balance creativity and motherhood, and how to be taken seriously as a writer. The question is, why is the modern mother-writer fighting the same battles her literary mother fought nearly two centuries ago?

Even well into the last century, it was widely accepted that women's minds were at the mercy of their wombs, that women couldn't think and be female at the same time. Women were encouraged to be procreative rather than creative—to choose babies over books. By the 1970s, society had changed, and for the first time, literary women were urged to choose books over babies—to deny their procreativity. It was believed the social constraints of motherhood limited creative potential. Regardless of the century and the prevailing attitude, determined mother-writers chose—and continue to choose—books *and* babies: a maternal *and* a literary life, not one or the other.

But many of the mother-writers of the past have been largely forgotten, their legacy lost for their creative daughters, who must readdress the problem of books and babies in each generation. Then, as now, many editors, publishers, reviewers, and scholars did not view motherhood as a theme, or mother-writers as having literary merit. Their works, if published at all, were rarely kept in print. Nor were they made available in the marketplace, taught in universities, stocked in libraries, or represented in bibliographies. This is as true today as it was in the 1850s.

Whether the mother-writer is Fannie Fern or her modern-day counterpart, motherhood literature is not considered literary. A web search of motherhood literature brings up a host of how-to parenting books. Bookstores shelve literary memoirs about motherhood in the "Parenting" section. Mother-writers often are told by publishers that the market is flooded with mother books; that mothers don't read or buy books; that motherhood is a "trend" that is already "played out."

Is the market really flooded? Or do the works of contemporary mother-writers seem ubiquitous because of general attitudes toward the mother's voice in literature—namely, that "motherhood" and "good writing" are incompatible? As one mother-writer put it, "There are 907 books about Ronald Reagan. You would think we could stand a few more about motherhood." At *Literary Mama*, we've been developing a bibliography of memoir, fiction, poetry, and critical commentary on motherhood that is fairly complete, and it hasn't reached 907 entries. The market can't really be flooded.

In the academic world, the reception to motherhood literature hasn't been much better. When today's students encounter motherhood in the classroom, they tend to be assigned texts that depict motherhood and art as being incompatible (e.g., Elizabeth Stuart Phelps's *The Story of Avis*, Kate Chopin's *The Awakening*, or Charlotte Perkins Gilman's "The Yellow Wall-Paper"). A recent check of the major bibliography used in literary studies reveals a strong preference for books that mine the incompatibility of motherhood and art, not their synchronicity. Motherhood is not viewed as a theme worthy of literature, unlike uniquely male stories (such as traditional war stories). Some mother-professors report that colleagues react with ambivalence about the seriousness and quality of motherhood and literature. Motherhood makes many academics uncomfortable, and thus the academy doesn't always work to keep literature about motherhood in the cultural memory.

Despite all this, mother-writers have always written and always will, and we've found supporters within the publishing community and academia. A recent flurry of publications about motherhood suggests that as the first generation of women writers raised by feminist mothers now become mothers themselves, they are making inroads into the publishing profession. The proliferation of women publishing work on motherhood has even given rise to the term "momoir"—a dismissive label applied to memoirs that focus on the psychological, spiritual, and emotional development of a woman through motherhood. Memoirs by Anne Lamott, Louise Erdrich, Naomi Wolf,

Lisa Belkin, Andrea J. Buchanan, Anne Richardson Roiphe, Phyllis Chesler, Susan Kushner Resnick, Junee Waites and Helen Swinbourne, Faulkner Fox, Spike Gillespie, Brooke Shields, Annie Spiegelman, Ariel Gore, Katherine Arnoldi, Lauren Slater, Ayun Halliday, Martha Brockenbrough, Jan Waldron, Francesca Lia Block, Cherríe Moraga, Ann Leary, Michelle Herman, Isabel Allende, Eleanor Vincent, and many more use humor and pathos to explore motherhood as a journey of heroic proportions. Anthologies—such as *Child of Mine* (2000), *Mothering Against the Odds* (1998), *Wanting a Child* (1998), *A Mother's World* (1998), *Bigger Than the Sky* (1999), *Mothers Who Think* (2000), *Room to Grow* (2000), *Breeder* (2001), *Pregnancy Stories* (2001), *The Bitch in the House* (2003), *Toddler* (2003), *Mamaphonic* (2004), *You Look Too Young to Be a Mom* (2004), *Because I Said So* (2005), and *Rise Up Singing* (2005)—offer personal narratives that challenge and question social constructions of motherhood. In addition, we have seen the publication of the multigenre anthologies *Cradle and All* (1989), *Double Stitch* (1991), *Mother Reader: Essential Writings on Motherhood* (2001), and *Birth* (2002); an anthology of poetry, *Mother Songs* (1995); an anthology of fiction, *Mother Knows* (2004); and an anthology of critical and personal essays about women as both mothers and poets, *The Grand Permission* (2003). As more women who are editors, publishers, and professors become mothers or gain interest in motherhood, we find more literature about motherhood in the bookstores.

Even the glossy parenting magazines, which traditionally feature only personal narratives about motherhood that fit a narrow formula, are expanding their approach. Many editors are encouraging writers to submit "edgy" pieces (although these same writers report their "edginess" tends to get edited out). The magazine *Brain,Child* regularly publishes high-quality literary writing about motherhood. Websites such as HipMama.com, AustinMama. com, Mamaphonic.com, and others create an online outlet for writing about motherhood that is immediate and current. Their popularity reflects the large number of mothers who want to read other mothers' literary writing. And the number of weblogs focusing on motherhood suggests a whole new group of writers and readers. Many mothers choose to blog because web self-publication lets them write and read the work of other mothers. Bloggers also receive the immediate gratification of seeing their work published without going through a long submission process, and have the freedom to explore topics that are often taboo in other venues. The large audience for these blogs suggests that the vein of voyeurism that is often a part of motherhood—observing children, teachers, other mothers—leads women online, often late at night, between feedings or diaper changes, to seek out other mothers' stories. Clearly the market for motherhood literature isn't played out.

However, will the mother-centric books and weblogs be there for our daughters? Will our daughters have access to mother-writers of previous generations? When we at *Literary Mama* first discussed reviewing *Mother Songs*, the only collection of poetry specifically about motherhood, many of our editors hadn't heard of it, even though it had been published in 1995. In some ways, our cultural memory is already fading. We're not nominating twenty-first-century mother-writers for the endangered species list at a time when it seems they are coming into their own, but there may be reason for concern. Fanny Fern and other mother-writers of the 1850s, like mother-writers today, challenged the status quo. They thought they had won the battle. But who knows them now?

Literary Mama was the brainchild of women writers frustrated by what they perceived as a lack of readily available literary writing about motherhood. A group of us began a quest to find more mother-writers like ourselves. We found that most of the available contemporary literature on parenting fell under the categories of nonfiction journalism and how-to books, much of which had not been written by mothers. But we did discover an easily accessible medium being used by mothers speaking in their own voices about their experiences: the Internet. On parenting websites and bulletin boards, on sections of sites like *Salon's* "Mothers Who Think," and later on blogs, women were writing, talking, exploring the honest and sometimes-uncomfortable truth about motherhood. Still, those avenues proved less satisfactory than we had hoped: *Salon's* "Mothers" section was eventually transformed into something less mother-specific called "Life"; parenting bulletin boards were dominated by chat and shoptalk, which is vital toward growing a community but not in crafting writing; the blogs, while often well written, offered individual voices and isolated experience rather than the digested perspective of literature. And while many of our favorite sites published stellar creative nonfiction, few included poetry and fiction by mothers.

Given the dearth of outlets for motherhood literature, we decided to create the place we wanted to find, with the kind of writing we wanted to read: *Literary Mama*, an online literary magazine of writing about motherhood.

With twenty or so editors—mothers who are writers or aspiring writers—volunteering their time and effort, the site has become the only literary magazine on the web to publish exclusively mothers' voices. Since its launch in November 2003, *Literary Mama* has grown from a small hobby site to a nationally recognized online magazine that each month attracts more than 35,000 unique visitors, a half million hits, and hundreds of essay submissions. Literarymama.com was chosen as a Forbes Favorite in Forbes.com's "Best of the Web" picks for 2005; and *Writer's Digest* named us one of its "101 Best Websites for Writers," saying, "Don't let the site's casual name fool you: These writers are serious."

Some *Literary Mama* contributors are well-respected authors; others are women who are discovering themselves as writers for the first time. All of the writers speak to their own unique experience of mothering in a way that is compelling, literary, and unsentimentalized. As we say on the site, *Literary Mama* aims to publish work that is "too long, too complex, too ambiguous, too deep, too raw, too irreverent, too ironic, and too body conscious for other publications. . . . At *Literary Mama*, writers explore ideas and emotions that may be outside the usual scope of commercial writing."

This work is continued and exemplified in *Literary Mama: Readings for the Maternally Inclined*, which features standout pieces published on the site over the last two years.

We knew that mother-writers had craft and style. We knew that the theme of motherhood could inspire writers to explore the depths of the human psyche and the complex web of human relationships. We knew all of this when we started *Literary Mama*. But with this volume, with the work laid out on paper instead of hyperlinked, we are seeing new trends and patterns that we didn't expect. And what we are seeing is blowing us away.

The first section, "Creative Acts," emphasizes an important theme: the birth of a child as the birth of the artist/writer. In these selections, the creative acts of pregnancy, becoming a mother, caring for a young child, writing, and art come together on equal ground. Because mother-writers in the past often subscribed to the traditional opposition between books and babies, "Creative Acts" suggests a new generation of mothers that recognizes the ranking of (pro)creation of the body as less significant than creation of the mind for the gender propaganda that it is. The mother-writers in this section claim that creativity is creativity, whether it comes from the physical body or the mind.

"Pregnancy," the first poem of this section and the book, is a perfect example. Male writers have often used pregnancy and birth as a metaphor for creative acts of the mind. This poem uses pregnancy and birth to reject the artificial binary of the mind and the body, and details the physical symptoms of pregnancy in the shape of a pregnant body, with the content matching the body part. Other poems in this section also explore the pregnant, birthing, and nursing body, transforming these private creative acts into art.

Creative nonfiction pieces in this section, such as Joanne Hartman's "Evolution of a Muse" and Nicole Cooley's "Thirteen Ways of Looking at Being a Mother and a Poet," describe the writers' transformations into motherhood as inspiration for, rather than impediment to, their writing. Hartman uses an innovative form, employing key moments with her child as the impetus for writing and detailing her writing process. Cooley's piece mixes poetry and prose in stanzalike sections.

This coming together of writing and motherhood is not without uncertainty. Barbara Crooker's poem, "The Blue Snake Lies Curled in My Bowl Like Oatmeal," employs an extended metaphor that links the child with a creative product, exploring the conflict the poet feels between her writing and her mothering work.

Mothers of older children, too, discover personal illumination as well as ambiguity about motherhood and art. Lizbeth Finn-Arnold's "Out of the Woods" explores how Walden Pond and Henry David Thoreau help her to see her children as valuable to her creative work. Karen Vernon's "The Gift" and Jennifer Lauck's "Not So Perfect" address the ways in which family members can discourage creativity. Both pieces encourage mothers not to squelch their own or their children's artistic impulses, even if it means being different from those around them.

The second section, "Mothers Raising Women, Defining Mothering," begins with the poem "Casi's Face," by Gabriela Anaya Valdepeña. The poem introduces a theme that appears often in women's writing about their daughters, the girl child as a mirror for the self: "I see me, but taller; me but prettier, / and with your father's chin." The poem "LiLi," by Laura A. Lopez, celebrates a daughter caught in song, using the daughter's moment of creation for poetic inspiration.

Many of the writers in this section investigate how raising their daughters inspires reflection on identity and transformation. Deesha Philyaw Thomas's "The Girl Is Mine" explores how motherhood is defined as the author grapples with issues of adoption and nontraditional family structures. The speaker in Rachel Iverson's "nighttime with dorothea" navigates the boundaries between mother and daughter, sometimes collapsing them, sometimes holding them firm. The dangers and joys of a daughter's growing independence appear in the two fiction pieces in this section: Cassie Premo Steele's "Chocolate" and Peggy Duffy's "The Girl at the Side of the Road." And the poems "Eclipse," by Marguerite Guzman Bouvard, and "Beautiful Daughter," by Mary Moore, detail the separation mothers feel from their adult daughters—even as the mothers admire their children's independence. All of these writers use setting—specifically the outdoors, with its elements of danger—to highlight themes of separation. These pieces illustrate how as children grow, mothers grow, forcing both generations to confront the larger world in new ways.

The third section, "Mothers Raising Men, Exploring Mothering," shows mothers grappling with the ambiguity of their concurrent closeness to and distance from their boys. Ona Gritz's poem, "Boy Child," and Jennifer Eyre White's nonfiction piece, "Analyzing Ben," attempt to reconcile the writers' stereotypical views of boys with what they see in their growing children.

Many of the writers in this section see themselves as outsiders in their boys' worlds. In "When You're Ten," Lisa McMann tries to reconcile the image of boys holding weapons in war-torn countries with the vision of her son taking his first shooting lessons. She, like Amy Burditt in "Albion Street," sees the dangers inherent in learning to be male in a culture that defines manhood in narrow ways.

Two poems, Linda Lee Crosfield's "Packing the Car" and garrie keyman's "Son of a Bitch," explore the separation the poets feel between themselves and their sons. Crosfield begins her poem with a metaphor that links her son's removal of boxes from her home to the removal of evidence from a crime scene. Keyman also experiences separation, but with a bittersweet anger: "they never told me / to stop pushing." The poem's title suggests that she blames both herself and the traditional role of mother for the distance between them.

In contrast, "How to Make a Meat Pie and Other Tales of the Ambitious Mother," by Lisa Rubisch, sets up a parallel experience where the mother and son both have temper tantrums over something they cannot have: The child longs for someone else's toy, and the mother wants both to have a career and to be with her son.

In the "Sex, Fertility, and the Body" section, writers challenge the duality between the virgin and the sex goddess, the angel and the whore. Most people balk when asked to discuss the sexuality of their mothers because mothers are supposed to be sexless and utilitarian. KerryAnn Cochrane's poem, "Matermorphosis," demonstrates how even mothers themselves internalize these social messages. Jennifer D. Munro's "The Dogs of Sayulita" and the Naughty Mommy's "Becoming Mine" reveal settings outside the house, away from where mothering takes place, as allowing liberating moments that enhance sexuality, as if the home itself stymies mothers' libidos.

The fiction piece "Camping," by Barbara Atkinson, and the poem "Sanctuary," by Peggy Hong, both explore longing and desire—again outside the home—for unattainable men.

In the next section, "Mothers, Fathers, Parents," mothers learn to be parents from their own parents. Whether they reject or accept what they have learned, mothers recognize that their past families shape their present families. The section opens with "The Impatient Mother," by Ona Gritz, a poem that collapses the past and the present, the mother and the mothered. The speaker portrays herself as being possessed, demonlike, by her mother's impatience—thus becoming her mother—then shifting to align herself with the child forced to endure the impatience.

Kimberly Greene Angle writes in the nonfiction piece "Forecasts" of her father's love of rain and tornadoes, and how she survives the storms of her parents' alcoholism. "Nebraska," by Holly Day, "Eyes in the Back of Her Head," by Gayle Brandeis, and "Blueberries for Mom," by Meagan Francis, each explore the effects of growing up with mothers who were wounded, lost, missing, or otherwise displaced. Suzanne Kamata's "Gan" explores a cross-cultural relationship when a mother-in-law's health emergency sparks a marital crisis. In "Mama's Orange Robe," Cathleen Daly uses a 1970s housecoat to symbolize her mother's powerful ability to make her father's absence (and their family's difference) bearable. "Word-Girl," by Mary Moore, offers an extended metaphor in which the generative acts of speaking and creating children become one, as the speaker explores how her mother's words shaped the child she once was. And in "Motherkind," S. A. Miller attempts to understand her abusive mother when she encounters a warm, loving mother figure so different from her own.

The final selections in this section address illness, death, and secrets. "Gray," by Sybil Lockhart, and "Mitzraim," by Liz Abrams-Morley, show women of the so-called "sandwich generation" struggling to be caretakers to both children and aging parents. The narrator of "Acts of Contrition," by Lisa Meaux, finds secrets hard to bear; she refuses to continue the family tradition of not speaking of mental illness, choosing instead to support her son's recovery. "Dad, in Red," by Sonya Huber, traces generational patterns when the artist narrator attempts to fulfill her father's last wishes: to have his ashes mixed into her paint. Genetics matter, these writers tell us, as does early socialization. How much they matter is perhaps never more apparent than when we are raising our own families.

The sixth section, "Surviving Illness and Loss," highlights what is at stake in the journey of bearing and raising children. At the most basic level, the job of mothering is to keep another person alive. It's the struggle between life and death. Women often write about miscarriage and loss, but Megeen R. Mulholland's "Miscarriage of an English Teacher" reveals the writing process as part of the poem's structure. The speaker revises her writing as she struggles to capture the essence of her experience with miscarriage, illuminating the distance between creative body and mind. "Johnny," by Heidi Raykeil, explores the death of a newborn son and the writer's battle to come to terms with her loss. The poems "Namaste," by Rachel Iverson, and "Hospital Quartet," by Phyllis Capello, and the essay "Dear Friend," by Vicki Forman, detail the vigils mothers keep with ill children. And finally, Rebecca Kaminsky, in "Down Will Come Baby," confronts postpartum depression in a story that rings true for many mothers and fathers who suffer from this serious and life-deadening illness.

The work in the final section, "Healing the Past to Live in the Present," examines the connection with nature or with other humans in a wide range of settings—homeless shelters, concentration camps, mental institutions, music conservatories. The opening poem, "Answers," by Lisa Suhair Majaj, asks us to consider what we carry with us from the past, how we remember the past, and how that past leads into our futures. Cindy La Ferle's "Fragile Season" tells the story of a mother, struggling to define herself after her grown son has left home, who finds solace working in a homeless shelter. In "Why My Garden," Ericka Lutz, prompted by the need to understand the Jewish heritage she is attempting to pass on to her daughter, goes on a journey to the ruins of Birkenau and Auschwitz. After confronting the quiet evil of humankind, she considers planting fragments of the ruins in her garden, assimilating the enemy.

The fictional piece "The River," by Amy Hudock, is also about a journey, but one into and out of madness. This story reworks the tale of the mother-artist who kills herself—like Edna in *The Awakening*—to reveal greater possibilities for mothers who write, paint, create. "The Plant," by Andrea J. Buchanan, explores the notion of nurturing—plants, ourselves, our children—as something that can be learned in her story of grappling with the nature of pain. All of these stories celebrate the heroic internal work that must be done to overcome the past and fully embrace the present.

The basic story arc of motherhood is the same as it always has been. In fact, it might surprise those who think of motherhood as a nonuniversal experience to recognize in that arc the classic hero's journey: separation (the physical transformation of the pregnant body marking a gestating woman as different from other women), initiation (giving birth, the identity-shift of motherhood), and return (rejoining society as a mother, with all the cultural expectations that status carries). What's different about the mother writing of today versus centuries ago—such as the current preference for frank honesty about mothers' previously private experiences, from birth and breastfeeding to sex and anger—has more to do with the cultural zeitgeist than with anything fundamentally new about the story of motherhood itself.

However, one crucial difference between Fanny Fern's world and the world of today's mother-writers is that of access. Contemporary mother-writers around the world can easily and quickly share their work. *Literary Mama* is produced entirely via email and the web; many of the editors who communicate with each other every day have never met in person or even spoken on the phone. We've never met the majority of the writers we publish. Yet through the immediacy of the Internet, we are able to know one another—to read each other's stories, to collaborate on large-scale projects, to encourage and inspire one another.

Our goal at *Literary Mama* is to take writing about motherhood seriously. By publishing writing exclusively by mothers, we assert that motherhood as a theme is worthy of great literature—and that mothers are capable of writing it. Our literary foremothers began this work generations ago. With *Literary Mama: Reading for the Maternally Inclined*, we hope to further our role in midwifing the literary mothers of the future. For these are writers who do not deserve to be forgotten.

Andrea J. Buchanan and Amy Hudock
September 2005
Philadelphia, Pennsylvania, and Summerville, South Carolina

I.
Creative Acts

Pregnancy
by Lori Romero

mood
swings
piqued
euphoric
morose
pooped
blue
pink
pale
anxiety
keenness
breasts blossom
small ring of color
caresses the areola
hypersensitivity
nausea
heartburn and indigestion
shortness of breath and backaches
frequent urination, abdominal cramps
tiny amounts of hCG enter bloodstream
food cravings, fatigue, bloating, back pain
    incessant urination, constipation, irritability
      triple fudge sundae and pickles, navel pushes out
      ohwowsomethingismovinginsideyesicanfeel
      youmoveandnowyouarekickingandpunching
owwtherewewillbothshifttoamorecomfortable
position I wonder if you'll have my mother's
eyes or the soft curl of my sister's upper lip
should I name you Elizabeth or Samantha
Samuel or Caleb or wait until I see you
spider
veins
fluid
edema
ankles
swelling
feet feel
tight and shoes
don't fit quite right

Third Month
by Sarah Pinto

Lucknow, India

Forgetting—like nausea—is a matter of
waves
and walking
into this new remembering strangles narration
and its
false beginnings.
What should be a thing of insides and interiors,
hanging drapes and gluing paper in a new room
where secrets can be told in the glow of sunlight through velvet curtains

feels more like
a demolition of
walls and windows
into crumbling bricks and glass.

I am onions and spices, the
tang of men's urine spritzed casually on building sides,
a dizziness grander than these narrow, faulty walls of skin.
Like those snowbound Eskimos,
I am a dictionary of the thousand words for smoke,
a story about other people's joys and sadness.
I am an Indian city on the plains in summer,
a great invisible oven with shiny knobs and dials—
tubes and corridors of shivering heat under a sun meant for no woman.
Bake me and I shrink,
in rain
I will swell,

I am the clay miniature toasting into readiness
which the town has become.

Instead of one-two-ness I become an infinity of things not even human.
In this way the world decimates me
and collects and collides and merges in my bloody depths.
In this way the world becomes human.

I had read that in the highlands of a certain island
a child is not made by connecting it to a world of named others,
but by separating it, stretching it away
tediously
from all and all and all that is.
But I wonder now if before the child can be

made not to merge with the slippery world
the world must coagulate,
all that is sticky and moist and
sharp and sugary and soft and loud and persistent
must first crash through the well-maintained boundaries of
someone already made.

This is what it feels like
from the heart of a barrage of everything.

And what should smell of time
and the sweeter side of impermanence
is a vertigo of stopped seconds.
My amazement stands ready for use
like a regiment tired of weekend drills.

thirty-seven weeks
by Rachel Iverson

sunglasses
disappear
from their perch
on my head
somewhere
in the block
between the
coffee shop
and dry cleaner.
the fifth button
of my shirt
is agape exposing
my tight-skinned
belly until i feel
a breeze.
keys dangle
from the knob
outside my
front door
as i dream in
the mezzanine
of the afternoon.
i forget to
feed my baby;
he shrivels
and shrinks to fit
faceless in my two
cupped hands.
my mother
whispers promises
this baby will never
let me forget.

Evolution of a Muse
by Joanne Hartman

The developing muse:

I have a great story idea one night as I try to go to sleep. But there is no paper of any kind in the room, no writing instrument nearby. I'm eight months pregnant, too big and too tired to get up, so I tell myself I'll remember it in the morning.

This is what I remember in the morning: that I had a story idea the night before. No searches in my cranial hard drive are able to retrieve it. I did not write it down: Therefore, it does not exist.

I must, must, must write things down.

I start a pregnancy journal and leave it in my bedside table drawer. I want to remember how it feels to be heavy with another life inside of me, the responsibility and care I feel for something I can't even see and someone I know so little about.

The muse is born:

After we bring our sleeping newborn daughter home from the hospital and set her on the couch in her car seat, and after the dogs have sufficiently sniffed her, we have that "Okay, now what?" moment some first-time parents recall.

I stare at her and wonder what I'm supposed to do now. My exhausted husband has already fallen asleep on the couch next to her. My new job description must be in one of my baby books. But instead of looking through the books, I find myself propelled to the computer, where I start to write her story, recording the first hours and days of her life, the way new motherhood makes me feel.

Whenever motherhood is too overwhelming or too quiet, the love too amazing to hold within, when she sleeps and I can't, I write. I write for her, so she'll know what I felt. I write for me, to remember my journey.

The muse exhausts:

Sleep deprivation makes for esoteric poetry and illegible journal entries. Writing comes in starts and spurts, and it's difficult to sustain a thought or idea, even though the muse inspires me. I write when she naps, but it's not so much real writing as it is the jotting down of words and phrases on the proverbial paper napkin, even once on a disposable diaper. Mostly, I write on the back of old Yahoo! driving directions that litter the car and diaper bag, those many maps and directions I printed out to get me to a park, a museum, or a playgroup member's home. The writing is a sort of mother-shorthand I later transcribe to my computer.

This mommy job isn't as easy as I thought it would be. I'm constantly guessing, consulting books and more experienced mommies, and I feel just like I did my first year teaching: not sure, a bit off balance, but loving it and knowing I'm doing something incredibly wonderful. My writing takes the form of lots of questions and responses, as if I'm writing a Q & A interview with myself. Will she ever sleep through the night? Of course, they all do. All of them? Will that include mine?

I write at night in the dark when I should be sleeping, keeping the lights off so as to not wake the baby or my husband. In the morning, I find words are layered upon words.

The muse speaks:

My daughter is two. She is a poet, unknowingly masterful at allusion and metaphor.

"The moon is a sleeping ball," she tells me on our night walk and points up to it, full and round, low in the sky. As if that isn't enough to make me want to run home and write it down, she says to the night sky, "Come down, down, down, moon, into my arms, and I will hode you." She reaches both arms skyward, stretching her tiny palms up toward the huge white orb that bathes her small face in its glow. I want to freeze this moment in time.

I write in a manic bit of insomnia. I discover, through writing about it, that she is my moon—in orbit around me, close and full like the moon was that night. I publish the moon piece in a local parent publication. I paste the printed piece in her baby book and show my daughter her name in print. Several phone calls and emails arrive from mothers who have read it. They are sending copies to friends; they hope that's okay. I save the messages for a long time as concrete proof that I am a writer.

At the annual neighborhood picnic, I'm introduced to a new neighbor who has a son my daughter's age. The woman's a writer who has sold a fantasy novel, a completed book that has an actual publication date. I tell her about my little essay. I don't feel like a real writer now.

Later that night, my daughter tries to dress herself. "No, Mommy. Go away. I can do it!" She pushes my arms away dramatically as she attempts entry in her one-piece pajamas, confusing the arms for the legs, writhing with frustration on the floor when she is twisted in the fabric like a pretzel. "Help me, Mommy! I am inside out!" she screams through tears, and I go to her from my not-so-distant orbit. I help turn her right side in, gently guiding her left arm in the proper place and letting her find the right sleeve herself.

I decide I am a writer, that I must go and write it down.

The muse is restless:

As I sit down to finally write after so many long months of not doing so, I have to remove from the computer keyboard a stuffed animal named Domino, a hefty Dalmatian who is resting upside down with an entire roll of Scotch tape wound around his middle. The tape is also wrapped around the mouse. A dozen Post-it notes with swirly hearts and asymmetrical drawings stuck on the monitor and the surface of the desk, a pink barrette attached to a pink ribbon, and a small white plastic horse inhabit what is supposed to be, and what was long ago, my writing space.

In my writing group, before I had a child, we discussed our Zen-like approach to clearing the clutter around us before we could truly focus on writing. Now I laugh out loud at that thought. I must write amidst the distractions, with the continuous and concrete reminders that I have a young child. Perhaps if I can become one with the clutter of her childhood, I can still focus on my craft. But it is a challenging task and something I cannot yet master.

The writing life and mothering life are so similar: Both are unpredictable, isolating, and they pay poorly. With both, I try to follow gut instincts, I constantly revise ideas and expectations, and, with limited opportunity for feedback from my peers—someone to say, "Hey, that was well done!"—I have to be creative and confident. After all, these are two professions where critics abound.

"You're a bad mommy," my daughter tells me when I explain that chocolate pudding is not a choice for breakfast. And then I go to write. My husband is watching our daughter; it's the only time I'll have. But my own critic tells me the writing isn't flowing; it's clogged, backed up. I'm way out of practice, but I try to write anyway.

My daughter is screaming that she wants me, not her daddy anymore. Breakfast time has passed, though she still hasn't eaten, and I'm tempted to give in to chocolate pudding (there is protein in the milk, right?). Laundry is piled as high as our dog. We're out of OJ and low on milk. I don't have the time or energy to be a writer. What made me think I did?

The next day, I find out an essay I wrote almost a year ago will be published, and I'll be paid close to $300. My daughter is in the story, of course. She's there when the editor calls to tell me the good news. "Terrific," I tell the editor. "I'm so glad you liked it." I yell to be heard over my daughter's whining. After I hang up, I explain to my daughter why I'm doing the twist when no music is playing in the room. "Well, I want to write a story," she says; this dance of excitement is something she desires, too. She tells me a tale of a unicorn and a cat and a girl. I grab the fat orange felt-tip pen from her art supplies, and I begin to write it down.

The muse is unpredictable:

I write a lot since my daughter is more independent now. She has many friends and playdates, and her formerly workaholic father is now home with her. He shares much more of the parenting and has taken over the exhausting role of Head Question Answerer. He is more qualified, since most questions are of a scientific nature. What's the difference between a comet and meteor? What are eyeballs made out of? He makes me write them down.

I send more pieces off to magazines and anthologies. I start a column. I write while she happily entertains herself crushing flower petals to make perfume. I stop my writing to help her catch butterflies with the huge gold lamé net her father has made for her. White flutterings bounce and hover from bush to bush like fairy wings.

She has her first loose tooth. The tantrums come—periods of intense frustration and neediness. It's not pretty or easy. I don't write much of it down. There are the jokes she makes up and songs she sings of butterflies and old vine swings that I record in writing, but I miss her free-flowing thinking out loud, when she told me everything she was thinking, all the time. She's more reflective now; there are private thoughts that she doesn't want to share. This should come as no surprise. I taught middle school, I know all too well that my days of knowing her every thought are numbered. I just didn't think it would happen when she was only five and a half.

I find myself writing about loss, about the changes that are taking place as my muse struggles with growing up. Graduating from preschool made her cry, and I don't know if she's worried about starting kindergarten; she's not talking about it, not asking any questions. When I bring it up, she doesn't say much.

I write about her growing independence being wonderful to witness; I feel some relief that she no longer needs me in the constant way she has before, but I miss the easy ways to comfort her: nursing, picking her up and rocking her, rubbing her tiny back. Her babyhood is over. I'll never again carry her strapped in the front pack, her head resting above my breasts, her heart beating on top of mine as she falls asleep, connected, cocooned.

The summer is punctuated with days of bliss among the steadiness of her intense frustration. I so want her to open up to me. Is she wondering if she'll ever see her preschool friends again? Is she afraid that kindergarten won't be so fun?

One summer day, I drive her to the playground of what will be her new school. We run around through the redwood grove and kick high on the swings to the top of the canopy of branches that frames the cool blue sky. That night she says, "Mommy, I'm very confused about something."

Aha. Finally. Here it is; my answers are ready for what I think she needs to ask.

"Maybe I can help," I tell her and push the mail aside and invite her into my lap. She climbs up the tall kitchen bar stool and wraps her arms around my shoulders.

"Mommy, what it is that I don't understand is—what is the difference from a quesadilla and a tortilla?"

I try so hard not to laugh at my expectations, or trivialize her question. I don't want to risk future conversations when she might actually need me to help navigate deeper issues of confusion. "Cheese, sweetie," I answer. "A quesadilla is a tortilla that has cheese inside of it."

"Oh," she says with furrowed brow, her head nodding as she files the explanation in the Mexican food section of her brain. She smiles and climbs off my lap.

And then I go and write it down.

Thirteen Ways of Looking at Being a Mother and a Poet
by Nicole Cooley

1.

A confession: I was one of those people I shake my head at now, a woman who thought having a baby would not change my life.

2.

I was thirty-four and living in New York City when my daughter, Meridian, was born, and I had lived the majority of my adult life with—though I did not realize it at the time—total freedom. Freedom to spend weeks at artists' colonies, to travel with my anthropologist husband through Europe and Southeast Asia, and most of all to set my own schedule for each day. I had published a novel and a book of poetry while getting my PhD, and I was very good at balancing and keeping separate all the different aspects of my life. Having a baby, I told myself, would just be like adding another genre to my writing repertoire.

I felt confident about having a new baby, writing, and teaching because I thought of myself as someone who was very good with time. For most of my life, I'd counted my writing time down to the minute. As an undergraduate, I calculated how much each creative writing class cost based on my financial aid package so I would feel too guilty to miss a single session. In graduate school, I tallied how many hours I read and wrote each day to make sure they added up to at least eight hours. At artists' colonies I counted time as well—it would only be worth it to be there if I could spend eight hours each day writing. For years, I punched an absurd, imaginary time clock in my life as a writer.

3.

A scene: My daughter is three days old and absolutely beautiful. My husband and I could look at her all day. Her dark, shiny eyes hold my gaze, and her mouth puckers then widens into what I think is a smile.

Yet I am holding a three-hundred-page book open above her head as I sit admiring her. I am making my way through *The Collected Poems of Muriel Rukeyser* so I can get a start on my own poetry again, stalled for so long during my pregnancy because I felt so exhausted and sick for the whole nine months.

She is three days old, and I think I am planning my third book of poems. I believe it will be no problem to write it, since the baby seems to sleep so much. She has slept the majority of the seventy-two hours she's been home from the hospital. "Look how much I can accomplish!" I tell my husband, while breastfeeding ten hours a day, my daughter on my lap in the rocking chair.

4.

Before Meridian was born, I searched literary history for examples of poets who were successful parents. First, I could only think of father artists: Rilke locked in a tower writing *Duino Elegies* and refusing to attend his daughter's wedding, Robert Lowell in McLean Hospital suffering alone while his wife cared for his young daughter at home for months. All of the poets who were fathers seemed too absent. I searched through book after book in my poetry collection looking for references to their children and found very few. I t was easier to think about the fathers because the mother poets were more disturbing to consider. Two of my favorite poets, Sylvia Plath and Anne Sexton, were especially unsettling examples. They killed themselves. They left their children behind.

5.

Just as, in the first few weeks with a newborn, you can convince yourself you can survive indefinitely on three hours of sleep a night, for a little while after Meridian's birth, I managed to hold on to my belief that having a child would not change my life.

Of course after the first week of constant sleeping, she woke up, snapped to attention, and began to cry. She cried for hours. She refused to sleep. My husband and I took turns trying to comfort her, with little success.

Home with a baby all day, I found myself consumed with the desire to escape. To stand on the street corner with the local teenagers, drinking from a paper bag and smoking. To disappear into the city alone. Having lived so much of my adult life doing whatever I wanted to do and whatever would be good for my work, I felt trapped in a way I had never envisioned. The strains on my body from the birth and breastfeeding were overwhelming. The baby's all-consuming needs felt relentless. "Motherhood is the gradual extinction of self," I wrote in my journal. No one had ever needed me like my daughter needed me. Paradoxically, there was no one I wanted to be with more, yet no one I wished more to escape.

Although motherhood was isolating, at the same time, what I missed most was my solitude, the freedom to leave the apartment whenever I wanted, to read without being interrupted, to look out the window and just think. Whenever I was able to get out on my own, rather than meeting friends I would walk the streets of midtown Manhattan and revel in the wonderful feeling of anonymity. Out of the apartment, down the wet, dirty winter sidewalk, over the unshoveled snow against the curb, onto the train, its tiled floor muddy with everyone's tracks, through the tunnel—this was such a pleasure that each time I rode the subway alone I felt terribly guilty.

My daughter would teach me the most crucial lessons about my work and self, but I was not yet ready to receive them.

6.

My understanding of myself as a mother and a writer was forever changed when my daughter was ten months old.

On the morning of September 11, one week after I had returned to teaching, I was at home with Meridian napping on my lap, holding a book in one hand and preparing my afternoon classes, when the first plane struck the World Trade Center. For the next few weeks, like most New Yorkers, I walked around in shock, trying not to breathe the burning smell that floated through the streets, that hung in the air, that entered our apartment no matter how we sealed the windows shut. All barriers against that dangerous outside world were futile. The terror invaded our apartment through the smell of the burning and the TV news we were unable to turn off. The phone kept ringing with out-of-town friends asking if we were okay. In front of the endless TV coverage of "America's New War" that fall, I held my daughter as tightly as I could, grateful that she was too young to understand the world she would have to live in.

This moment quite literally snapped me out of myself. It shattered my resolve to focus only on my work, drew me closer to my daughter.

7.

A scene: After the World Trade Center attacks, I force myself out of the apartment, back into the world. More than anything, I want to stay home, where I feel safer, but I know that impulse is dangerous to both Meridian and myself.

My daughter and I walk for hours through the streets of Queens. I carry her against my chest, in her BabyBjörn—we both hate the stroller. Crossing and recrossing the long avenues of our Greek neighborhood, we adopt a new rhythm together. If I stop walking even for a moment she will wake up. Walking, thinking, rolling words over and over in my mind, remembering fragments of poems, dreaming up images, I find myself, for the first time in nearly a year, playing with language in my head. Past the souvlaki trucks and cafés where men sit smoking, watching Greek satellite TV, we move through the world together. I think my own thoughts, and yet there she is, held close against me, safe. For the first time, I feel a flicker of the old freedom.

8.

A week after the September 11 attacks, my husband and I took our daughter down to Union Square, where round-the-clock vigils and protests against the government's handling of the event were being conducted. As I circled the park, my daughter held against my chest, I read the posters telling of the "missing," with names and phone numbers and physical descriptions of tattoos, scars, and birthmarks, identifying features. Beside these posters were poems, hundreds of poems, written by children, relatives, coworkers of the victims, and people who wanted to express some feeling about the attacks. For hours, crowds filed through the square reading these poems.

Meridian stirred and pressed her cheek against me. This was the moment when I began to return to poetry, to thinking about it, to writing it, to understanding what it could do in the world. I gripped her small hands. These poems, "good" writing or not, deeply mattered. They were being read by thousands of people. Poetry, in this context, had a clear social purpose, beyond the latest literary magazine or university reading. The poems displayed on the fence and taped on trees were deeply personal and at the same time publicly displayed.

9.

Contrary to what everyone told me, having a child did not make me more efficient. "You'll get more done in less time," they said. "You'll have to because you'll have no time!" But what having my daughter really did was slow me down in a way that was good for me and my work. I began to pay attention, in the way you must when you are walking down a street with a toddler who wants to touch every crack in the sidewalk and examine every broken bottle. And this quality of persistent, close attention to the world in its smallest aspects is very much what you need as a poet, and it was what had been missing from my work during all the years I actually had time.

10.

In the aftermath of the events of September 11, as my daughter became a toddler, my own writing was stalled and difficult. Slowly, I began to write new poems, but they made me uncomfortable because they seemed to violate the borders I'd set for myself in writing: Never invoke the self directly. Walking to a poetry reading on campus in early October, another poet said to me, "Oh God, I hope people aren't going to read their September 11 poems today." Inside my folder was my own new poem about September 11 that I planned in fact to read. But, I was hesitant to read it for a different reason: It seemed too personal—it even mentioned breastfeeding—and focused on motherhood, on having a young child in the wake of violence.

For the past five years, I had been writing a book of poems on the Salem witch trials, proud of the fact that the book was based on "research," a legitimating search for truth located outside myself. Now for the first time, persona began to seem like a disguise. I felt I was escaping into someone else's history, trying on other people's pasts like borrowed clothes. Strangely, persona had become a kind of self-imposed silence.

My new poems were explicitly about myself. My new manuscript, *Stabat Mater*, took on subjects I hadn't seen in poems before—with titles like "Amniocentesis," "Cesarean"—and in these poems I blended my intimate, bodily experience with my daughter with what was happening outside our apartment window in New York as the world seemed forever transformed.

11.

A scene: My daughter is two and a half, sitting on my lap in my study with me, and we are writing poems. She dictates, and I write her words down. "Once upon a time there was a Mama and she swim in the breeze."

Her arms flap up and down at her sides, her whole body visibly excited by our project. "Write poem!" she shouts over and over. Until now I never brought her into my tiny room, my allegedly sacred work space. The borders of all my old ideas about writing and motherhood start collapsing, divisions between parts of myself are breaking down. My husband and I set up a corner for her in my room with an easel and a box of crayons so she and I can write together.

12.

In the fall of 2001, with a new baby and an uncertain world situation, living in a city that we all feared—and still fear—would be attacked again, teaching classes of students who were bereft and grieving, all my old ideas about my identities fell apart.

After having a child, I could not keep writing poems about worlds I had never inhabited. Unable to compartmentalize any of my experiences, the domestic space of my apartment and my family merged with the larger world outside the window. The structures I had set in place to dictate the careful order of my personal and professional life collapsed. A new vista opened: For the first time I began to write poems about my own experiences and my own life. The experience of having a child became significant material for my own poems. But it could not be explored without an acknowledgment of the larger landscape.

My daughter forced me out of myself, demanded that I live in the world, and made me pay attention, and yet at the same time, she made me look more deeply inward than I ever had before.

13.

Now, nearly three years after Meridian's birth, pregnant with my second child, I can't even remember that person who tried to write poems for eight hours a day and was too afraid to write about herself.

As Meridian falls asleep at night, I hold her close and remember the words I read early in her life from Muriel Rukeyser. A mother and a poet who lived through much of the twentieth century and who bore witness to so much horror in the world around her, Rukeyser wrote these words that I now, finally, understand: "What three things can never be done? / Forget. Keep silent. Stand alone."

The Gift
by Karen Vernon

Keegan digs in the dirt, making spherical mud pies adorned with twigs and rocks. Occasionally she unearths a prized bottle cap, and she crowns the ball with much ceremony. Keegan does everything with much ceremony. Living with her is being treated to a never-ending series of performance-art pieces.

The first one I remember was when she was two. We were walking along a wooded path leading to the park carousel when she began to twist, gyrate, then freeze, and begin again. A contortionist's dance with brief interludes of motionlessness. As she began to attract stares from passersby, I asked, "What are you doing?" "It is," she replied, drawing herself up from a frozen pirouette, "the Sound of Leaping."

More recently she has adopted a stage persona, the "Great Ballerina Seena." The name itself may be a sort of postmodern commentary because I have never seen her perform any ballet. The Great Ballerina Seena travels with a grandiose British announcer who always provides her introduction. "Ladies and gentlemen, tonight a rare spectacle will meet your eyes! The Great Ballerina Seena, recently arrived from her latest European tour, will perform for you an act which has delighted and amazed audiences the world over. Never before have you seen such daring! Such beauty! Such sheer talent! Acclaimed from Munich to Minsk, and seen here tonight only by special arrangement, I present to you, the one, the only, the Great Ballerina Seena!"

Last night after her customary introduction, the Great Ballerina Seena came on with a pink nightgown and guitar. She began a sort of flamenco dance routine, accompanying herself on the guitar, which she had tuned to an atonal scale of her own devising, more than you'll see on most Spanish stages. But the Great Ballerina Seena is about so much more than just entertainment. She quickly broke down the "fourth wall" of the stage and instructed every audience member to also take up guitars and play along. It became a participatory art event reminiscent of early Yoko Ono. Unfortunately, after the audience had joined in, the Great Ballerina Seena became dissatisfied with the stage lighting and demanded accommodations the venue was unable to provide. (Keegan like so many other writer/director/performers has a tendency to be somewhat tyrannical in pursuit of her vision.) Unnerved by the lighting, her directions to the audience escalated from artistic choreography to abuse, and the authorities had to close the show down. The Great Ballerina Seena decried the censorship, yet made no apologies to her public. I think she courts this kind of controversy.

Keegan is not always performing, of course. She has quiet, introspective times as well. These she narrates in the third person. When she is alone in her room, I can hear her talking quietly to herself. "And the girl leaped [soft thud] across the water. 'I will never give you the child!' she said." (The girl Keegan also speaks with a somewhat affected British accent, à la Wendy in Disney's *Peter Pan*.) "The girl *swept*—" (she draws out the word as she grabs the doll and tosses her across the room) "—the child across the river to the castle."

When she experiences a block and cannot come up with words to match her dramatic inner dialogue, she is not thwarted. She will simply babble nonsense syllables with the pace and inflection of narrative. When things fall dangerously silent, I will peek around the corner and see her looking down, head tilted to the side. Her lips move rapidly, and she rolls her eyes, purses her lips, changing expression repeatedly. This dialogue is punctuated with appropriate hand gestures. I am sorry I can't know what she is talking about now. But this part of the story is not yet meant for public consumption.

Of course it is difficult at four years old to always use your powers for good and not for evil. I might ask Keegan to pick her coat up off the floor, and, if ignored, lightly lay my hand on her shoulder to emphasize my second request. She will fall to the ground, clutching the offended area, keening in pain. "Owie, Owie, owie, owie, ooowwwie, oooowwwie, ooowwieeeee." Left alone, the owies will escalate into great wracking sobs, and such is her dedication to her craft that ice and Band-Aids must then be administered. She will also create stories to justify her behavior when she knows she has violated the rules. She is a method actress, and once she has created these backstories, she believes them completely no matter how unlikely they may be, or what obvious inconsistencies we might point out. She will argue with us with passion and conviction, and though she protests vehemently she will accept banishment rather than admitting the truth.

Last summer I watched a group performance of Keegan's theater camp class. They played in a drum circle, did an African dance, and then improvised during a brief poem. At least I watched all the other students do those things as a group. Keegan came onstage with her class in each act and proceeded to do something completely different from everyone else. She participated, enthusiastically. She dismantled her drum and wore it as a hat. Beaming and panning at assembled parents, she marched in jerky circles while the other students danced. In the improvisation activity, as twelve of the thirteen girls proceeded, one after the other, to leap to the left, leap to the right, pirouette, the Great Ballerina Seena came on in a spider walk, a modified back-bend, walking on her hands and feet. For the finale she planted her butt on the stage and extended all four limbs straight to the sky, balancing on that tiny bottom. After the performance the teacher approached me. "Are you Keegan's parent?" I nodded. She looked at me intently, eyes widening, and clapped her hands together in front her. "So . . . unique. So . . . different. So . . . always doing her own thing." She was earnest, and I smiled, but my stomach tightened. Fear filled me. Keegan would start kindergarten in a little over a year. What was a school going to do with her? What would the world make of her "uniqueness"? And what would she make of it in the world? But I contained these anxieties that threatened to overwhelm me. I thanked the teacher. I praised my daughter, and I told her grandparents how great she was. And my heart broke a little, and not really for Keegan, this proud girl parading her backward-dancing, spider-walking, storytelling self to the world, but for me.

I remember the hours I spent working out fantasies in the in backyard, conversing with lions or riding aback dragons, and the books I consumed under the covers of my bed each night. I imagined myself an author, writing down the fantasies I constantly inhabited. Only last week I caught myself grimacing and gesturing as I walked down the sidewalk in the Financial District through lunch-hour crowds. I had become so engaged in the conversation I was having inside my head with people who were not there that I had forgotten not to let it show.

My father was a creative man, although I didn't realize it until later. When I was about fifteen and going through a closet of my father's childhood artifacts, I came across a drawing of a frog on a lily pad. The colors were brilliant, greens and blues and purples. It was really beautifully done, even though he was young, maybe nine or ten, when he did it. I took the drawing into the family room where he was watching TV. "Dad, you did this? This is really good." My father looked at it and grimaced. "Yes, I used to like to draw." He looked at the picture a minute more, then shifted his eyes to me, staring at me intently. "You know, Karen, when I was young my teacher pulled me aside and told me that people who are really talented—who really can do art—they are born with that kind of talent. It's a gift. You either have it or you don't. And he let me know I didn't have it." My father paused and looked away. "Best advice I ever got. I could have wasted a lot of time on that. Best thing anyone's ever done for me." I was appalled. Aghast that any teacher would say that to a student, and horrified that my father viewed it as the best advice he'd ever received.

My father wasn't unkind. He loved me. He worried over me. He agonized over each decision I made. In each achievement, though he would praise me, he would then point out the problems, the potential pitfalls, the ways things could still go wrong. I realized later he had a basic belief that things would not work out. And I was left with that underlying anxiety that what you desire you will not ultimately get, and, if you do, there will be something essentially flawed in it. I took his teacher's horrible advice. I believed it. "Real talent is born in you like a mark you and everyone else can see. If you had the gift you'd know." I repeated it like a mantra to myself. If I really had talent, I would have written that novel by now. It would have just flowed effortlessly onto the page. Not like these halting words that shuffle clumsily along the line, tripping on their loose ends. I crumple the paper after the first sentence, embarrassed. How sad, I'm an aspiring writer. One who wants desperately to write, but doesn't have the gift. Pathetic. I became suspicious of my own dreams. And I left them behind.

Yesterday Keegan declared, "I'm a cowboy princess." I was unsure if this was her job, her gender, or a philosophical statement. But I said, "Yes, yes, you are." I smiled as she stomped away in cowboy boots and butterfly wings to caucus with the fairies under the dining room table. I thought to myself, "She has a certain something. She was really born with that bent for drama and fantasy." And suddenly I put a hand to the wall to catch myself as my knees went momentarily weak and my mouth dropped open. A gift. She has a gift. This is what the gift looks like. It's not the Mozart sonata at age five, not the perfectly formed novel. It's this, this flair, this love, this inclination. This is what it is, and I had it, and they knew it.

My father's words, his piercing eyes when he said them. I realize how clearly I have remembered each time he talked about it. How these moments stand out, preserved in detail from a blur of other childhood experiences. These were meaningful moments in a family mostly ruled by silence. He could see the creativity in me, as plainly as I can see it in her. But he had abandoned his own gift, left it behind. And he feared for me, that I would feel disappointment like his own, for what he saw as an impractical existence. And, to be honest, I have begun to know his anxiety as I watch Keegan venture further out in the world. I worry for her. While other parents are up in arms over the reading programs being used or the test scores at different schools, I shrug. Keegan's hunger for stories will drive her to read if all the school can offer is a set of alphabet blocks. But the neat rows of desks and the rooms of silent children scare me. The older girls walking the hall in carefully coordinated outfits, patrolling their peers for any kind of variance. How will the Great Ballerina Seena continue her performances in her cowboy boots, fairy wings, and construction worker's hat? Can she continue to let that gift show, with the weight of her peers' disapproval, her own doubts, and my fear and regret pressing down upon her?

So here I am, caught between my father and my daughter. An awkward midwife for something unborn in him, something burgeoning in her, and in me . . . a new and tenuous sense of possibility. When Keegan was born, the moment I held her, I was overwhelmed by a powerful elation unlike anything I had ever experienced. For the first time in as long as I can remember I had something that I truly desired, something that really mattered to me. And there was no downside. I began to ask, what else? What else really matters? And I began to believe that perhaps I could have the things I truly desired, and they could be good and worthy rather than dangerous and misleading traps. For her sake, I realize I must contain my fear, and not visit my disillusionment upon her as my father did upon me. I must cultivate faith. Faith in her. Faith in myself. Faith that this world will have a place for both of our gifts.

I have begun to write. I am sending my own ungainly words spider-walking out on to the stage. I have to show her how to nurture that gift, rather than abandon it. It's the least I can do. The Great Ballerina Seena deserves at least that much of an introduction.

The Blue Snake Lies Curled in My Bowl Like Oatmeal
by Barbara Crooker

Coffee sticks like syrup in my throat.
I cannot let you go, my child, my love,
eyes liquid as marbles.
Tears hide in each cheek,
about to rain.

Your hand is as small as a wish,
waving to me,
who has belted you in securely
on each voyage all these years,
tightened the cord,
must I give you up so easily
to cold steel, flashing lights,
the teacher's chalky smile?

I hand you over;
time is given back to me:
two hours to fill
with black snaked lines
on fine, blue-veined pages,
while your stubby hands sweat
on crayon covers;
trying to redo, with circles and lines,
the spangled world behind your eyes;
making fat clay worms
that tangle and break.

Time that is mine alone,
yet my arm crooks to hold you

young and babied once more.
My hand fights the discipline
of the page, and the cold snake within me
squeezes though to burst.

Are we always to be wanting
what isn't:
the greenest grass
accord and principle
motherhood and career?
Yet our age lies to us
like an asp,
whispering, "Both."

But to work is to abandon
to indifferent, casual hands,
what I, the potter, have worked
this demi-decade to achieve in you,
soft claygirl.
You respond to my words
like a cobra to a flute,
like the wooden chimes on the porch
dance to the soft music of the wind
from our lake.

But these five years are spent, idle, and gone
with but a handful of poems to show.
No publications from Antaeus to Xanadu,
but you, my poemchild,
whose smile is all my sonnets.

Not So Perfect
by Jennifer Lauck

It's a Saturday morning in Portland. The sky is full of low clouds that send down a fine mist of cool rain. Being outside is like being under the spritz in the vegetable section of the grocery store. It's the kind of mist that stings the skin, but we don't care. We're floating in the hot tub.

My almost-three-year-old daughter, Jo, has decided to forgo her Barbie one-piece and is in the buff. Spencer, who is seven, is at the control panel. He adjusts the aeration knobs, double-checks the light switch, and starts the pump for the jets.

"It's a hundred and two," Spencer says. "Just right."

The jets churn the water into foam, and we're all grinning at each other. I start to hum a little song, and Jo stands up, her round baby belly pushing forward enough to make her belly button pop out.

"What's that?" she says.

"It's that song," I say.

"What song?"

"That one I'm playing on the piano."

"You know," Spencer says. "The one she keeps making mistakes on."

Jo nods in this big way, like it's all so clear, and sinks down into the water again.

"Oh, that song," she says.

Spencer's observation stings more than the misting we're getting from the sky. I want to say, you get in there and play that piece without making mistakes, you little cretin; but he's right—I do make a lot of mistakes on that song, heck, on all songs I attempt. More amazing than any error I make on the piano is the realization that he's been paying attention.

In the divide of time just after my mother died and before my father died, we had a piano. It was an upright that came with the woman my father was dating and later married. It was more for show than function, though. After being around her and her kids for a while, I saw that no one actually played the thing. I remember cautiously making my way to the keyboard, wondering if anyone was going to tell me to leave the piano alone. When no one did, I started to play a couple of notes with my index finger. After a while, I'd hum songs like "The Entertainer" and "Sunrise, Sunset" to myself. Through countless hours of trial and error, I figured out which keys matched the tune. Somewhere in the midst of this exploration, I began to long for real lessons.

Then my dad died. Just eighteen months after the death of my mother and less than a year into his new marriage, he had a heart attack. Any idea of lessons was replaced by a storm of change during which my stepmother sold the piano, along with most everything else she owned, and joined a cult in L.A. She left me in a commune to fend for myself and took off to live somewhere else in the city with her own kids. By the time I was ten, I didn't have parents or a home, much less a piano. In the years that followed, I was rescued from the commune by an aunt and uncle, sent to my grandparents, and then sent to live with another aunt and uncle. By the time I was eighteen, I had moved twenty-seven times and been in a dozen different schools. That kind of transient, often-impoverished life wasn't conducive to the study of music.

Things didn't change when I was in my twenties, either. I was married, then divorced, and worked as a television reporter in three states. Finally, in my thirties, I settled down in Oregon, got married for a second time, and had my kids. I was blessed to write and publish a book that made enough money to indulge in something as luxurious as a piano. I bought a pretty baby grand from a friend. Three thousand bucks later, it was in the living room, and two hundred dollars after that, it was tuned and ready for my hands.

I found a teacher, too. Her name was Annette and for the first few lessons, I'd hear a piece of music and begin to cry. Annette would pat my knee with an indulgent smile and say sweet things like, you can teach anyone to play the piano but you can't teach a student to feel music; good for you.

She was right; I did feel it, in the very core of my being. To my heart, nothing was more sublime than beautiful music. When Annette guided me to play the notes with my own hands, I was in love. Playing those notes was so incredibly intimate and tender. I couldn't say what was so intimate about it; I was just overwhelmed by this intense sense of vulnerability. It was so tender to play, I could hardly do it in front of my own teacher. More often than not, my hands got all sweaty, my body shook from the core, and I'd even ask her to stand in another room while I played.

Over the holiday season, I was mastering a version of "Norwegian Bells," which required me to make the piano sound like hundreds of bells ringing. I was having the best time, commanding the keys under sure fingers while pumping my sustain pedal like an organist, when Jo started screaming.

"IT'S JUST NOISE!!!"

She stood in the middle of the living room, hands pressed to her ears until I stopped.

I was so embarrassed. Was I really bad when I thought I was good? If Jo couldn't take my playing, what about the neighbors? Were they covering their ears too, hoping I would stop?

It took a while to recover from Jo's critique, but I'd since gotten a little confidence back. Now there was Spencer, offering his thoughts on my playing, and I saw myself being embarrassed once again and even defensive. Exactly what was so important about a seven-year-old child's opinion of my playing, anyway? That's when it hit me that I was seven years old when my own mother died. I was the age Spencer is now when my childhood came to a fast and bitter end. The person playing the piano today is that little girl, very much alive, who has been hiding away in wait for this moment of calm. She's timid and insecure. A big part of her doesn't really believe that she deserves to play the piano at all. As the woman holding onto the spirit of that child, I'm hardly helping her heal herself by expecting perfection after just a year of study.

We'd been in the hot tub long enough, evidenced by how our fingers were wrinkled like raisins. Spencer jumped out first, running through the cold mist and into the house.

"Please dry yourself off at the door," I said, only he slammed the door on my words.

"Carry me up, Mommy," Jo commanded.

I lifted her slick, naked body against my side.

In the house, Spencer left behind a big puddle of water and tracked a mess of wet footprints through the kitchen.

Any other time, I'd be "the mother" and call him back to clean up after himself, but I didn't feel much like a mother at that moment. I didn't care about doing the right thing as a mother or teaching him some lesson about being tidy.

I started humming my song again, hearing the notes lift and fall in my head. I dried off Jo and let her run after her brother, screaming at the top of her lungs, "Spencer, I'm going to get you."

I wrapped myself in a towel and padded my own puddles through the kitchen, the dining room, and the living room. I sat down at my piano, put my fingers on the keys, and played the song again and again, trying to get it right, while my kids chased each other through the house, naked and happy.

Out of the Woods
by Lizbeth Finn-Arnold

> *I find it wholesome to be alone the greater part of the time. To be in company, even with the best, is soon wearisome and dissipating. I love to be alone. I never found the companion that was so companionable as solitude.*
>
> —From *Walden, or Life in the Woods,* by Henry David Thoreau

I am a solitary person. Where others may seek out company, I seek out secluded places of thoughtfulness and self-discovery. My early appreciation for solitude may spring from the fact that as a twin, I began my life sharing the most intimate and private space of all—my mother's womb. I am also the fifth of eight children, and there was barely ever a quiet moment during my childhood. Early on, I learned to appreciate private spaces and uninterrupted quiet time.

Perhaps I also crave solitude because I'm a writer, and like most writers I'm at my best alone in a room, inside my head, thinking and creating.

Once upon a time, I imagined myself staying at home with my babies and writing in my spare time. However, I quickly discovered that motherhood is not conducive to the solitary life of a writer. Babies and small children pretty much preclude any possibility of solitude. They have the tendency to interrupt the creative process that, like children, needs constant nourishment.

When Thoreau wrote, "Our life is frittered away by detail," he could have been talking about the life of any modern mother. I love my children dearly. However, by the time my daughter Olivia was three and my son Jared was one, I was suffering from complete and total "mommy burnout."

Taking care of my two toddlers had become exhausting and unwelcome work. I was overtired from lack of sleep and at times felt isolated and alone in my role as stay-at-home mom. I craved adult conversation, intellectual stimulation, and a break from the tedium. I also was frustrated by endless negotiations with demanding, illogical children. The house was never clean, and I could no longer muster the energy to put away the toys and "other little people things" that seemed to overtake every nook and cranny of our home. My life suddenly seemed like an overwhelming, out-of-control, endless to-do list.

Henry David Thoreau had wise advice from his two-year excursion in the woods at Walden Pond: "Simplicity, simplicity, simplicity."

But Thoreau wouldn't have lasted ten minutes in his tiny cabin with my two tots. And Thoreau had no idea how busy and complicated life is for a modern mother.

Besides, just like Thoreau, I too viewed myself as someone on a sojourn. I believed I was simplifying my life when I decided to eschew a career in order to stay home and raise my babies. In fact, after Olivia's birth I was riding an unbelievable emotional high. Every movement and milestone were closely observed and celebrated with great enthusiasm. To me, there was nothing mundane about being my baby's caretaker. I reveled in it all, enjoying every minute detail. I was testing and challenging myself like never before.

I went to the woods because I wished to live deliberately, to front only the essential facts of life, and see if I could not learn what it had to teach, and not, when I came to die, discover that I had not lived.

Isn't this the same reason I had decided to become a mother? I had a secret yearning, a desire to give birth and to nurture something other than my own personal ambitions. I was willing to take time off the fast track in order to nurture my children.

But I was totally unprepared for the physical and mental challenges of caring for two young children. I felt pulled in a million directions, and there was never enough time to do everything that needed to get done. I tended to chores while the kids were napping; played with my toddler while the baby nursed; and skipped meals, exercise, and sleep in order to accomplish more tasks from my to-do list. I fell into bed each night, exhausted and stressed.

When we are unhurried and wise, we perceive that only great and worthy things have any permanent and absolute existence, that petty fears and petty pleasures are but the shadow of reality.

How I would have loved just one night in my own secluded cabin during this time. However, unlike Thoreau, I was a mother, with unrelenting responsibilities and no escape hatch. I began to rely on afternoon naps for my very sanity. If I could get both kids down at the same time, then the afternoon would be a good one. If one refused to nap, there would be hell to pay by the time my husband walked in the door at dinnertime. If both refused to nap, I'd morph into the "crazy, mean mommy"—the one who screamed, cried, threatened, and cursed. I became a monster.

> *However mean your life is, meet it and live it; do not shun it and call it hard names.*

Trapped in the stifling reality of my domestic life, I began to resent my children. It all seemed like a harsh punishment, a prison sentence with no parole. I could no longer derive any pleasure out of motherhood. I tried to deny my unhappiness, or told myself it was normal to feel this miserable. But after one too many freak-outs, I could no longer bear to see the fear and confusion in my children's eyes. I could tell they still loved me immensely— but they were becoming afraid of me.

I went into therapy to confront my demons head-on. At that first consultation, I was practically in tears as I frantically described my terrible failures as a mother: "I'm always moody and depressed. . . . I'm not enjoying these children, who were planned and wanted. . . . How come motherhood is so difficult for me? Why am I unhappy? Why am I failing?"

Seeing how clearly overwhelmed and stressed I was, my therapist asked me what I did for enjoyment. I answered that I took the kids to the beach or park. She then asked me what I did alone, just for me. I told her that I occasionally snuck out to a Sunday matinee while my husband watched the kids.

She probed deeper by asking me about my life before motherhood. What did I do before I had kids?

"Sleep," I joked. She laughed, too. I told her that I used to exercise several times a week, go out with my husband every weekend, sleep in on Sundays, read as much as I could. As almost an afterthought, I added that I used to write screenplays and work on local independent films.

She was impressed by the writing and filmmaking, and curious to know why I had given them up.

I explained that I had decided to stay home and put my children ahead of my writing and filmmaking, a career as time-demanding and undercompensated, I now realized, as motherhood. I complained that I barely had the energy to get out of bed, and that I couldn't imagine adding the stress of a job into the mix.

My therapist encouraged me to make time for myself, to carve out a little space so that I could revitalize myself. "Time for me" was a foreign concept. When I wasn't feeling guilty about falling short with the kids, I was feeling guilty about not meeting the needs of my husband. I had become low man on my own totem pole. The thought of having time to myself seemed selfish and unrealistic. I even felt guilty about taking an hour a week for these Saturday morning therapy appointments.

It is remarkable how easily and insensibly we fall into a particular route, and make a beaten track for ourselves.

I had fallen into my own beaten track, a mommy rut. I was so used to the pattern of my life that I could no longer step outside of it and find an alternate path. It was my therapist who helped me sort out my conflicting ideas about motherhood, identity, success, and happiness. I had become stuck in a maternal pattern of nurturing others before myself. I was following the only model for motherhood I had ever been shown—my mother's.

My mother was from a time and place completely foreign to me. She was raised in the fifties, during an era that would later be studied by Betty Friedan in *The Feminine Mystique*. My mother and father were strict Catholics—hence the eight kids. My mother believed that mothers gave up everything for their children. She'd often quote from a song, "I gave up the good life to become an ordinary housewife."

I don't remember my parents ever going out on a date, holding hands, or even really having a private conversation. With eight kids, they rarely slept alone in their bed, which still makes me wonder when and how they even found time to make babies. My mother believed in laundry, vacuuming, and perfectly made beds, as if they held the key to absolute success in the universe. But my mother also was a contradiction. She was smart and creative, and she had her own dreams and ambitions too. Somehow, she found time during our naptimes for her own escape—she wrote and illustrated children's stories that were magnificent and beautiful to us, her children, even though they never found a publisher.

My other maternal role models came from popular magazines and entertainment, but I didn't recognize myself in those representations either. I wasn't the all-glowing "Natural Mom," content to stay home and give up all other facets of my life for the sake of my babies. Yet I also wasn't "Super Mom," who could attend to a high-powered, exciting, and demanding career at the expense of any personal life. In fact, I wasn't comfortable with any of the labels doled out to mothers. And I didn't understand why everyone, including me, expected and accepted that motherhood should completely annihilate my individuality.

If a man does not keep pace with his companions, perhaps it is because he hears a different drummer. Let him step to the music which he hears, however measured or far away.

With my therapist's help, I began to listen to my own drummer and ignore the din from the generic masses. An antidepressant helped lift the thick fog from my brain. I made time to read again, and realized how much enjoyment I had always derived from such a simple pleasure. I signed up for a yoga class and began to recognize the powerful connection between the mind and body. I learned how to meditate to clear my mind of negative thoughts. Gradually I came to realize that I was a creative person who needed to express herself.

I couldn't do motherhood exactly like my mother, my sisters, my friends, the experts, or movie stars. I had my own personality, my own needs and desires, my very own strengths and weaknesses. I had to make my own path in the mommy woods.

. . . if one advances confidently in the direction of his dreams, and endeavors to live the life which he has imagined, he will meet with a success unexpected in common hours.

Over the next year, I continued to make peace with the war that raged inside my mind and body. Through reading, yoga, and meditation, I had gained coping skills that helped me remain calm, despite the often-chaotic and pressing demands of my life as a mother. The "time for me" was paying off. I was beginning to enjoy the everyday details of my life again.

During this time I planned a mini-getaway: a much needed change of scenery and a chance to escape the mound of chores inside my home. With kids in tow, I headed to my twin's home in Massachusetts during the midst of a crisp New England autumn.

On the last day of our visit, I insisted that we stop at Walden Pond in nearby Concord. I hadn't been to Walden since I was five, the same age as my daughter. Because of my developing interest in meditation, I suddenly felt drawn to Thoreau's transcendental woods.

My children were only mildly interested as we peeked through the windows of the replica of Thoreau's cabin. It was windy and unseasonably cold for early October, and Jared was cranky and ready for a nap. Olivia humored me by posing for photos by Thoreau's statue, but she was more interested in chasing her little cousin, Lucas. I didn't expect the children to care about Thoreau's contributions to our modern understanding of natural living and Transcendental Meditation. However, I knew they could at least appreciate Thoreau's (and my own) simple love of the woods.

We slowly made our way over to Walden Pond, a vision that Thoreau described as follows:

In such a day, in September or October, Walden is a perfect forest mirror, set round with stones as precious to my eye as if fewer or rarer. Nothing so fair, so pure, and at the same time so large, as a lake, perchance, lies on the surface of the earth. Sky water. It needs no fence. Nations come and go without defiling it. It is a mirror which no stone can crack, whose quicksilver will never wear off, whose gilding Nature continually repairs; no storms, no dust, can dim its surface ever fresh; — a mirror in which impurity presented to it sinks, swept and dusted by the sun's hazy brush. . . .

On that bitterly cold October day, I was immediately struck by how breathtaking and awe-inspiring it was. Even my children seemed impressed by the magnificent sight. I took a moment and tried to connect to Thoreau's thoughts, as well as to those who had visited this spot before me. For a minute, I was jealous of Thoreau's experience. How could he enjoy years of solitude in these majestic woods, when I could not find two minutes of uninterrupted silence in my own home?

I snapped more photographs of my children playing in the shadow of the magnificent woods at Walden Pond.

The greatest gains and values are farthest from being appreciated. We easily come to doubt if they exist. We soon forget them. They are the highest reality. Perhaps the facts most astounding and most real are never communicated by man to man. The true harvest of my daily life is somewhat as intangible and indescribable as the tints of morning or evening. It is a little star-dust caught, a segment of the rainbow which I have clutched.

It was while looking through the lens of the camera at the wonders around me, as if connected to the ghost of Henry David Thoreau himself, that I had a moment of clarity: There is no greater beauty in this universe than that of my children.

I had been so lost in the dark grip of depression, frustration, and personal anxiety that I often overlooked the most precious gifts before me. Yes, my young children were loud, demanding, and exhausting. They robbed me of even a moment's peace and constantly assaulted me with their needs. But they were also the source of my deepest comfort. My children reminded me of my place in the universe and showed me how to slow down and appreciate life. In that moment, I realized that my children were my greatest inspiration . . . my Walden Pond . . . a mirror into my very own soul.

> *I left the woods for as good a reason as I went there. Perhaps it seemed to me that I had several more lives to live, and could not spare any more time for that one.*

I left Walden for a simple reason: It was time to drive back to New Jersey and get back to my home, my chores, my life. It was also freezing, and Jared clearly wasn't cooperating with my need to commune with nature. Like Thoreau, I had visited Walden Pond and felt its awesome power. Unlike Thoreau, I didn't need an additional two years of seclusion in these woods to fully grasp its lesson. As I drove home, I realized that I could leave the woods physically, and yet still live there spiritually. It was up to me to bring the peace, beauty, and simplicity of Walden home with me.

> *I should not talk so much about myself if there were any body else whom I knew as well. Unfortunately, I am confined to this theme by the narrowness of my experience.*

When I decided to start writing again as a creative outlet, I was initially frustrated by my lack of time and inspiration. It was difficult to commit fully to an idea when other important details crowded my mind. It was hard to feel poetically inspired, isolated as I was at home with a life consumed by pooping, puking, and peeing. I believed that great writers wrote about great things and thrilling adventures. Yet, my life was without adventure, at least as defined by our society.

Thoreau had said, "How vain it is to sit down to write when you have not stood up to live." And during this time I began to wonder, was I truly living? Were my domestic pursuits and my maternal struggles worthy of contemplation and writing? What, if anything, did I have to say?

Blocked and unproductive in my stolen moments to write, I stepped away from the computer and began to satisfy the few bursts of writing energy I had by scribbling away in the journal I had begun while pregnant with my first child. Some days I just recorded mundane events: a doctor's visit, a baby's new tooth, or some other milestone. These were boring details to the rest of the world, yet major events in my family's life. Other days I recorded my frustrations, desires, or other emotions. It wasn't a lot. But it fueled my creative juices.

Something exciting happened just about this time. I discovered a community of women on the Internet. I found women struggling with their identities as mothers, discussing the "dark side" of mothering. There were writers out there, brilliantly capturing the essence of the complex and confusing world of motherhood. I suddenly found that not only did I have something to talk about—I also had something to write about.

I do not propose to write an ode to dejection, but to brag lustily as chanticleer in the morning, standing on his roost, if only to wake my neighbors up.

I put my journal aside, and began mapping out short maternal essays in my mind. Then, in short spurts of time (naptime or school time), I fleshed out these thoughts into real, organized essays. I found I had a knack for it. I found that I truly enjoyed writing about what had become the greatest passion in my life: my children. I discovered that the challenges of motherhood were not mundane or insignificant.

And as a writer, I finally discovered both my confidence and my passion. My children, it seems, gave me an authentic voice.

Now I write, and write, and write. People ask me how I do it. I tell them that I squeeze it in whenever I can. I write while there is chaos swirling around me. I write in fits and starts, between making lunches, wiping butts, getting drinks, kissing boo-boos, folding laundry, playing basketball, cleaning up broken glass, giving baths, checking homework, feeding the dog, and breaking up fights between two stubborn siblings. It is my life and my best material: loud, full, unpredictable, and always an adventure.

Still, I have not given up completely on solitude. I steal snippets of it when I can. It has become easier to reclaim some of my former self, as my children get older, become more independent, and spend more time at school. I have also learned to take the time to nourish my soul, mind, and body— without feeling guilty.

And like Thoreau, I have come out of my woods with a deeper understanding of my world and better appreciation for the simpler things. I try not to sweat the small stuff, or get caught up in the music of other people's lives. I try only to "live each season as it passes; breathe the air, drink the drink, taste the fruit, and resign yourself to the influence of each."

II.

Mothers Raising Women, Defining Mothering

Casi's Face
by Gabriela Anaya Valdepeña

Sometimes, I take your features for granted,
the constant shape of your eyes.

When you were born, everyone said you looked
more like your father, though I insisted your chin was mine.

Tonight while we wait for the macaroni to soften,
we dance in the kitchen to the symphony of a priest.

As I recuperate from an ungraceful spin—
a second stilled in the light of your face—

I see me, but taller; me but prettier,
and with your father's chin.

LiLi
by Laura A. Lopez

she wears a plastic pink beaded necklace
to match red-hearted pink pajamas

her brassy four-year-old laughter
breaks the winter morning silence

and her white kitty slipper sways carelessly
above a yellow crayon on the floor

her tiny hands draw warmth
from a magical mug of hot cocoa

as she sings a silly rhyming song
on the merits of a marshmallow

nighttime with dorothea
by Rachel Iverson

1.

the room is dim,
light peeks out from the closet
vertical slats across the carpet.

i tromp over the dog bed
wearing last year's big-heeled boots

baby in one arm
shrugging, flinging.
my jacket falls to the floor.
i rip a velcro zipper apart and
step out of speckled pants.

she twitches in my arm.
her back arches. she squirms
to burrow her mouth into my
still shirt-encased chest.
she pitches her head back, with a grunt.

dog's ears perk into a couple
of triangles, and he scoots under the bed.
he too doubts i'll be fast enough.

plop onto the bed. i'm on my side, she's on her back,
lips pursed, cheeks twitching. her head lurches backward.
maybe six seconds left before her writhing and groaning
will shatter into screams.

i roll my tight tank top above my breasts.
no time to take it off. her neck is getting red.
her arms make a football goalpost and her hands ball into
fists. she snorts. i move closer, and waste half a second
wondering whether there's time to look for the t.v. remote,
but she whips her fist toward her mouth, and i tuck in beside her.
my head on a pillow, my palms against her cushy back, i shove her closer.

her round head bobs spastically,
her face crashes into my chest and i feel
her groping lips fumble and then she pulls
my nipple into her mouth.

i rub the soft tufts of hair on her head in circles.

she sucks. her body loses its rigidity.

so does mine.

2.
my husband sleeps in his territory.
it's almost another room
on the other side of the king bed.

i want to wake him up.
he should know what's going on.
he should see the way her mouth fits
perfectly around my nipple and sucks
with exactly the right pressure.

she's a genius. her dad should know.
who cares if it's past one in the morning.

i reach over to poke at him with my right foot
but i can't quite reach. i toss a pillow toward him,
but it sails over his back onto the floor next to the bed.
he stirs but doesn't wake. i grope for something else to lob
his way, but the only thing i find is an old copy of *People* magazine
wedged into the crack between the bed and the wall. it slips down
all the way underneath and the dog darts out with a yelp

i rest my head on the pillow again.
oh well, probably wouldn't be worth it anyway.
he'd wake, roll over, look at me, look at her and say
"yeah genius . . . amazing . . . see you in the morning."

just like he did last night.

she peeks at me from the corner
of her upturned eye,
single iris staring into my face
through the darkness.
her eyes crinkle,
she doesn't want to let go
to erupt into a full smile.
but i do. and now she
can't stop herself. her lips
disengage. she smiles a mouth
full of nipple and a single drop of
milk rolls down her chin and drips on
the sheet. i laugh. she squawks and
kicks the covers from her feet.
i lean over to kiss her cheek,
but she moves away and her gums grab my
nose. she smiles and shakes her open mouth

back and forth, finding my breast again.

until we're one person again
for tonight,

almost.

The Girl Is Mine
by Deesha Philyaw Thomas

On a rainy pre-Christmas December day, my friend Kristan and I strolled down the book aisle of Sam's Club, making gift selections and gifting ourselves with a few titles that had languished far too long on our "get" lists. Somewhere between *The Life of Pi* and *How to Cook Everything*, we ran into Kristan's aunt, whom I'd never met before. After introductions, the aunt (whose name I promptly forgot) peeked at the tiny baby snuggled in the fleece sling draped across my chest.

"Ohhhh! She's beautiful. A little peanut. How old?"

"Five weeks," I said.

"Five weeks?" the aunt sputtered. "But . . ." She gave my body a not-so-subtle once-over. "You look—great! How did you do it?" A real mystery: How had I managed to squeeze back into my button-fly not-too-low-riders so soon after giving birth? Where was that telltale postpartum bulge?

My shopping cart certainly attested to a recent addition to the family, even if my waistline didn't: a jumbo box of size 1–2 Pampers, a canister of Similac, enough baby wipes to last until the child went to kindergarten. Verdict: After several years' hiatus, I was back to baby days. Only this time around, it was minus the nine months of pregnancy, twenty-one hours of labor, and round-the-clock breastfeeding.

To Kristan's aunt, I explained, "I . . . didn't *have* her. She's . . . adopted."

Wait. That didn't come out the way I'd rehearsed it. What was with the pauses? And where was my proud, megawatt smile? This was not the way I'd intended to explain how my younger daughter came to be mine, in response to "I didn't know you were pregnant" and similar comments. I'd planned to be matter of fact about it all: I was this child's mother.

The story: A D&C in the wake of a miscarriage, and surgery to correct a cornual ectopic pregnancy three years after that, left me with only one Fallopian tube and more than a little scar tissue. My ob-gyn assured me that with a costly surgical procedure he might be able to remove the scar tissue adhering my one tube to my pelvic wall, and maybe after that the tube would work properly. Too many maybes for me. Besides, I'm no fan of hospitals, and my husband and I had already been blessed with a child (in between surgeries). We told the doctor, "No thanks," and immediately began discussing adoption. From the experiences of friends of ours, we knew of the joys and pains of the adoption process. We shared our friends' belief that as black people with the resources and desire to give a child a good home, we should consider the many black children whose childhoods are spent in foster care.

Still, it would be a few years of trying to find the "right" time to grow our family before we contacted an agency. One failed adoption followed that initial contact, but the experience actually strengthened our resolve to adopt and ultimately led us to our daughter.

When she was thirteen days old, two days after her birth parents surrendered their rights, we brought our baby girl to a hotel room in Chicago and, with her thrilled new big sister, made our first home together. We stayed at the hotel and then with friends until judges in Illinois and Pennsylvania agreed to let her leave and enter those states, respectively. We arrived home in Pittsburgh greeted by excited relatives and friends bearing Classic Pooh sleepers, tie-dyed receiving blankets, and frozen lasagnas. We told everyone it felt as if she'd always been with us, how she'd slipped quietly into our lives, blessing us and changing us forever. And we changed her name.

Five years ago, my husband, Mike, had named our first child Taylor Nicole. This time around, it was a joint effort. Peyton Imani—he chose "Peyton," I chose "Imani," which means "faith" in Kiswahili. I like "Peyton," though I primarily associated it with the movie *Peyton Place* and the line from Jeannie C. Riley's song "Harper Valley P.T.A.," in which the saucy mama tells off the town busybodies: "Well, this is just a little Peyton Place and you're all Harper Valley hypocrites!"

Mike's eyes had glazed over when I shared this bit of late-seventies trivia with him. He was otherwise engaged, preparing his "Manning—not Walter" explanation for the proper spelling of Peyton to interested parties and football aficionados.

Peyton Imani is the same name we'd chosen for another baby a few months earlier, a baby whose birth mother suddenly decided not to place her for adoption just as we were about to bring her home. Though the name is a reminder of that painful experience, we liked it so much we opted not to retire it like a sports jersey. Peyton I (Peyton the First) was a cute, chunky newborn who my mother-in-law now says never seemed like "ours," based on the pictures sent via email. I don't know. I thought Peyton I had my nose. She definitely had my big eyes. She looked like ours. But I understand where my mother-in-law is coming from. This is her way of embracing Peyton II, of welcoming her into a family and community with a rich history of formal and informal adoption. In fact, with Peyton's arrival, the adopted children now outnumber the biological children at certain gatherings of family and friends.

The hesitant words I spoke to Kristan's aunt that day in Sam's Club did not reflect the joy Peyton has brought to my life and to others. Though my body does not tell the story of her birth, I could not love her more if it did. I inhale her new-baby smell, marvel at her tiny fists gripping my fingers, and adapt to her warm presence against my chest in the sling, my constant companion.

And I believe the feeling is mutual. Peyton's almost immediate preference for me is destined for family lore. In the beginning, many nights found Mike, defeated, handing a wailing Peyton to me, only to have her settle down immediately in my arms. Now, at three months old, she still prefers being in my arms than anywhere else. When I'm not holding her, her eyes follow me constantly, with an occasional smile erupting across her sweet face.

I must confess that not long before Peyton's arrival, I'd grown cranky listening to new parents spout such things as I've just written in the two preceding paragraphs. With my preschooler Taylor under my belt, the cynic in me avoided people who assumed the minutiae of their babies' lives were as interesting to others as it was to them. But I'm glad to be back among the gushing. Now when I have occasion to explain Peyton's adoption, the words flow easily, and the message is clear: The girl is mine, and I am hers.

Chocolate
by Cassie Premo Steele

Margaret suddenly had a yearning for cake. Chocolate cake. She had six boxes of cake mix to choose from in the pantry. She took two from the shelf and set them on the counter. One looked very dark, and that was attractive. But the other said "pudding in the mix," and that clinched it. No woman with a hankering on a hot Saturday afternoon in summer could resist the promise of pudding in the mix.

So Margaret put the dark one back—she might make it for a special dinner for the man she'd been seeing. Dark chocolate was rich enough that you wouldn't eat too much and fall into bed in a chocolate stupor; it also pumped you up to stay awake for any late-night activities that might be on the agenda.

"Mom?" Jane was at the back door, dripping slightly in a bathing suit. She'd been swimming at the neighbor's pool.

Margaret decided not to say anything about the water.

"Yes?"

"Can I talk to you?"

Margaret smiled to herself. The girl was in the mood to talk. Nagging about the water dripping would have shooed her away. "Good save," the boyfriend would have said.

"Sure."

Jane sat down on the cushioned bench in the kitchen. Again Margaret said nothing about her wet state.

"I was just talking to Christine." Christine was a fourteen-year-old who lived down the street. She would start high school in the fall.

"Hmm?" Margaret poured oil into the cake mix.

"Christine says you don't usually like it your first time."

Margaret stopped stirring. There were still light brown, dry lumps in the batter.

"Does she know that for a fact?" Margaret's voice came out more jagged than she'd meant.

"No. She said her mom told her."

Margaret resumed stirring.

"So?" Jane asked.

"I wouldn't necessarily say that," Margaret said, not looking up.

"Well, what would you say?"

"Hold on." Margaret measured the water carefully, then added it to the batter. "Okay." She started stirring again. "I would say that it depends on how much you care about the person."

Jane stared at her, unblinking.

"I mean, for a woman, it seems to be important to care about the person you're with. And the more you care, the more you like it."

"There are girls at school who do it with all the boys, and they say they like it. They can't care about all those boys, can they?"

Margaret thought about this question while adding two eggs to the mix. It seemed to her that it was a sort of wet-swimsuit situation. If she freaked about the fact that girls at her daughter's middle school were having sex, the conversation would be derailed. Finally she said, "You're right. Not all girls have to care about the guys they are with. But I did."

This was a wild swing, she knew. It was a popper to the right field where she'd never hit one before. She must be spending too much time with Gary, she knew, to think of it this way.

"You did?" Jane's eyes were wide.

"Yes. I did. When I had sex, before I got married—a few times, not a lot—it would vary for me depending on how much I liked the person."

"You did?"

"Yes. I did," Margaret repeated.

"So, Mom," Jane said slowly. "Did you care about Daddy the most? Is that why you married him?"

Margaret put down the pan she was greasing. To answer this question meant going back in time, in a kind of warp speed, before she and Tom had achieved the amiable distance they now had, before the charred feelings developed the first year after the divorce, before the sour taste of the two years when she felt the split coming but was too afraid to say anything, before the happiness—yes, that's what it was, plain and simple—of the early years of Jane's life, back to the beginning.

"Yes," she said, honestly. "I loved your dad more than I've ever loved any other man."

"Even Gary?" Jane gasped.

"Yes." Margaret looked at her daughter plainly. "I like Gary, but . . ." Gary was a lawyer with two sons. He insisted on paying whenever the five of them went out for pizza or to a movie, and this annoyed Margaret. Sex with him was good, but she really couldn't imagine moving into his house, full of boys' baseball uniforms and model airplanes and posters of the solar system. And he wasn't the kind of man to move into a woman's house. Margaret knew, in that moment, that it would be over with Gary, and soon. "But I don't love him."

"So," Jane began. "Then why aren't you with Dad now?"

It had been years since Jane had asked this. The therapist had told them, when they split up, that she would come to understand it in new ways every few years.

"Did the sex get bad, Mommy, at the end?"

Clearly, when Jane was five, Margaret hadn't envisioned *this* conversation.

The simple answer was yes.

But Margaret wouldn't say it.

Instead, she took the white plastic spatula she was using to scrape the brown batter into two metal cake pans and held it out to her daughter.

"Here," she said. "Taste this."

Jane jumped up. "Really?"

"Yes, go ahead."

The girl brought her mouth down around the thick liquid clinging to the soft plastic and closed her eyes.

"Good?" her mother asked.

"*Mmm*," the girl moaned and smiled.

"There are raw eggs in there. Did you know that?"

Jane pulled it out of her mouth with a jerk.

"But you like it anyway, right?"

The girl hesitated.

"That's how sex is. Sometimes it's sweet. Sometimes it's dangerous. Sometimes there are things about it you don't want to know."

Margaret took the spatula from her, filled it up again with batter.

"But you know when you like it," Margaret said, and then flung the viscous mix at her daughter. It landed in her light brown hair.

"Mom!" Jane shrieked.

Margaret did it again. It landed on the small mound of her swimsuit top, covered its orange hibiscus flowers in chocolate.

"Here," Margaret said, passing Jane the bowl with one hand after filling her other hand with the dark sweet stuff. "Get me," Margaret said, smiling. She licked her index finger and waited.

Jane stood up and threw a large wad right at her mother's face. Margaret laughed and came closer, grabbing her and smearing her daughter's arms with it.

They both dove into the bowl again and again until all the batter was spread over them.

"Now lick your arm," Margaret said seriously.

"What?"

"Go ahead. Do it."

Jane did, tentatively.

It was warmer and waterier than it had been before. Jane could sense the tang of chlorine and the salt of sweat on her own body, too, underneath the velvet brown. There would always be, for the rest of her life, the memory of this taste in her mouth whenever she would make love.

"Jane, honey," Margaret said softly. "It doesn't matter what's in the batter as long as you like it. As long as it tastes good to *you*."

Jane took another lick.

"That's the important thing. It has to taste good on your own skin."

The Girl at the Side of the Road
by Peggy Duffy

I spotted her when I rounded a bend. She was by the side of the road, in the shadow of trees that line old Route 19, a slow narrow route into town. The road itself had swelled and cracked so many times as to be beyond repair. I used it as a shortcut because there were no traffic lights and no real traffic to speak of. The tree branches overhead had grown so close, their leaves an awning from the hot sun.

I slowed the van almost to a stop both because of the oncoming truck and the surprising sight of her. She was walking toward me, but not against traffic like I'd taught my own two girls. She was on the other side of the road. Her lips were painted deep red, her eyes outlined in black. It was early June, the air already thick and sweltering, almost palpable, and she had on short shorts and a skimpy black shirt, so tight I could see the outline of her breasts beneath the cloth.

The truck driver honked his horn, and she stopped and turned to follow his path, angling her head so that her long, dark hair swung across her face in harmony with the tilt of her hips. A flash of red as she smiled and waved. The leaves moved ever so slightly and she stood for a moment in the mottled light. A sway of her hips and she began to walk again. Despite the heavy makeup and the well-developed breasts, she appeared still a child, no older than my own twelve-year-old.

"Isn't that the girl on your soccer team?" I asked Kate.

She was in the back of the van, a spiral notebook on one knee and an open math book on the other. Her sister Ellen bounced from seat to seat in spite of my earlier warnings to sit still and wear her seat belt. Kate leaned into the glass and peered through the window. "Yeah, that's Sarah," she said.

I heard the sulky displeasure in her voice. "Why do you say it like that?" I asked.

"It's just that she thinks she's better than everyone else," Kate answered.

I debated with myself. Should I stop and offer her a ride or just drive by?

I looked through the window at this Sarah, my eyes searching out hers for a hint of what I should do, but the girl outside tossed her head away from my van and avoided my gaze.

I was left with a parting glimpse of her in the rearview mirror, a child playing at being a woman. A dangerous game. All the words of warning that should be spoken came into my head, all the things I would say to my own Kate if she were on the side of the road flirting with the drivers of passing trucks. I drove into town, windows closed, protected by the air-conditioning from the heat of the day.

Kate was such a good child, an obedient child, who rarely gave me a moment's grief. She did as she was told, I always knew where she was, and she didn't test the boundaries of our rules to see how far they would stretch, the things that cause a parent real grief.

Ellen was only seven, but already I worried about her. She had far more energy and friendliness than could be contained in such a small body, and she tended to release them in all the wrong places. She fussed in church, and when I eased my hand onto her shoulder, she reached up and yanked it off as if even the slight pressure of my touch was too much restraint for her to bear. She could not sit for an entire meal in a restaurant, not even McDonald's, and roamed the aisles while the rest of us finished eating. I would find her sitting with some lone diner who seemed cheered by her presence, chatting away while nibbling on her new friend's french fries. Once again, when we were back in the car, I would try to explain to her about strangers.

I pulled the van in front of Rowe's Department Store that day, and we went inside in search of a few things for Kate. She had grown so quickly over the past few months, nothing she owned fit anymore. But it was difficult to find new clothes for her. She was too tall and a bit wide for the larger girls' sizes, too straight for juniors.

Kate and I headed for the sale rack while Ellen went to play with the stuffed animals at a nearby display. She was rushing back within minutes to show me the dark green turtle puppet she'd found and had slipped over her hand. In her excitement, she bumped into a woman studying price tags at the other end of the rack. The woman was one of those middle-aged types who had forgotten what her own grown-up children were like when they were younger, remembering only their perfection. She eyed my imperfect child through a disapproving scowl. Ellen glared back at her.

I made my way to where they stood and mumbled sorry, adding something about her high energy level that I always hated myself for afterward. I pulled Ellen to me, repeating that tired, worn-out phase that always passes between us, "When are you going to learn to watch where you're going?" As we turned, I felt the woman's scorn on my back. She had to overhear me bribe my youngest daughter into submission.

"Ellen, if you can stand here quietly, without moving, for just five minutes, I'll buy you some ice cream."

I knew she wanted that ice cream, but she couldn't stay put even for the small amount of time it took me to figure out there was nothing in the store suitable for Kate. Before I knew it, Ellen was no longer by my side but crawling under the rack, clothes falling from hangers in her wake.

"I thought I saw a dollar bill," she said as we were leaving the store. I knew I was going to buy her the ice cream anyway, like I always did, because I wanted to believe she really tried.

We placed our orders beneath the pink and white striped canopy at the window outside Sally's Ice Cream Palace, then seated ourselves at one of the tables on the sidewalk. Ellen licked the chocolate ice cream leaking over the top of her cone and onto her hands, while Kate contemplated the colored sprinkles in her cup. I sipped my coffee and found myself searching my memory through the lineup of parents at the Saturday soccer games, trying to pair the girl on old Route 19 with the adults she belonged to.

"How well do you know Sarah?" I asked Kate.

She stirred the sprinkles into her ice cream, then piled as much of the mixture as was possible onto her plastic spoon and popped it into her mouth. "Why do you want to know?" she asked through puckered lips.

"Just curious."

"Why?" she repeated.

It amazed me, although it shouldn't, how children always seemed so protective of one another, even when they didn't like each other. "I was just wondering, that's all," I said. "I mean, she's on your soccer team, but I don't know anything about her. I don't even remember meeting her parents."

"She's one of the popular girls at school," Kate said.

They were in seventh grade. I wasn't too old to remember what popular meant in seventh grade. "With the boys?" I asked.

"I guess," Kate said. She spooned another huge glob of ice cream into her mouth.

"Kate has a boyfriend," Ellen said. She clutched the soggy remains of her cone in one hand, raised it above her head and slurped the leftover drips of chocolate ice cream out the bottom with a satisfied sound.

"Shut up," Kate said to her sister.

"You do?" I asked, truly surprised. Too surprised to remind her how much I disliked her using those two words. "Since when?"

"Mom, it's no big deal," Kate said.

I watched her raise another spoonful of ice cream to her lips and thought about Kate having a boyfriend, a nameless boyfriend who was no big deal.

"How come I didn't know you had a boyfriend?"

She looked annoyed. "I said it's no big deal."

I took a sip of coffee. "Well, does he have a name?"

"Mom, I don't want to talk about it, okay?" Kate angled her head and gave me a sideways, arrogant look, eyes defiant, which lasted just a few seconds, before she turned her attention back to her ice cream. I watched her finish eating, all I should have said left unspoken, silenced by the window of trust she'd closed between us.

I missed the first half of the soccer game on Saturday. It was the last game of the season, and Kate's team was undefeated. So was the other team. The winner would be the league champion.

I was locking the car door when Ellen took off ahead of me. I followed the trail of her footsteps over to the soccer field, the limp blades of grass flattened by the soles of her sneakers. The sun shone above my head through a haze of midday heat.

The girls were scattered along the sidelines, some drinking water, others pouring it over their heads. I scanned their faces searching for Kate and spotted Ellen's short, blond hair, someone's water bottle already lifted to her lips. I saw Sarah talking to a woman I had never seen before, her mother I guessed, and headed their way. The woman wore knee-length tan shorts and a loose-fitting, white cotton, button-down shirt. I'd pictured someone taller and younger, in black stretch shorts and crop top perhaps, not this shapeless, older mother with salt-and-pepper hair and spidery varicose veins creeping up the back of her legs.

Kate was standing beside the coach, and I waved at her so she'd know I was there. The coach called the rest of the girls over. Sarah said something to her mother I couldn't hear, tossed her water bottle onto the ground, and joined the team for some last-minute instructions. This Sarah bore no resemblance to the girl I'd seen at the side of the road. Her black baggy Umbros hung halfway to her knees, in stark contrast to the tight jean shorts which had barely covered or concealed the curve of her from behind. She looked like the child she was—dark hair pulled into a ponytail, face flushed from the heat of the game.

"Do you know the score?" I asked her mother.

"Zero–zero," she said without looking my way.

"I'm Joan Adams," I said and waited for her reply. She turned toward me, but didn't say anything. "Kate's mom," I added, but it was clear from the blank look she gave me she didn't know who Kate was.

"Susan Wilson," she said, extending her hand. "Sarah's mom."

"Nice to meet you," I said. The girls were lining up on the field, our team in red, the other in yellow, ready to start the second half of the game. "How'd the girls play first half?"

"Well enough, I guess."

"I hate missing any of the game. I promised Kate I'd be here, but my little one is so pokey and uncooperative. . . ." I had that apologetic tone to my voice that I dislike so much.

"I work at the hospital most Saturdays," she said, with warmth and understanding. "I don't get to see many of the games myself. My husband usually comes." I tried to visualize her husband, a graying man, slightly overweight too, but I couldn't recall having seen anyone who fit that description.

The referee blew his whistle, the other team took the kickoff and with a swiftness that always caught me by surprise, the girls and the ball were all in motion at the same time. Sarah intercepted the ball and ran toward the goal. A girl in yellow came at her from behind, and Sarah kicked the ball across the field to one of her teammates.

"Sarah's a real good player," I said.

"Is she?"

"She's one of the best players on the team." Susan didn't say anything. It was clear she didn't know this either. We watched the game for a while. Sarah was all over the ball. My own Kate wasn't nearly as fast or aggressive. She played left fullback and tended to stay back, waiting for the ball to come to her.

"She's our youngest," Susan said. "None of the others ever played." She stated it as fact, without excuse. I felt comfortable with her and found myself liking her.

"How old are your other kids?"

She laughed. "Oh, hardly kids anymore. My two oldest girls are married. One of my boys is at Cornell and the other's in the army stationed over in Germany." She looked at me and in a confessional tone, one mother to another, added, "Sarah was a bit of a surprise, as you can imagine."

Sarah had the ball again and was running with it up the field. She took a shot on goal, but the ball hit the corner of the goalpost and bounced out of bounds. A player on the opposing team ran to get it and their goalie took the kick, a nice high one. The ball flew halfway up the field.

"Five children. I have a hard enough time with two. I couldn't imagine five," I said.

"It was a lot of work. First four were real close in age. Of course, I was a lot younger then," she said. Sarah had possession of the ball again and was outrunning the other team's defensive line up the field. "Hard to keep up with that one sometimes."

I thought about whether I should tell this woman I'd just met, who'd successfully raised four children, about Sarah. "I saw your daughter the other day, on old Route 19," I ventured. I figured I'd work my way up to the waving and flirting.

"Yeah, it's a good hike into town from our house, about a mile or so, but she's at that age where she wants to go shopping, and with work and all, I can't always be there to drive her." She looked at Sarah, who was running free of interception toward the goal. "They have to spread their wings before they can learn to fly, I always say. Before you know it, they've left your nest and are off building their own."

Sarah was just outside the goal box. The other parents on the sideline were screaming, "Shoot, shoot"; but Sarah waited and her timing was perfect. When the goalie came out, Sarah dribbled around her and shot the ball into the corner of the net. The parents cheered, and out on the field our girls jumped up and down, one by one high-fiving Sarah as they took up their positions again. I looked at Kate. She gave me a triumphant smile.

"Okay, just hold them off," the coach yelled. "There's only five minutes left. You just have to hold them off."

And they did. When the referee blew his whistle signaling the end of the game, the score was still one–nothing and our team had the league championship. The girls came flying off the field, ablaze with victory, yelling and screaming and hugging each others' sweaty bodies.

It was a league ritual for the parents of the winning team to congratulate the girls by making a human tunnel for them to run through. We took our places on the center line, two parallel rows of parents. I stood facing Sarah's mother. Arms held high, we reached across and clasped our hands together, the heat of the sun pressing down on our bent backs. Her grip was strong, sure of itself. As the last girl ran under our arms, yelping a celebratory cry, and the coach asked the girls to meet him under the large oak tree at the top of the hill to hand out the trophies, I realized I had no idea where Ellen was.

I missed hearing the coach praise Kate's performance that season and seeing her get her first-place trophy because I was walking the park, looking and calling for Ellen. And though she always turned up somewhere, I couldn't help but feel during those moments of fear that this time she was lost for good. When seconds dragged into minutes and soon the notion of time itself began to lose all meaning, and the sound of panic became audible in the quiver of my voice, I swore to myself I would never, ever get impatient with her again if only I could find her.

This time I found her at the other end of the park, sitting on a bench by one of the baseball fields, watching a little league game. She sported a baseball cap that she swore someone gave her for keeps. At any rate, nobody claimed it as I took her hand and led her back to the hill overlooking the soccer fields where one of the mothers was passing out ice pops from her cooler.

The trophies were huge, more than two feet high, each with a marble base and the figure of a girl kicking a soccer ball perched on top of a gold cup. Susan stood with her arm around Sarah, their faces beaming, Sarah's trophy held high between them. I went over to admire Kate's and give her a hug. Her skin felt hot and sticky, but her arms remained cool and limp by her sides. I pulled my arm from her shoulder. "What's wrong?" I asked, and at the same time felt Ellen's hand slip from mine. She darted to the front of the line of girls, elbowing a few aside, and grabbed a handful of ice pops from the cooler.

"Nothing," Kate said in that voice a mother knows means everything.

Ellen handed me the crumpled wrappers from her ice pops and went to run down the hill. Kate rolled her eyes and stuck out her foot. Ellen stumbled and, in recovering her balance, dropped one of the ice pops on the ground. She shrieked, and Kate said "sorry" in the most sarcastic tone imaginable.

"What's gotten into you?" I said.

"Like you don't know." She slapped the trophy into my hand. "Here, take it."

"Kate . . ." I started, all I should say coming into my head.

"I don't want to hear it, okay? I'll meet you at the van," she said and stomped off. Even in her baggy soccer shorts I could see that the thickness of her waist had moved downward and was settling in as budding hips. I'd been missing a lot with Kate.

I sensed the pause in activity that often accompanied these confrontations. A few of the mothers turned and watched Kate. Susan merely caught my eye and winked. Then she and her daughter turned and headed toward the parking lot, the grass below their feet already flattened from the footsteps of all the parents and children who'd crossed the field that day.

I should have told her about Sarah. About how she'd looked and acted at the side of the road. I could list so many reasons why I hadn't. Who was I to tell a woman with four grown children, who surely knew better than me, not to let her daughter walk alone on a little-used road into town? Who was I to judge her mothering when she hadn't judged mine?

Ellen ran over and wrapped her skinny arms around my waist. "Come on, come on," she sang and grabbed my empty hand. She pulled on one arm and the weight of Kate's trophy pulled on the other. Halfway to the parking lot, Ellen let go and skipped ahead, the sticky remains of her ice pops clinging stubbornly to my palm. I made my way to where my two daughters waited, unlocked the van, and we climbed inside. But when I started it up, the air-conditioning wouldn't come on. We drove home in silence, the afternoon heat through the open window like a fresh bruise rising against the side of my cheek.

That's an image that would remain with me always—their faces beaming, Sarah's with success and her mother's full of pride. Because three months later, on a hot and humid August afternoon, when the mercury hit a high of ninety-six, Sarah disappeared. According to the newspaper account I read and the gossip that spread with suburban speed, she'd last been seen around noon walking on old Route 19.

I asked around and found out where Susan lived. I let a few days pass before I drove over alone late one afternoon, a freshly made chili casserole on the front seat beside me. I came to offer solace and hope in the only way I knew how, although the general consensus by then was leaning toward hopelessness.

When I pulled up to the house, there were cars in the driveway with out-of-state plates. Her older children, no doubt. I sat in the van, gazing through the window, thinking about what I would do and say when she answered the door. I hadn't seen her since the day of the soccer game. Would she even remember me? Yet I felt a kinship, a sharing of grief and guilt with this woman I didn't really know. I could imagine her pain, the moment when panic gave way to fear and that timeless sense of loss.

I was ashamed to admit, I had judged her. When she told me she allowed her daughter to walk alone into town, I'd viewed her with that same self-righteous eye as those women who watch me with Ellen, forgetting for the moment what my own children were like. Because it could just have easily been Kate or Ellen at the side of the road, testing the boundaries, seeing how far they would stretch before they might burst, like hips pushing against the side seams of a pair of shorts.

What was it Susan had said that day?

They have to spread their wings before they can learn to fly.

Yes, I would tell her, but they learn to crawl before they walk, too, and then they can get up and walk away. How long do we hold on to them, and how tight, and how do we know when to let go? Perhaps we never do. All we can do is watch, hands clenched over our hearts, praying they find their way back.

Beautiful Daughter
by Mary Moore

The birch shadows compose and loosely
rein in the red-gold light-shards her skin
throws off. One shadow branch almost bridles
the powers arcing their shoulders inside her,
bristling their lion-colored manes. They are
barely contained. This gives her skin
the effulgence of adobe, smeared with sun.

Some days she is braiding her hair when I
look, making two puma-colored ropes she
coils around her head; but loosened, her hair
is lithe and fluid as rain. She shies
away from his eyes, whose corners graze her
with their green lights. Some of her flies away
at the least touch like wild horses; some of her stays.

Eclipse
by Marguerite Guzman Bouvard

This strange dusk at noon, masking
a fire that can sear our vision
with its intensity, the radio warning us
to shield our eyes.
It is noon for you also,
my daughter, and darkness travels
across your fierce light.
I make a pinhole for a few words;
"How are you?" I ask lightly,
as if I could journey through space,
as if I could touch that raw
flaming. I am your mother
but I cannot pull the moon
down from the sky.

III.

Mothers Raising Men,
Exploring Mothering

Boy Child
by Ona Gritz

The stray ballpoint, a gun.
Umbrella, a sword.
Hands empty,
the air gets a roundhouse kick.

Is this typical "boy" I want to ask.
Or just typical of this boy?
Past bedtime he's enacting battles,
strategies elaborate as chess rules.

Finally, he crash-lands beside me,
seeks my shoulder, slurs "Mommy . . ."
I stroke his sweat-damp hair
until, shifting position, he sleeps,
arms thrown back in surrender.

When You're Ten
by Lisa McMann

In the summer, my brother put on his wooly brown-bear coat and black ski mask, ran around in the front yard, and we took turns shooting at him with a BB gun.

I learned guns and hunting with my father and Sandy, our cocker spaniel. First with a paper target on a hay bale from thirty feet, then with real-life targets on four feet, or with wings. I stomped on pricker bushes with tall, green boots. I held my gun pointed up and away, clenching it tight enough to make my knuckles ache. Four giant steps behind my father, I knew I would not shoot until he said it was okay.

At my father's urging, I took my first shot at something I would have taken home as a pet the day before. The thrill of a moving target became instantly more exciting than Atari. I smelled the gamey scent of warm, dead pheasant and rabbit, and hardly flinched when my father shot final bullets into their brains to stop the tremors.

Back home, I showed my mother the swollen, red-prickled skin on my shoulder—a result of the gun's kick. She touched it gently and smiled, then turned back to the pot of boiling water on the stove.

"Rabbit stew," she said.

I nodded, swallowing hard.

I am not ready yet.

"When you're ten," I replied, every time he asked.

Twice, three times a year, that question again. It seemed so far off. I shivered at the thought, displaced it. Until now. He's ten.

"Be calm, don't jump around."

"I know."

"When is a gun loaded?"

"Always."

"Listen to Grandpa and Dad."

"I know."

"If you kill yourself, I'll kill you, you know."

"I know."

"Be careful."

"Mom!" He jiggles in too-large boots. "Can I go now?" Eagerness pools at the rims of his wise eyelids. He measures a proud fifty-six inches, only an inch and a half shy of his grandmother. I nod and he's off.

I wonder what makes me so shy of guns now. Is it Columbine? Is it the man-and-child sniper team? Constant images of a war-torn Middle East? The media that drags us through every sickening action a hundred times a day from a dozen different angles?

Perhaps my shyness stems from apprehension. If my child touches a gun, perhaps he'll be branded as a potential killer. If he speaks proudly in eavesdropped hallways at school about shooting a gun, will we be called to confer with the principal? Will other parents shield their children from mine? After so consciously avoiding all toys resembling weapons during my son's early years, have I talked myself into a state of such political correctness that I would consider stripping my child of a pastime I treasured?

Perhaps it's his cool, soft boy cheeks and my own eyes staring back at me. I remember shooting at my brother in his furry coat, and imagine the tragedies that could have resulted, tragedies I never considered at the time. We were reckless and lucky. I think of the trust my father had in me, to allow me to walk behind him with a loaded weapon. I don't think I have that trust yet for my child, not now, maybe not ever. I wonder if my parents should have had it for me.

I turn on the TV and blow-dry my hair, but I can still hear the popping sounds outside the window. I pull aside the curtain and see my son standing tall between his father and grandfather. My husband catches my eye, and assures me with a crooked smile and a nod.

When my boy comes in, I know he will proudly show me his battered paper target, and I will be impressed. And then we will have hot chocolate with marshmallows while he tells me in a suddenly deep voice about the coldness of the steel, the roar of the shot, the thrill of the bull's-eye.

In anticipation, and to take my mind off the worrying, I search through the box of photos marked "1978." I find the right one just as I hear cheering from outside, and I pull it out. It's fading, but clearly I see a long-haired girl standing in a yellow-gray field of corn stalks, wearing a baseball cap, a .22 at her shoulder, and a smile as wide as Tennessee.

Ten felt so much older back then.

Albion Street
by Amy Burditt

I see him from the window of my son's room. He has good bones and paper-white skin and dark, greasy hair. I bet he smells like sweat and smoke and unwashed hair. He crouches between the parked cars with his needle and a crumpled brown bag. I'm not entirely sure of the process although I've watched it dozens of times from my second-story window. His arms are waxy and his backbones poke out when he pulls the black sweatshirt over his head to get at his arm. People walk by, and this isn't an unfamiliar sight on my street, so they just pass. He gives them a half-apologetic smile if they look too carefully. It seems to my eye that it's a lot harder to get a vein than it ought to be. He stabs, when it seems like it should slide under his skin.

Sometimes I pound on the window. He looks around, but never up. I watch his head fall back, and after a minute he gets up, scans the pavement to make sure he hasn't left anything and scurries off.

I see him in the early mornings as I drink my coffee. Chubby little Mexican girls in Catholic school uniforms run past him, and I can hear the *slap, slap* of their sandals on the sidewalk. Sometimes I'm out walking my dog with the baby strapped to my chest, and I see him crouched in the familiar way between cars. I cross the street rather than get the apologetic smile.

At bath time, I run my hands over the baby's silky, warm skin and think of needles and dirt and God knows what he has to do at night for that crouched morning pleasure.

He looks like the kind of guy I used to date. I would wake up cotton-mouthed on his futon. I'd knock over the full ashtray with my bare feet on the way to the bathroom. I would have to resist the prissy urge to hover over the filthy toilet seat and it would sting when I peed.

I see him with his shirt off in the park—long skinny arms and visible bones in his chest. The sweatshirt is spread on the grass next to him like a black jellyfish. He has his head back, face toward the sun, same position as after the needle push, only now he can hold it, linger in this warmth. There are lines around his eyes. In the yellow summer light, he looks older, more solid. Less like a scurrying kid, less like some furtive skateboard punk. He looks adult. His pale skin shines, and I think absently of the sunscreen I now carry in my bag.

The baby's skin is smooth and pink and is so soft that there really isn't a word for its touch. I rub his back and his fat legs, creased and dimpled. I kiss his knees and put his little hands in my mouth and suck each finger. I know as he grows his body will become his own, and I'll never have this tactile pleasure again. His skin will change texture, and he'll have scabs on his knees, then hair on his legs, and then I'll have to remember that this is the same person, the same body.

I see him pull his pants down and shoot into his thigh. He's scavenging for needle entrances. His face is covered with scratches and scabs.

I picture him clear-eyed, working at the video store. He smiles at the baby while he rings me up. We discuss the movies I've picked out. He's seen them all. Or I imagine the paramedics coming. They never hurry, like they do in the movies. At least, not on this street. They step down from the van, no break in their conversation. They stretch him out on the sidewalk.

I jiggle the baby on my hip while I consider both scenarios. They both make me feel lighter. I realize I don't have enough love to save him, to make him well. I want him out of sight. Gone, it doesn't matter how. I resent his dirty intrusion into our soft world of songs and milk and warm water. My new-mother love isn't strong enough to embrace the world. Instead, I hold the baby so tight he cries.

Analyzing Ben
by Jennifer Eyre White

Before I had Ben, I wondered if the gazillions of mothers who claimed that boys are massively different from girls were exaggerating. And even if they weren't, it seemed to me that this difference would probably show up around puberty. A mere sixteen months after the birth of my son, however, I've been able to empirically determine that, in fact, boys are massively different from girls.

As an engineer with a fondness for data, I've been preoccupied with trying to quantify the differences I've observed between Ben and his big sister, Riley. Now I admit, my sample size is small and I have no control group, but after extensive observation I have concluded that Ben is 15.3 times more likely to do something dangerous and/or violent per hour than Riley was at the same age. Or at any age. They do not appear to be from the same species. She cuddles and tickles him; he yanks her hair and tries to poke her eyes out. Her first word was "book"; his first (and so far, only) word was "uh-oh." I've compiled a few additional stats on my kids, and I'll share them with you here:

Instances of:	Riley, 16 mos.	Ben, 16 mos.
Eating dirt	None	Uncountable
Hitting	A few	Uncountable
Plugging things into other things	A few	Uncountable
Sitting in my lap, being read to	A lot	Two
Engaging in acts of wanton destruction	A few	A billion

Other relevant data:		
Number of words spoken	About 15	About zero (does "uh-oh" count?)
Objects used as hammers	Hammers	Just about everything

In the process of compiling this data, I have come to identify strongly with the famous primatologist Jane Goodall, who spent years living amongst chimpanzees in the jungles of Africa. As I sit on the couch watching Ben and Riley, I think of Jane squatting in the forest, scribbling in her notebooks, trying to unravel the mysteries of chimp behavior. She spent hours observing her subjects in their natural habitat; me too. Jane's subjects had much in common with human beings; mine too. We are not so very different, Jane and I.

Certainly I had expected to see personality differences between my two children; what's come as a shock is just how closely their behavior differences align with common gender stereotypes, and just how early these differences manifested themselves. From what I can tell, however, Ben appears to be fairly typical of youthful masculinity. I recall, for example, when the six-year-old son of a good friend earnestly told me what he had learned in school one day, with his own special interpretation: "Safety first," he told me seriously, then added with a grin, "danger later!" I remember watching Ben go on a destructive breaking-banging-hitting-screaming-whirling-dervish episode a few months ago, and shaking my head as I asked my husband afterward, "How do you people [men] function in society when this is what lives inside of you?"

He knew exactly what I meant, and he had no answer.

I can't help but notice that, unlike my daughter, my darling son is inordinately preoccupied with Things That Plug into Other Things. I can see, in my mind's eye, his interview with his high school counselor, trying to determine what to study in college. "I like to plug things into other things," Ben will say. "Ah yes," the counselor will respond, checking a box, "you must go to engineering school." Because that's what all the really good engineers are like. My engineer husband, for example, has only the thinnest veneer over this primal urge to plug. Ben once observed his dad using an electric drill; and as soon as the little guy had the chance, he grabbed the drill, successfully plugged in a new drill bit, and tried to turn the thing on. I was somewhat appalled by this episode, but my husband and son could not have been more pleased. I caught the two of them exchanging smiles that bordered on the maniacal. "Yikes," I said softly.

In another example of the plugging thing, Ben recently discovered how to stuff his finger up his nostril. As he walked around with his forefinger rammed in up to the second knuckle, I could see a glow of happiness ("So *that's* what it's for!") suffusing his face. My little cherub.

And if fingers are fun, penises are even better. If you have a boy child yourself, you must have noticed that they really like to play with this particular appendage. Apparently penises, like fingers, need to be explored and experimented upon by their owners, though I assume that it will be years before Ben understands how they fit into the grand plugging scheme. From Ben, I have learned that penises are—in terms of elasticity, anyway—not that different from rubber bands. He recently spent an entire bath time yanking on his, and after one particularly hard tug I could swear it went *BOINGGGGG!* when he let go. He's not gentle when it comes to exploring body parts, whether they belong to him or to some unfortunate bystander (me, for example).

I have found it to be extremely difficult to discourage Ben from engaging in active (and often destructive) exploration of the world around him. In this sense, I think that Jane Goodall had it easy. She only had to observe her subjects, not try to control the little beasts. There is virtually no area of our home that has not been thoroughly investigated, and I do not say this with great joy. I remember when my daughter was a baby I scoffed at the toilet-seat-lock thingies—what kind of pathetic parent, I wondered, can't teach her child not to play with the potty? With Riley, all it took was a firm "no," and that was that. Ben, in contrast, considers the toilet his personal spa. It does not matter how many firm "nos" there are, how many times I dump him in his crib to make my point, or, for that matter, how many times he crunches his own fingers by dropping the lid on them.

Just today, for example, I noticed that he had been playing quietly in the bathroom for about ten seconds—and with Ben, quiet is never good. I walked into the bathroom and saw that he had lifted the toilet lid and was up to his elbows in potty water, cackling wildly. "Benjamin!" I growled in my most dangerous tone, which made him swish all the harder and chortle all the more joyfully. "Are you aware that you're possessed by Satan, or does he do it without you knowing?" I muttered as I dragged him away.

In yet another exciting episode, the little guy pulled a step stool up to the kitchen counter (this was before I realized he actually knew what stools were for—you'd think the drill episode would have taught me something, but apparently not), climbed up, grabbed his box of dry oatmeal cereal, and dumped the entire carton on the floor. I found him sitting in what looked like a pile of snowflakes, grabbing handfuls, and dumping them over his head. When I changed his diaper later, he had sticky oatmeal goo smeared all around places where oatmeal really should never be. Maybe I've just forgotten, but I don't believe my daughter ever managed to get breakfast cereal pasted on to her private parts. She simply didn't have the requisite drive to climb, grab, and dump that so strongly propels Ben, and that so often yields unfortunate results.

Now don't get me wrong; my daughter is far from passive. Riley's actually a soccer-karate-tetherball-tag-playing tomboy. She's certainly not a girlie girl, and until I had Ben, I never thought of her as being particularly feminine (in the dainty, froufrou sense). So I had expected that having a boy wouldn't really be that much different. It's only by having the contrast of Ben the Boy Baby that I've realized how many gender stereotypes are being played out in our household.

Until now, I had never noticed the way she has always been able to sit for long periods of time with her hands quietly resting in her lap. How she could admire a flower without mashing it into little pieces. How she was always more interested in watching my facial expressions and communicating with me than in trying to stick her fingers up my nose. How she went through her entire babyhood without, to my knowledge, plugging an extension cord into itself more than a couple of times. I understand her; we instinctively connect. She's a normal person, after all. And Ben—my baffling, infuriating, adorable Ben—is a boy.

Packing the Car
by Linda Lee Crosfield

he packs the car with memories
his, not mine
in crates and boxes he takes
from the house like evidence
removed from the scene of a crime

I watch as he stands back
surveys his work
his eyes narrow
and he leans into the car
adjusts a box this way
turns another on its side
making everything fit
making room for
just one more

as I watch him I remember
the first jigsaw puzzle we did together
I kept putting his hand on the right piece
showing him how best to place it
here
or here
until he frowned and said
he could do it himself
and did

I stand aside
watch helplessly
as books stream from shelves

into boxes, out the door
and I envy them their invitation
to accompany him on this journey
to the rest of his life

gradually I'll notice little things
the phone will stop being for him
there'll be one less toothbrush
by the bathroom sink
and milk will last longer than a day

but right now
the dog who's famous
for her big brown eyes
closes them tight
when he says goodbye
and her tail droops
lower than my heart
as tires crunch
against the gravel in the driveway
and he drives off
into the late summer morn

How to Make a Meat Pie and Other Tales of the Ambitious Mother
by Lisa Rubisch

Making a meat pie for your infant requires love, patience, and every pot you own, but yields unexpected delights.

First, broil a gorgeous piece of meat. It should cost the price of a new pair of shoes. Then gather fresh vegetables, about sixty different kinds. Peel, de-seed, chop, and roast. Next, make mashed potatoes from scratch; you know the drill. Since your infant lacks teeth, locate the Cuisinart, which you have never used, dust out the stray hairs and dead bugs from its container; try to figure out the blade while avoiding amputation. Place all of the ingredients into its belly and push go. Feel terrific about this milk shake of meaty love you've created for your son.

Later this afternoon, feed it to him in spoonfuls at a downtown café, ignoring stares from the People Without Children, those lucky enough to have only recently awakened for the day. Just don't be too surprised when the meat milk shake is barfed out at such violent velocity that later you will be picking this meat pie from your bra in the restroom. How did it get in there, you will wonder, and why does it look exactly the same coming out as it did going in? Try not to be secretly thrilled about the horrified faces of The People Without Children, as, not unlike the prom-goers in the movie *Carrie*, they get sprayed with the creamy, beefy puke.

The meat pie is just one example of what happens when I do not work. The workaholic self creeps, ghostlike, into the body of the mothering self. And when I work, the mothering self raises her eyebrows, hands on hips, and wags a guilt-inducing finger.

Working and mothering create a devastating dance. The question is, how can I be perfect at both?

As a commercial director, I am lucky. When I work, I work hard. But days go by where the only time spent with Owen is when he is asleep. My jobs last a month. This is exquisite torture. When I am not working, I am home. We reconnect like long-lost lovers; we kiss so passionately and so often, my husband says, "That looks weird." But the transition between the two is never seamless.

Here is what happens when I *am* working:

About six months ago, I took Owen to a music class. I was in the middle of a big job but snuck out for one precious hour. We were sitting in a circle, in an echoey, blond dance studio, my son shy and clingy, when in walked another mother-son duo. Owen's eyes went wide and he said, "Mommy?"

This mother looked a little like me—dark hair, big eyes, a red sweater like mine. I smiled. Shrugged at the other moms.

Until he got up, toddled over to her, and shrieked, "Mommy!"

His tiny voice was suddenly large, looming in the hall. A little amused, a little embarrassed, I pulled at his arm—"No, sweetie, *I'm* your mommy." He shook his head. He pointed to her.

"Mommy!"

He climbed into her lap and buried his head into her bosom, her pillowy, full bosom—my own bosom having long since melted into candle-wax drippings. She was the better version of me—softer, rounder, available. The other mother's son was busy strumming on the vent at the back of the room, so she said it was fine for Owen to sit with her, and she continued to cuddle my son.

It was a lonely walk back to my orange mat on the floor. Singing the *Lone Ranger* theme song with a group—a cappella no less—is impossible to do when your heart is broken. Owen howled when I pried him from her at the end of class.

That night, I called my pediatrician, Googled "reincarnation," and sobbed in the shower.

The other day, Owen and I entered Washington Square Park, where we stumbled upon a film crew. I ran into Reggie, the camera assistant from my crew.

"Whatcha shooting?" I asked him.

"A commercial for Puma," he said.

"Hmmm. Puma. I did a Puma job once." I tried not to sound, god forbid, jealous.

After we waved our goodbyes, I couldn't help but think of the great job I did for Puma. People said it was an especially good Puma commercial. Therefore, shouldn't I do all the Puma jobs? I mean, how could they, the Puma Corporation, do a job in my own backyard without me? With one eyeball on my son and one across the park at the film crew, I strained to relax and ignore that green ache in my stomach.

But when a little boy with a tiny Afro came into the park with Thomas the Train, my son went absolutely ballistic. My son covets trains the way I covet jobs. And Tiny Afro wasn't sharing. Owen picked himself up and threw himself to the ground repeatedly as though bouncing on a bed. He banged his head on the gravel. He screamed, "Thomas! My Thomas!" and did that thing two-year-olds do.

And as he flailed, with snot streaming down his neck, I suddenly threw myself to the ground and cried, "MY JOB, MINE! Mine-oh-mine-oh-MINE!" I stamped my feet. I banged my head on the gravel. And I screamed. I screamed for all the jobs I would do and all the jobs I wouldn't do. I screamed for the look on my little one's face when the nanny shows up. I screamed for the look on my mother's face, the way she raises her eyebrows when I tell her I won another job. I screamed for the lascivious producers who have asked me on break, "You gonna go . . . pump?" I screamed because there are too few hours in the day. I screamed for guilt and ambition, for love and for death. I screamed and bawled and flailed and thrashed. Then there was silence.

There is something to be said for a tantrum. My son and I caught each other's eyes lying there on the pavement by the slide, the gravel sparkly in the sun. We both sniffled, rubbed our eyes because we were tired, realized that maybe we needed a snack and definitely a hug.

Slowly, we got up and went to each other. I smoothed out my red raincoat. I helped him into his stroller. I wiped both our noses. And as we strolled past the shocked nannies and mothers, past the Puma ad agency and crew, it occurred to me that there is no perfect job and there never will be.

My son and I went home and had lunch. Since I was not working and we had the whole afternoon in front of us, I decided to make a meat pie, of sorts. This time, we made it together, out of hot dogs and string cheese and leftover spaghetti.

It just might be the most delicious thing yet.

Son of a Bitch

by garrie keyman

he slipped away
as smoothly
as he had slipped from my womb
when he had shot out
slick and flailing
small fists
cocked defiantly
at a world into
which he had
reluctantly
come

they never told me
to stop pushing
so by fourteen
he was completely
out of sight

IV.

Sex, Fertility, and the Body

Matermorphosis
by KerryAnn Cochrane

A candle flickers,
Shadows dance erotic on wall,
Curves sway, make waves.
Cloth is shed, left behind
Like skin from snake's body.
Arms and legs weave into
Kama Sutra poses,
Fingers stroke hair
Silk flowing down back,
And her breasts,
Her breasts
Are desire and passion.
Her back arches,
Two bodies
Now
One.
One, two
Buckle my shoe.
Three, four
Someone's at the door.
Calling, crying,
Crying
Mommy.
The candle sputters,
Shadows untangle and wither,
A frantic search
For flannel pajamas
Inside out on the floor.
Arms and legs weave into

Cradle rocking, swaying,
Fingers twist hair,
Soft, unruly curls,
And her breasts,
Her breasts
Are comfort and safety.
They fill with milk
Two bodies
Now
One.
Matermorphosis complete.
Lover to Mother.

Sanctuary
by Peggy Hong

Balding, with a holistic practice. He pulls his trousers over his mild
paunch, my dentist. In the bathroom of the nineteenth-century building he has
meticulously rehabbed is a calligraphic poster of "Twelve Signs of
Inner Peace," and at the receptionist's desk, an aquamarine bowl with
little cards that say, EXPECT A MIRACLE. I take several, tuck them into
my pockets.

The more I rush the more they balk. The oldest refuses to put her shoes
on, the youngest will not stop nursing, his teeth clamping down on me.
The middle child is still sitting on the toilet, waiting for a wipe.

It's been years since I've been to a dentist. In our two-hour new-patient
exam, Dr. O'Hara asks me in his lilting voice, "How do you feel about
your teeth?" I almost weep in his pastel examination room. "No one has
ever asked me that," I murmur. I flush and turn away.

Expect a miracle

The luscious scaling of each plaque-coated tooth. His tools are so
particular, so accurate. He always selects just the right one. Resting
in the rhythmic scraping, Enya over the speakers, the seagull mobile
and star garland. Like I'm at the beach, I could lie here for hours,
the children playing in the waiting room with strangers.

They wear on me like chronic diseases, hanging on my legs, so that I
limp. When one nose starts running, the other two noses quickly follow.
I barely manage to shower, what with all the noses to wipe, the crumbs
to sweep.

The scaling takes hours. We take four fifty-minute sessions just for this. The first week, the top right. The second week, the top left. The third and fourth weeks, the bottom right and left. He scrapes and scrapes until each tooth is smooth as polished marble, wiping his instruments on my paper bib and letting me rest from time to time. I've never been so thoroughly cleaned. I don't deserve such tenderness.

The baby sleeps with us. Between me and Jeff. Jeff watches TV in the other room until he falls asleep. "Are you asleep?" I ask him. "Huh? I'm resting," he says. Sometime in the night, he comes to bed. I hear his heavy mouth-breathing and smell his I've-been-out-with-clients smoky hair.

Dr. O'Hara sells me a special ninety-five-dollar toothbrush that can actually penetrate between teeth to remove plaque. He knows how busy I am, three little kids, my husband's never home; when would I ever find time to floss? He wants very badly for me to clean my teeth; he looks into my eyes and implores me to floss, to stop my gingivitis from worsening.

such tenderness
a miracle

If I can take fifteen minutes a day to meditate, he pleads, you can take five minutes to floss. He has kids too, he says. He knows. But you have a wife, I want to say. Instead I accept the toothbrush, write a check for it at the reception desk. He hands me the electric toothbrush with a pearled smile, knowing that I will fail, that I will not floss, after all is said and done. He will keep meditating, and I will keep getting cavities. I take the toothbrush, MICHEAL O'HARA DDS, (262) 352-4220 embossed on the white plastic.

The two oldest sleep across the hall in a queen-size mattress on the floor, but most mornings I wake with one or more curled at my feet or nestled under my arm, the yeasty smell of damp diapers, sweat, milk.

Because I love him. And because he loves me. Because I love him, I let him work on me without anesthesia. He doesn't bother with gloves. The mask is tossed aside.

the yeasty smell

Without anesthesia. "Are you sure?" he asks. "Oh, yes," I insist. I want to feel, to know every spin, every whir of the drill. His short fingers in my mouth comfort me.

Without anesthesia.
Without gloves.
Without masks.
Without children.

His fingers without the gloves taste slightly metallic. I accept his touch, his high-pitched drill, his lovely composite fillings. I let him remove each mercury-sodden amalgam filling and repair each tooth with white porcelain, remaking me, pristine and white.

a miracle

It hurts for only a moment, I tell him when he stops the drill to look at me with his funny magnifying spectacles and ask if I'm all right. "I've been through childbirth," I say to reassure him.

Jeff says, "He's not a baby anymore." I say, "He's still nursing."

"Three times," I add, three kids, three births. I can't see his eyes
through the telescoping lenses. Only a moment. With my tongue, I poke at
my hollowed tooth.

the drill whirring like hummingbird wings
seagulls circling above me

Every six months I am back, for more probing, more scaling. I ask him
about his family. He takes off his magnifying glasses and his eyes
look moist. "My wife moved out," he murmurs, taking their daughter.

such tenderness
a miracle
the children playing in the waiting room with strangers

When he tells me this, I love him more, his hair graying at his temples
and his manicured beard. I lie there in his mercy and goodness and
project my love to him as he works on me. I wish I had more cavities
for him to repair.

Only a moment, his fingers probing my mouth.

They're selling their house, he tells me, and he's buying an even older
house. He will spend his evenings and weekends rehabbing it. I imagine
him with his very small, meticulous tools peeling paint and applying
grout, sanding and finishing original woodwork. He will work a sill, a
cornice, a single molding at a time.

I say, "Do you want to be the one to carry him over when he wakes up
crying in the night?" I keep the baby in the middle, away from the
edges of the bed.

I ring the angel chimes at the receptionist's desk after I make my next appointment, leave with the brackish taste of my dentist's short fingers. I toss the electric toothbrush on the car seat next to me and rushing to get home and cook dinner I get a seventy-five-dollar speeding ticket.

the drill whirring like hummingbird wings
seagulls circling above me
such tenderness

Camping
by Barbara Card Atkinson

Zoë slept like an old drunk or a well-run dog, mouth open, completely surrendered. Though it had taken fourteen rounds of harmonizing "Pop Goes the Weasel" with the worn-out sing-along tape, now her bare big toes were intertwined, two thick fingers hooking the corner of her mouth. They were already an hour into the drive, so the timing was just right—she'd probably stay asleep the rest of the way there. Abbie watched Zoë sleep with a mixture of pleasure and thin anxiety. It wasn't even that Zoë trusted the world to inflict no harm; at a mere eleven months, she was unaware harm lurked in the corners. It was an obliviousness for which Abbie was both grateful and greedy.

Gary smiled to himself and turned the radio back on—he was an inveterate talk-radio fan. Abbie strained against the seat belt awhile longer, twisting backward to wipe the teething drool from Zoë's chin and pluck hard biscuit chunks from her lap.

Abbie turned to face forward again, catching from the corner of her eye another passing minivan. Gary drove too slowly. The pace was eating a hole in her belly.

The plan was to meet old college friends in a campground in upstate New York, four hours of driving from Boston. Shelly, Connecticut-based therapist and three-year roommate of Abbie's, had organized the long weekend, down to assigning cabins and meal duty among the ten friends, their spouses/partners/lovers/"for nows," and children. So many children. Most of the couples coming had a child or multiple children in tow. Abbie thought it was slightly unreal and secretly bittersweet. The last time the group had gotten together, it was gin and tonics, flirting, and bad poker. Now there would be graham crackers and whole milk and naptime, and not just for the youngest.

Abbie had always loved road trips; in high school and then college she took them as an opportunity to talk out issues both mundane and life-changing, balancing takeout coffees on her knees and dutifully feeding the driver jellybeans or fries. It was like traveling in a bubble, moving forward in space while hovering between worlds, unaffected for a short span anything outside the contents of the car. She hoped this could be the case with Gary, that the next two hundred miles with Zoë here/not here might allow them to recapture some of the ease from before, when every decision wasn't a parenting pass/fail or a marital slight.

She looked at Gary, watched him listening to the radio. The BBC World Service was detailing a dead despot's old war crimes and Gary nodded, ticking off some list in his head. What was it she wanted to say?

She settled back in her seat and willed herself silent, watched the road. Gary gently smoothed the fabric along her leg.

Abbie had Zoë, and she no longer needed Gary. At least, that was Gary's fear. Abbie tried to reassure him, calling him every day at the office with some helpless, new-mother concern ("The furnace seems to be making a weird noise," "Do you think we should start Zoë on solids?"), but in her heart, she worried, too.

It just seemed so complete, the circle she and Zoë made together. Abbie to Zoë, A to Z. Gary, a G—not even a B, which would have at least made him next in line, given some feel of a natural progression—was a hitch, a tangle of leaves and small twigs that threatened to snarl up the stream between her and her girl. Abbie hadn't realized how fuzzy the connection was between herself and Gary until Zoë came and popped the world into sharp focus. Suddenly "kind of" being happy with someone wasn't enough, wasn't even close to being enough, and she mused how it might be better to leave before Gary's detached Otherness eventually closed the rivulet off completely and she was lost with Zoë on the far banks.

Abbie watched Will from the safety of the picnic table. He shifted logs onto the fire with tongs, startling up wheeling sparks. Shelly sat down beside her.

"Damn," Shelly laughed under her breath, "if he doesn't still look good."

They watched him in silence, and Abbie could see the self-conscious set of his jaw, the way he angled his chin. He knew they were there. He kept a steady rhythm, lifting and shifting the wood until the fire was high and hot and lit to the edges of the site. When he was satisfied, he tossed the tongs onto the woven blanket at his feet and turned to look directly at Abbie. He met her eyes with a pleased smile, the slightly cocky grin of a man at ease in his environment, but something in Abbie's face made him shift. His smile drew inward, his eyes grew hooded, and although he still smiled, it became something private, a confirmation. Abbie saw this shift and knew that he had seen on her face a piece of what she had been thinking. She had been thinking about him.

After the babies were tucked in and the partners less desperate for company (Gary, of course Gary, and Will's Emma with their twins) had retired for the evening to the Scout cabins with the mildly rude graffiti and the lingering scent of mildew and mice, the die-hards stood near the campfire, banking it yet again, unwilling to let the night end. Abbie stumbled her way to the bathrooms by the parking area, but the two glasses of wine gave her night blindness and enhanced her fear of small, wild things in the dark. She gave up, found a quiet patch of trees, and crouched low, feeling foolish and exposed.

She buttoned her pants and found their car with the others tucked in under the pines, in the darkest shadows. She sat on the hood, listening to the laughter on the hill, and was suddenly swept by a deliciously syrupy-slow, lonely ache like in high school, the kind that made you feel weepy, intensely important, and terribly overlooked. She heard the crunch of someone coming through the pines. Will stepped close, moved into the space her feet made where they rested on the front bumper of the car. She could feel the warmth of his hips radiate against her thighs. His jeans and hers whispered as they just barely brushed together. She waited for him to look into her eyes, but his face was in shadow. He didn't look up. His eyes and then hers as well watched his hand as he placed it on her waist.

His hand rested there, just along the curve of her hip, and they both looked at it as if it had moved there on its own and they didn't know what it would do next. He glanced at her then and slid his hand up to cradle the fullness of her breast. As their eyes met she felt a tingling and a dampness and realized that he had triggered her letdown reflex.

The front of her t-shirt was wet, two warm heavy circles. He didn't notice until she let out a tiny gasp, almost a sigh, really, and shook at the front of her shirt, frowning to herself as if flapping madly would erase the moment. Will took his hand from her slowly, letting it slide away, as if he wasn't put off or embarrassed, for which she was grateful.

She chuckled a little, not meaning it, and reached into the car for the extra diaper bag and fresh bra pads.

"I didn't even get to kiss you," he whispered. Abbie leaned forward then, cradled his face between her hands, and caught just the movement of herself reflected in the dim of his eyes as she bent toward him. She stopped just shy of his mouth, their lips a mere breath apart. She knew exactly how he would taste. She inhaled, deeply, loudly, smelled coffee and clove and the coolness of the night in his dark hair.

It was one of those slate gray downpours, where the rain was painfully cold by the time it hit and the lights inside the house made everything look unnaturally bright. Abbie was driving home from her Tuesday afternoon Mommies' Group with Zoë in the front seat, even though it wasn't as safe as putting her in the back. Zoë whined and dropped her chewy dinosaur where Abbie couldn't reach. Abbie was cautiously passing the slow, old-woman traffic on the main street, thinking about what was available for dinner makings even though it was only three in the afternoon, when she felt something tickle the nape of her neck. It felt like her collar was curled under; she brushed at it without a thought, and suddenly the right side of her neck and part of her cheekbone were shockingly hot—nettles?—and she swerved to the side of the road. There was a wasp writhing on the dashboard, and Zoë's damp crook of a thumb slid out of her mouth as she watched Abbie gasp and claw at her neck in panic.

Abbie turned to Zoë and said in a high, misty voice, "Mommy's okay. A bug bit Mommy." Zoë looked as if she couldn't decide whether to cry and a red Subaru behind them honked and that's when Abbie knew she had to choose to stay with him. Zoë would never be completely safe with just her. Abbie might fall down the stairs or have an allergic reaction to strawberries or just simply go mad, walk off, coffee mug still in hand, and forget Cheerios and diapers and sticky toys. Zoë would be bleating in her crib for days until she slowly faded and stilled and curled back in on herself. With Gary, even just Gary, there was someone else, a low, solid bumper for her failings to catch against.

The Band-Aids kept peeling off, and Abbie felt foolish anyway, could feel the eyes of the women at the supermarket slide over the crisscross of colored patches along her neck and cheek. Zoë, strapped in with a frayed red belt, banged her legs against the shopping cart in a discordant rhythm; it rattled and shuddered as Abbie wedged her foot against the bottom rack to keep it from tipping.

She pushed her fingertips along the fragrant melons, searching for a pliant flesh, and felt the round Barney Band-Aid along her jaw loosen. She smoothed it back with one hand while the other tickled across the pyramid of melons. Her finger suddenly broke through the rind, plunged into damp, green rottenness. The wet smell and the obscene flesh insisting itself against her fingertip were enough to make her bolt. She unbelted Zoë, swung her up and then under her arm, carried her in a move her father had always called "sack o' taters," Zoë's face slack with surprise. Abbie thought about the cart, abandoned in the produce aisle, about what she might make for dinner now that shopping was an impossibility, about how quiet the house would be. She strapped Zoë in her car seat and belted herself in as well, and as she cried, she told herself it was a delayed reaction to the stings.

Becoming Mine
by the Naughty Mommy

wean (wēn) tr.v. **weaned, weaning, weans 1.** *to accustom (the young of a mammal) to take nourishment other than by suckling.* **2.** *to detach from that to which one is strongly habituated or devoted.*

—The American Heritage Dictionary of the
English Language, *fourth edition*

When my daughter was a little over a year old, she made her first real joke; she grabbed my boob in her chubby paws, grinned hugely, and announced, "Mine!"

I might have found this funny and cute, if she hadn't been up all night, leisurely grazing on breastmilk. Or if I hadn't just spent an hour of precious naptime arguing with my sad and neglected husband about our sex life (or our lack thereof). Or even if I hadn't, just minutes before, yelled uncharacteristically at my sad and neglected dog to "GET THE [BLEEP] AWAY FROM ME," just because she laid her head on my lap for a long-overdue petting session.

The problem is, in my daughter's first devil-inspired try at humor, she got it right. Contrary to what my husband might hope for, my breasts *do* belong to her. And that's just the beginning. My heart, my attention, my devotion, my very most important reason for living now all also belong to her. It is her scent I inhale at night. It is her skin I polish with kisses. It is her body I know better than my husband's now, better than my own.

At the time she made that joke I was well beyond "touched out," that catch phrase parenting books and magazines love to use as an explanation of new mothers' lack of libido. Yes, I was tired of being touched and pulled and scratched and stretched. And yes, there were times I wanted to fling her off me like some parasitic bug. But most of the time I just wanted the world and all other living creatures to leave the two of us alone so I could hold my daughter and count her toes and stare at her like she was my high school sweetheart.

I remember the first time we left her. I knew it was time; I could sense my husband drifting away, tired of begging after the scraps of intimacy or connection I could muster up to throw his way. But the whole time we were out I thought only of her. I smiled and held his hand and plotted with him to be naughty if she was asleep when we got home. But even after two drinks and a stroll through the adult section of the local video store, I was about as hot as day-old bathwater. I wanted to want to be naughty, but really, all I wanted to do was rush home and kiss my baby.

As a lifelong intimacy junkie, mothering an infant was the ultimate fix. I'd float around in my own clockless world, bathed in a "Madonna and Child" afterglow, satisfied in a deeper way than even the best sex can produce as a by-product. I swam in a world of maternal preoccupation that left me needing sex about as much as—to borrow that famous phrase about how much a woman needs a man—a fish needs a bicycle. Forget being "touched out"—I was touched just enough, thanks.

At two and a half, my daughter is weaning herself. She pulls away when I reach for her. She squirms when I kiss her. She berates me, using the same tone I use on the dog: "Get OUTTA here, Mama!"

We spend the days not like lovers, but changelings. We are some sort of horrific half-beast with two heads, each trying to wrest control from the other. I am in intimacy withdrawal; I'm shaky, hormonal, and weepy. While she sleeps I steal deep whiffs of her once-baby breath, still laced with the sweetness of my milk. But I can't deny it. She is becoming her own person, her own body, her own heart. I am becoming, too: restless, unsettled, charged. My previously off-limits breasts begin to take on new life; my nipples tingle with long-lost sensation. I've had naughty dreams two nights in row; I've touched myself.

Her eyes mirror what I feel, fear and intoxication. Independence looms over every interaction, a lure, a shadow; the terror and thrill of freedom. I turn my back on it, but I know it's there, undeniable, firm, always knocking. She is not mine and I am not hers. We are our own.

My husband and I have instituted "Date Night." Tonight, we're going to hear live music, something we once enjoyed together, a lifetime ago. It's still hard for me to leave her. While the baby sitter gets settled, I panic and quickly scribble my last will and testament; I'm leaving explicit directions for the care of our daughter should we die in a freak accident.

We get drinks before the show, and, determined to rid myself of all kid thoughts, I pound two shots. It works. At the show we hold hands and weave through baby-faced adults so we can get up close to the baby-faced band. They are all beautiful and full of themselves and music and each other. I inhale the heat and energy from the crowd, sucking them down like an airborne drug. My husband is pushed into me from behind, and I don't push him back. He wraps his arms around my chest and yells something into my ear, but his words hit my neck instead. I shiver.

"What?" I yell back at him, the music pulsing through me like long-lost hormones and desires.

"Mine," he teases huskily, his lips on my ear, his hand discreetly grabbing my breast.

For the first time in a long time it makes me hot, instead of not. And for the first time in a long time, I know I am my own to give.

I giggle and tease him back. "No way," I say, turning my lips to his as we move together to the music. "Mine."

Coming
by Rachel Sarah

> *Once I ejaculate, the pillow looks better than my girlfriend does.*
> —*Mantak Chia,* The Multi-Orgasmic Man:
> Sexual Secrets Every Man Should Know

It's over. The longest relationship I've had since becoming a single mom has ended. I met forty-two-year-old Jim on Match.com a few months ago. He was emotional, like me, and seemed devoted to his two kids. But as the months went on, I started to think that maybe we weren't a match after all.

I was frustrated by a number of things: He was not divorced, even though he and his wife had been separated for years (unfinished business); he often showed up late for a date (lack of respect); and our parenting styles were radically different (whereas I'm like a therapist, he's like a commander in chief). In the end, however, what really broke me down was that he came too fast.

The first time I invited Jim over to my place, my four-year-old daughter, Mae, was having a sleepover at her girlfriend's house. (Her very first sleepover, mind you.) I had left her in tears. I almost dialed Jim's phone number to call it off.

During the drive home, I repeated various mantras to myself to alleviate the guilt: *It's okay if she cries a little. Tears are healthy, right? She's in good hands.* But the closer I got to home, the smugger I got: *It's about time I got a break! I deserve this. Don't I get one night off from being Mom?* I also tried to replace images of Mae in tears with ones of Jim seducing me. He was almost six feet tall, with dreadlocks and pumped-up biceps. I loved how gently he held my face when he kissed me.

Over the preceding few weeks, Jim and I had been all over each other, although not yet inside each other. We'd made out at the park in midafternoon, on his sofa after going to a jazz club, and in his car before a poetry reading. I was almost businesslike the way I'd prepared for the real thing. Did you get your HIV test? Check! Is my birth control prescription ready? Check!

At home, I slipped on my pink see-through lingerie under my dress. The phone and lights went off. I lit six candles. It was an unusually warm night, so I opened my bedroom window an inch. (My bedroom is half of the living room. Mae has the one bedroom in our apartment.) There was a knock at the door.

I flew down the stairs with a big smile. This was it! This was my night. It was my chance to forget about the day-old milk in the fridge, the dishes coated with macaroni and cheese, the Barbie shoes strewn across the rug, and the unbalanced checkbook. I was going to let myself go. True, I masturbated sometimes, but that moment of liberation just isn't the same solo. Nothing compares to having an orgasm with someone you adore.

Our clothes quickly fell to the floor. My world was wet and wide open. But just ten minutes and forty thrusts later, there was a loud groan. His head hit the pillow. His eyes were shut.

"What about me?" I said.

"Hmmm?" he mumbled.

I shook his shoulder. "What about me?" I asked again, annoyed.

Pre-baby, I was the kind of woman who came easily. But when Mae turned seven months old and I became a single mom, I shut myself off from men. Instead, I focused on nursing, bathing, playing peekaboo, editing textbooks, and mopping the kitchen floor. Having an orgasm was not part of my daily routine. Four years later, I felt that she was ready for a night away from home. No, actually, I was ready!

Night after night, I tried to guide Jim to relax and slow down. Part of the problem seemed mechanical: He was moving so fast that he wasn't really present with me. His hard-on directed the show: Sex became an overexcited monologue, instead of both of us playing complementary parts on stage. He told me that no other women had ever complained about being dissatisfied. But I wasn't trying to damage his male ego. All I needed was ten minutes, only ten minutes before he let the dam burst. Yet, time and time again, just when I was ready to go over the edge, he was gone.

I held tightly to my fantasies. I wanted to yell his name out loud as my body shuddered. I wanted to feel his sweat roll off me. But it wasn't just about sex. I imagined blending our families together one day, and buying a house with a backyard swing and a huge playroom. Still, each week, Jim came over, and boy, did he come. I didn't. My fantasies were flooded away by fury.

Then, one night three months into our relationship, it happened. It was the middle of the night, and he was half-asleep. Perhaps this made for less pressure to perform. Perhaps it was just luck. But I climbed on top of him. He hardly moved, and I actually climaxed. In that moment, every doubt I had disappeared into the darkness. I wanted to marry him on a mountaintop. I wanted us to take a bow together.

But sure enough, a few days later, he showed up an hour late for our date because he was dropping his kids off at his wife's place—"Uh, I mean, my ex-wife's place." For the next few weeks, I invited him over every weekend, eager to repeat our performance. But time and time again, he was coming fast and I was running high on frustration. The very last time, as soon as he started to snore, I was out of bed, on my knees picking up Barbie accessories from the rug. With that last plastic high heel put away, I knew this was over.

The Dogs of Sayulita
by Jennifer D. Munro

Dogs. Everywhere. Filthy, mangy, skinny mongrels. They pant in the scarce shade. They scratch at fleas in the pitted, dirt road. The taxi driver almost hits a few roaming mutts as they amble out of the way in the dusty heat. Used to operating on life's margins, like the villagers themselves, the dogs know exactly how slowly they can meander yet still avoid impact with hurtling bumpers. Lacking street smarts, several three-legged dogs miscalculated. Evolution would eliminate the faulty canine gene pools. But what, Emma wonders, did Darwin have against her and Devon's lineage? Will their marriage, a family tree with shallow roots, topple in the drought of childlessness?

The taxi driver speeds north from the Puerto Vallarta airport to the bayside hamlet of Sayulita. He passes on blind curves along the narrow jungle road. His bumper tosses a pedestrian's skirt. Emma sits mute in the backseat, hair flying like Medusa's snakes from the wind that whips through the open windows. She can't buckle the broken seat belt. Devon haggled this deal of a ride instead of paying full fare for an air-conditioned four-door. She wishes he'd splurged for her sake, but understands his frugality. They can ill afford this unplanned vacation, more a convalescence than a holiday. Though Amanda had lent them her vacation home in a town they couldn't locate on the tourist map, the last-minute airfare had been astronomical, and they had wiped out their savings on the unsuccessful in vitro treatments. They could hardly afford dinner at the local Taco Bell, much less a trip to Mexico.

The taxi driver almost clips a petrol tanker. Emma envisions, almost desires, a spectacular Hollywood movie blast. She wouldn't mind meeting her end in dramatic flame. At least it would be something. She's as numb as her anesthetized womb when the doctor inserted the fertilized eggs—all claustrophobic guppies who hightailed it downriver rather than bask on her welcoming shore.

Devon sits in the passenger seat babbling in bad Spanish with the driver, dredging up words from freshman year. Devon contemplates adventure, not mortality, a trait that both attracts and annoys Emma. She had worried about how he would adapt to fatherhood. He gesticulates wildly, as if he can grab forgotten words out of the air. He calls the small town they travel to "Salsalito," no doubt confirming the ignorance of all gringos in the driver's mind. But the driver encourages Devon's attempt to converse in the native language. Emma wishes her husband would shut up and let the man concentrate on the winding road rather than puzzling over Devon's garbled queries. Thrilled, Devon translates the driver's assertion that wild tigers haunt the jungle. Emma suspects he means house cats.

A stoplight provides momentary relief from the rush toward mangled death. A horde of dirty children swarms the car, begging. One kid is missing an arm. The driver barks something in rushed syllables that pile swiftly one on top of the other, and peels off.

They approach a military checkpoint, where guards with sweaty hands clutch bazookas. Belts of ammunition crosshatch their stiff bodies. Emma tries to look nonchalant, with her best *nothing in the trunk, sir* expression, then wonders if overtly acting not guilty causes suspicion. The driver mutters, but they cruise through without being stopped.

They drive up and down the cratered streets of Sayulita searching for Amanda's house. "Now, it's not a luxury resort or anything," Amanda had warned. They hadn't believed her. They'd seen what kind of wine she stocked at her lakefront home. She wasn't the type for rustic vacation shacks. But they bounce and jolt through the run-down town, chased by clouds of dust. Rather than snap at the taxi driver to take her back to the airport, Emma focuses on the dogs of Sayulita. They look content despite a miserable existence. They doze in lazy harmony, too hot and hungry to worry about defending meager territories. Odd Chihuahua mixes curl up beside strange Great Dane–like creatures. No breed segregation here. Rampant fornication has produced abundant, bizarre results. Emma pictures a miniature mutt perching his spindly hind legs on a splintered packing crate to reach his towering mate. Or, the other way around, how would a Lab penis fit in a poodle puss? Wouldn't it get stuck? How could they find the energy to screw in this heat, anyway?

What strikes Emma, though, is not so much the canine quantity and variety, but the balls. Countless swollen nuts sway between bony legs. Starving pooches haul ripe appendages, like stoic tramps dragging their bulging rucksacks. Emma is surrounded by an army of unsnipped doggie testicles. The obscene display of unchecked gonads transfixes her.

Only stray children outnumber the dogs. They wander the street or huddle under makeshift awnings, without adult supervision. Two boys in a crispy, brown field practice with lassos. The older child snares his patient dog, which doesn't budge as the rope tightens around its drooping neck. A naked baby crawls through the dirt. Emma the Mama Bandita could snatch the infant, *una desperada* propelled by an estrogen rush. But she doesn't have the will to open the car door, much less make a run for the border. She doesn't know what she wants anymore.

Amanda's house is, of course, lovely, once they find it, an oasis of luxury in the third-world town. A pure water dispenser protects them from bacterial harm. The three-room casa is a perfect setup for the perfect family vacationing in the tropics, with a king-size bed for the doting parents, a double bed for the sullen teenager, and twin beds for the two youngest. Emma shuts the doors on the two smaller rooms.

Ceiling fans beat a lazy tempo throughout the house. Two walls of the main living *sala* consist entirely of accordion doors that fold back like a giant fan, opening the house to the breeze. Emma tugs, but the salty heat has swollen the dark wood. Devon wrestles them open, and they step to the outside *palapa*. A thatched roof shades the patio. A bumblebee on steroids, ignorant of its carefree pollinating, flits from pink to red bougainvillea flowers that drape the walls. Heavy fruit loads the coconut trees lining the walkway. The warm waters of the Pacific Ocean slap at the beach mere steps away. With the doors open, their living room is practically an extension of the beach.

Later, dozing on the couch, Emma opens her eyes and sees a spout of mist in the distance. A second, smaller puff mimics the first. A mama whale, traveling back north with her newborn calf. Emma sits up. "Damn it, I need a drink. I don't care what kind of contaminated water's in the ice." Emma hasn't had a glass of wine in months, booze eliminated from her diet as one more possible conception-inhibitor. "I sterilize my laboratory with alcohol; it kills everything," the lab technician who mated Devon's sperm with Emma's eggs in a petri dish advised at their consultation. "You do the math."

Emma pads around the casa, nearly tripping over a stray mongrel that lies curled beside Emma's couch. The female dog blinks her weary eyes. Emma lets her return to her siesta instead of shooing her outside. Poor thing needs sanctuary from all those loaded pizzles.

She finds Devon napping naked on the side patio in the dappled shade, soaking up heat like one of the geckos chirping from the walls. He wore no underwear or socks when they met years ago, but these days he even suffers a necktie. A sun bunny misplaced in the Pacific Northwest, he rarely has the opportunity to indulge in carefree nudity.

Emma's forgotten how hirsute he is, with fine, black hair sprinkled across his back, chest, arms, and even his bum. When they first met, still teenagers, his long hair billowed about his head like a nuclear mushroom cloud. Now he cuts it short, controlling its electric mass. She had hoped a baby girl would inherit Devon's wild curls and swift metabolism—not her muddy hair and heart rate.

Devon's face sprouts a shadow seconds after he shaves, a Brillo Pad that chafes Emma's face when they kiss. In college, he shaved designs into the thick beard on his cheeks. Now he wears a close-cropped beard. As he sprawls in the sun, she sees that he'd let his pubic hair grow. Normally he kept the wild bush trimmed so that wiry hairs didn't poke up Emma's nose when she nuzzled his package. Guess he figured there was no point lately and let it go au naturel.

Emma hadn't been attracted to hairy men, although she'd liked the bohemian look of Devon's out-of-control locks. But his scent had lured her, its potent properties surely linked to his body hair. He wasn't stereotypically good-looking, not overly attentive, not stylish. He wasn't tall or muscle-bound, more a monkey than an ape. He wore flip-flops in winter rain, burped in the elevator, wore out-of-date spectacles that shrouded his eyes. Between the glasses and beard, one could make out little of his face under the black mane. He was odd and oblivious, not at all a coveted Aryan premed type, but he left jungle markings in the female dormitories of the tame and moldy Northwest.

Emma was no pheromone slouch, herself. The entire girl's wing followed her menstrual cycle; they all ovulated at the same time. Boys prowled the hall and were eagerly admitted, but choosing the wrong time of the month got them scratched. Devon suffered Emma's claws more than once before she granted him her estrus cave. She guessed, and feared, that once coupled together, theirs would forever be a shared territory. Once inside, Devon imprinted himself on her sheets, an odor not unlike cooking smells that lingered, not always pleasantly, but provoking hunger after satiation. After he left for early morning classes, Emma would cuddle into his pillow, intoxicated by his powerful musk. She couldn't get enough of him.

They couldn't have guessed that with their combined hormonal sparks, like match tips waiting for friction, they would not be able to conceive a child. It would be years before they made the sad discovery, when they finally decided that the time was right and stopped battling with birth control. And nothing happened.

Her periods continued, as regular as the moon. Then came the basal-body-temperature monitoring, the carefully orchestrated sex, the abstaining until ovulation to give him a higher sperm count, the chronic missionary position, hiking her butt up onto a pillow to aid the heroic journey of his sperm. Soon sex wasn't about the two of them. Always, the phantom of the third, the wanted child, hovered in the room, dictating when they mated. Then the doctors took over until, finally, conception took place while Emma and Devon were in separate rooms under fluorescent lights. Emma, her thighs and ass bruised from the daily hormone shots, lay spread-eagle for the doctor to retrieve her eggs while Devon hunched over a plastic cup with his dick in his fist. (Devonshire cream, he called it in a bad British accent when their lovemaking was still lighthearted.) At home, Devon moved to the couch. She was too sore and irritable to miss his smell on the sheets. Lying still on her back and getting up only when her bladder was about to burst, she struggled not to rock the boat as the fertilized eggs inserted into her womb decided whether to evacuate or cling to the life raft of her uterus. To help her pass the time during her required bed rest, Devon made up stories that wouldn't make her laugh. He concocted weird milk shakes and held the glass while she drank through a straw. But he couldn't disguise his doubt, and she now can't forgive him his lack of faith—perhaps his misgivings had jinxed them from the start.

Emma stares down at her husband. He looks better at thirty-five than he did at twenty. He's kept a trim figure, adopted contact lenses, tamed his mane. He's not so much quirky anymore, with that defiant desire of youth to be outrageously unique, as he is simply comfortable with himself. Devon has never worried about other people's opinions. Even now, a maid or yardman could round the corner and catch his nude snooze. Devon could care less. When was the last time she'd seen him naked? When was the last time sex between them had been about lust? About love and union? Just as one could forget the Seattle stars that lay so often shrouded behind clouds, she'd lost sight of the fierce attraction that had been the sparkling fabric of their marriage. Their passion burned out in the black hole of sterility.

Devon stirs under her gaze. As always, his cock wakes up first, stretching and seeming to yawn in the sun. Devon rubs his eyes, fists screwed up like a waking child, and looks up at her. His eyes are green in bright sunlight, with flecks of yellow. In the gray Seattle sky, they're dark and murky, inscrutable. He wiggles his fingers at her to join him on the lounge chair.

"Let's go get smashed." Emma turns back inside.

Devon pads behind her. He sweeps a sombrero off the shelf, places it on his head, clicks his heels together, and snaps his fingers. "¡Olé! Let's go!"

Emma points to his crotch. "Better cover that, instead."

"But, *chica*, the hat no ees beeg enough," he whines in a nasal accent.

Emma changes into a wrinkled sundress she hasn't worn in years.

"*¡Ay, caramba! ¡Muy bonita señorita!*" Devon rubs her arms, looking over her shoulder at her in the mirror. "I forgot you had skin under all those sweaters." He kisses her bare shoulder.

She dreads the lovemaking that Devon no doubt expects. Their vacations had always been about sex—odd, since they had no children to escape from. But she craves sun and solace, not passion. She wants a good book and a gentle breeze, not a lover's hot embrace. She feels dry and brittle, like a mummy that disintegrates when exposed to air. Devon would find nothing moist and welcoming about her barren body, her inner planes as uninviting as the vast desert across which the airplane had chased its shadow on the flight south. She would crumble into a pile of ash if Devon attempted to arouse her.

Emma turns in his arms and pecks him on the lips. "Let's get a margarita first." She steps away and into her sandals. "We'll make damn sure the hangover's worse than the food poisoning."

With no itinerary or map, they set off down the beach. Emma normally overprepares, but this last-minute trip left no time for studying travel guides or foreign language dictionaries. At Amanda's offer of her casa, they had booked the ticket, thrown their clothes into a suitcase, and made haste to the airport. Here, Emma could recover from the final in vitro round in warm and fragrant peace. No one could recover anything, most certainly not sanity, in the gray and soggy Seattle February they'd left behind. Stepping out into the cold drizzle one recent night and tipping her head back to feel the rain on her face, Emma wanted to drown on the spot like a stupid turkey staring into the watery sky.

The blazing sand burns their tender feet, and they cool them frequently in the surf as they mosey toward town. Emma fills her pockets with beach glass and shells. Two yellow pups argue over a coconut in the surf. A girl changes her bikini top behind a blanket held up by a proprietary-looking boyfriend. A few tourists, obvious by their generous bodies and red skin, mingle with the local families. A motorboat full of passengers without life vests cuts through a pack of bodysurfers. A fisherman dumps his fresh catch onto the sand. Emma looks away when he unsheathes his knife. Gulls swarm for the cast-off parts.

They choose an outdoor table at the first restaurant they come to. Under the shade of a Corona umbrella, they watch the waves inch toward their toes. The barefoot waiter looks too young to be out of school, much less earning a living by funneling *cerveza* down thirsty throats. He speaks no English—as, they discover, most of the locals don't—and they struggle to place their order. Margaritas and nachos he understands. Emma can't figure out how to request a double, and the boy brings her two drinks. Vendors sell junk hanging from poles across their shoulders, and Emma and Devon repeat, "No, gracias," a dozen times before the food arrives. Emma hands a twenty-peso note—a mere two dollars—to a crone who sells nothing but pity for her poverty.

The server stops frequently in his rounds to observe a surfing competition. One broad-shouldered surfer rides a handstand on his board all the way in to shore. The gentle wave carries him toward the beach as if it is God's palm delivering him to earth. The surfer flips sideways when he reaches shallow water, now standing on his feet with the board on his head. Water streams from his black hair down his face, down bunched shoulder muscles, down his brown belly and yellow swim trunks, down to where his ankles disappear in the white froth of surf and sand. He stands regally. The scattered beach crowd applauds.

"What are the old gods down here? Incan? Mayan?" Emma slings back her drink and crunches ice. "How American that I don't know."

"They worship Lord Quiksilver," Devon says, reading the logo on the surfer's shorts as the man jogs by, heavy board tucked under his arm as though he carries a toothpick. Emma had struggled through the soft sand as though she fought her way up a down escalator, but his bouncing sprint resembles a stone skimming across the water. Sand sprays from his heels like Mercury's wings. The surfer meets Emma's eyes, and he half bows toward her.

Emma licks salt from the rim of her glass. She makes short order of her margarita, glad she doesn't have to wait for a refill. Devon pushes up her skirt under the table and rests his hand on her knee. Emma tenses.

"Emma?" Devon squeezes.

She refuses to meet his eyes, turning away to watch the water-logged shorts cup the surfer's glutes, hard and round as two bowling balls.

"Emma, what's next?"

"*Los toros esta noche,*" the server says, setting down their bill (which would barely cover a bag of Doritos back home). He makes a riding motion with his hands and pantomimes horns.

"A rodeo's next," Emma says, something else to keep them out of the bedroom.

"That's not—"

"Tonight. With bulls."

Devon's hand retreats as he pays the server. Emma smooths her skirt.

Emma and Devon catch a ride to the rodeo with the three-generational tourist family vacationing next door. "We don't know how long we'll stay," the matriarch warns. "Carlie—my daughter-in-law—she's pregnant. It depends on the bathrooms. You know how it is."

Locals pack the raised bleachers overlooking the rodeo ring. Climbing up the rickety steps, Emma regrets her sundress. *Careful of Medusa's bush, boys,* she telegraphs to the men below. *She kills millions of sperm at a glance.* The crowd is an undulating sea of bright white, straw cowboy hats. Extended families blend into each other. The señoras wear frilly blouses with their pants. Toddlers wander where they please. Jack-in-the-box hands pop out from the dense mash of humanity to prevent unsteady tykes from toppling down the steps. Emma understands that the children in the street earlier weren't untended at all, but were looked after by the entire town. Even without coordinated Baby Gap outfits and personal DVD players in the back of an airbag-equipped SUV, the kids are adored.

Energetic mariachi music fills vast stretches of time between each cowboy's brief attempt to remain seated on bulls angered with painfully cinched balls. Man and beast battle in an arena stripped of safety. No ambulances, no clowns exist to save these crazy dudes if they fall. The bulls' horns are wrapped to prevent goring, but if any hooves meet skulls tonight, it will be a dark, bumpy ride to the Puerto Vallarta hospital in the backseat of someone's jalopy.

One tired old bull can't be bothered to protest the indignity of trussed-up testicles. He sinks to his front knees in the dirt and refuses to be provoked by the furious, flailing cowboy. Emma hopes the weary beast gets to retire to a field, nuzzling noses with a dried-up dairy cow, but suspects he'll end up on the wrong side of a McDonald's counter.

Devon winces. "Talk about callused *cojones.*"

Couples dance on the edge of the bleachers, heedless of no railing and a twenty-foot drop into the corral. Locked together, their legs press tight into the crotches of their partners as they bounce and sway. While inept handlers prepare the next beast, a white horse dances in the bullring. His rider, a portly man in a sombrero, clutches a Sol beer in one hand and the reins in the other, pulling the horse's chin tight to its chest. Its hooves tap out a fast rhythm as if it dances on hot coals. The rider sits still on its back, not spilling a drop of beer. A girl in tight pants climbs down into the ring. She straddles the horse, her back pressed tight to the rider's chest, her butt wedged into his crotch. The horse beats a swift rhythm with their bobbing bodies. Music pulses. Soon another tight-pressed couple bounces on a buckskin horse dancing nearby. The horses tap out a Morse code of desire that transmits up through an orgy of vibrating couples.

Devon flags the potato chip vendor. The cellophane bag crackles as the vendor slits it open with his knife. He sprinkles salt into the bag, squirts in red sauce, presses half a lime over it, and shakes. Emma doubts that's a food-handler's license crinkling in his shirt pocket. She crams thick and crunchy potato slices into her mouth.

Testosterone wafts through the stands like the fetid smell of the jungle surrounding them. Emma imagines wildcat eyes staring down at them through the surrounding growth. She turns to see Devon's eyes glowing at her in the dark. He licks her sticky fingers.

A black rain cloud threatens overhead. A few sprinkles drop, and the fair-weather crowd streams toward the exit, their hats like white water flowing downriver. Carlie needs to pee, and it's time to leave.

Emma stands at the edge of the dark water that she hears more than sees. The beach is pitch black and deserted. The ocean announces its advance toward shore with crashing thunder, something ominous in its constant battering of the earth. The sky echoes its boom. Cold raindrops *plink* on Emma's sun-hot skin. She looks up at the star-dense sky. With little electric city light to steal its shine, the sparkling and vast cosmos spreads out above her. An amber god surfs down the Milky Way—Lord, it's Devon streaking down the beach, his white ass luminous in the starlight.

"Somebody'll see you," she hisses.

He moves close in front of her. He's shorter than she is on the downslope of the beach. His crotch presses against her. The waves tickle his ankles.

"From what I've heard, you don't want to be thrown naked into a Mexican prison."

"Come on, Emma. Let loose. Nobody's around. Besides, I can hardly see you, even this close. We could tell them our clothes got ripped off when we struggled out of the undertow."

"Right, try saying that in Spanish." She backs up to higher, drier ground.

"Guess I'm not like that guy today. That surfer. Mr. Mexican Adonis." Devon steps back, his feet sinking into the softer sand and swirling water. "I saw the way you looked at him. Been a long time since you looked at me like that."

She looks down at him. "I'd understand if you found someone else. Someone younger, who could—"

"Are you out of your mind? You think I'd leave you for some other rabbit? Jesus, do you want me to?"

"Whatever's wrong is with me. We both know that."

"We don't know jack. All those goddamn tests, all that money, and still no clue."

"We've been over all this."

"But you haven't you been listening. I'd be happy with a goldfish tank."

"But I wouldn't!"

"You used to be. I don't even know who you are anymore." He turns around and wades in up to his knees.

She starts to turn away, back to the house, but a strangled yelp pulls her back. A rogue wave smacks Devon, knocks him down, grabs him in fists of current, and drags him back to sea.

Just as quickly, before Emma can yell or splash in after him, the ocean spits him back up, *patooey*. Spluttering, he crawls out of the surf. Emma grabs his arm and helps him up to dry ground. He plops his bare fanny on the sand, arms wrapped around his knees, face covered. Emma circles him like a frantic chicken. Without looking, he reaches out and grabs her hand, pulling her down beside him.

"You still blame me."

"I'm sorry. I don't know who I am, either."

She's a baby-crazed monster who can't purchase her own tampons, because the cruel supermarket gods stock feminine hygiene products in the diaper aisle, an emotional land mine Emma avoids. She'd like to go rabid amidst the diapers, shredding HUGGIES with her teeth and howling to the cruel fluorescent skies. Maybe then she can get the rage out of her system and reconcile herself to the injustice that millions of women so easily have what she can't have. Maybe then she can go on with her life. But she stuffs the grief down, showing up on time for work and smiling whenever someone asks her, "Why don't you just adopt?" instead of smashing their teeth in. She despises herself for such pathetic weakness, a twenty-first-century woman defining herself by her womb's failure. But she can not be rational about her all-consuming desire to be a mother. She can't fight with reason the hormonal hard-wiring of biology's millennia of procreation programming.

"You're my *wife*. My *lover*. That's who. That's the most important thing. That you're here on the beach with me, to give me a reason not to drown. That we're not alone. It's about what we *have*, not what we *don't* have."

"I know all that up here," she touches her forehead, then her belly, "but not down here."

"How about down here?" He sits beside her and reaches under her skirt. "It's where we started. Can't we start there again?"

She could call him a typical male, call him insensitive, get up and leave. But she understands that sex and communion are two different things and yet the same. She lifts her dress over her head and tosses it aside. She presses herself against his wet skin. She smells him, that intoxicating ripeness of his body mixed with the ocean's salt and seaweed. "This place gets your blood pumping, doesn't it?"

As if she's taken a dunk in cold water, she feels revived by Sayulita's acceptance of reality and its inherent dangers. No complicated legal system casts a tangled web of safety nets. No lifeguards, no life jackets, no rodeo medics, no seat belts, no minimum-age limit, no ambulance chasers because there's probably nobody worth suing. Dogs wander freely without leash laws or neuter clinics, and kids wander without hysterical newscasters warning of escaped pedophiles. It's not a perfect world, she can see that. Her understanding is dim after less than a day here, but there doesn't seem to be a false illusion that life is safe or predictable. In the States, the people operate under the illusion that accidents and illnesses can be prevented, and what's broken can be fixed with persistence and a charge card. When Emma could not get pregnant, it never occurred to her to accept her childlessness or to pray. She had gone to the doctor with the expectation that everything would be put right soon enough. The right medication, the right exercise, the right timing. She had lost any perspective about when to stop. Always, the solution seemed right around the corner. She had been poked and prodded until she felt like a skewed Picasso canvas. Treatment had altered her beyond recognition. Now what? A future as a dried-up hag with a pet poodle? Surely not, because she's got what no other woman has, and that's Devon. She's not alone, not barren, but a warm, welcoming ocean where he can relax his restless spirit.

Devon had said no, enough. Went down on his knees and gave up, and she'd continued to flail away at him to get up and try again. She'd hated him for his stubborn refusal. How could he know the next treatment wouldn't work? Now she grasps the truth. All along, he's accepted her as an off-kilter work of beauty, priceless art being damaged beyond repair in attempts to fix it.

Neptune might dislike Devon's flavor, but she suddenly craves him. She wants to pop him into her mouth like sushi, that sea-flavored saltiness lingering on her tongue.

He kisses her. His beard stubble chafes her face. "Sorry. I'll shave."

"I've missed it." She nuzzles her cheek against his.

And then they join like the dogs of Sayulita, knees and palms in the still warm sand, the cool waves of the incoming tide lapping at their heels, the breeze on her breasts and raindrops on his back. Unlike the odd mongrel combinations populating the streets, they are perfectly matched, two puzzle pieces snugging together in a confusing world where very little fits together so perfectly. Her rump is still bruised from the last round of hormone shots, but she welcomes the soreness of Devon pressing into her. The pain brings her alive. She's glad he can't see the bluish skin, or he'd be solicitous and careful. She wants it like this, just two animals without past or future, a necessary and urgent coupling. Raw and simple, the two naive youngsters they used to be, going on instinct and trust. Devon's hand covers hers, and their wedding rings clink.

Later, Devon steps over the dog to turn off the bedroom light. They lie in the moonlight that claws its way through the clouds and spills in through the hacienda windows. Emma sees that Devon has three scrapes across his cheek from his ocean tumble. She also sees that he's shaved a heart in the newly trimmed pubic hair on his low belly.

"Is that for me?"

"It's been yours all along."

A thought flits through her brain like a butterfly. If ever they were to conceive, it would be in a magical place like this, with steaming fecundity permeating the air. Surely Sayulita would provide the miracle that science could not. Maybe, just like that, her period won't come in two weeks. But she chases the wish away, snapping at its wings. For now it's just the two of them, Emma and Devon, and that's enough. The phantom baby takes heel, and the only third party in the room is the panting dog, curled around her own tail.

V.

Mothers, Fathers, Parents

The Impatient Mother
by Ona Gritz

I know it in my teeth when I become her,
the way they tingle, tighten against each other,
and in my sudden rod-straight spine.
Beside her at the table, my son twists away
from a sheet of questions on Lincoln.
He scuffs the floor with a squeak of sneakers,
whines, *This is hard.* She feels the pitch of his voice
on her scalp and, though I have poured tea,
wrapped her fingers around the heat of the cup,
she will not be calmed. *You're not trying,*
she accuses, barks *think!* then marches to the sink
to wash dishes, clattering them onto the rack
to show what accomplishment sounds like.
Behind her she can hear sighs and the tick
of a pencil hitting wood. *Such an actor,* she thinks.
But when she turns to him again his shoulders
are shaking, his face wet. This is what it takes
for her to leave us alone. I dry my hands,
hold him, rub slow circles on his back.
He is still such a small boy. *Shhh,*
I whisper, as if I could erase her work.
You can do this. You can.

Forecasts
by Kimberly Greene Angle

My son was born redheaded, wide-eyed, and crying. I was prepared for his crying. I'd read all the books, and I knew that it was normal, even healthy, for him to cry a part of each day. But then he was born, and I learned that his crying was not just an audible sensation in my ear, it was something I heard with my whole body.

Every nerve in my whole being reacted, my mind went blank, my breasts leaked milk. *I knew that I must stop the crying.* I would put him to the breast again even though my nipples were sore and bleeding. Even though the pain was so intense when he latched on that it sent an aftershock tremor that shot all the way down my leg to the big toe of my right foot. *I would do almost anything to stop the crying.*

But he would cry again.

One time it was my husband, Michael, who'd had enough. He picked up our tiny baby and said, "I'm giving him a shower." I'd always thought we would bathe our child in his little white tub, but this sounded like a good idea. In his daddy's strong hands, our son calmed down as the warm sprinkling water washed over him. Then, like a little bird, he opened his mouth to let the water drip onto his tongue. At that moment, I realized that my baby was made to survive at this particular place in the universe—that he was a child of this earth. And that he came expecting rain.

Growing up, I spent a lot of time at my grandparents' house. It was a family fallout shelter for me. In that house, my grandmother always finished washing the last dish in time for the evening news. The climax of this broadcast was the weather forecast. My granddad's garden was really only a hobby for the enjoyment of fresh vegetables, but he behaved as if our lives depended on it. When the weather came on, everyone focused on the TV. No one even answered the phone. The heat and humidity of a Georgia summer oppressed in the same way day in and day out. But we watched the weatherman with intensity.

Of course, on some days, just when it seemed the air itself would combust, a little cloud would move in the sky. The lush summer growth below would shimmer in response. Then the humidity, on cue, would gather itself into a dark ceiling of clouds that blocked out the relentless sun. The trees and grasses were finally quenched with cooling rain. But the earth itself still betrayed its thirst for fire. Even in the midst of a rain shower, our planet still demanded varicose veins of light and heat from the clouds.

My grandparents did not like these summer storms. Storms caused the electricity to go out so that we could not watch the forecast on the evening news.

When I was about six years old, my brother, my two sisters, and I were running around the dining room table at home. Our dining room table was round. It was the nucleus of our house, and we screamed and ran around and around it like so many electrons. My mother eyed us. "A storm must be coming," she said. We laughed and continued our play even more frenzied, wild to be part of the angry atmosphere that shot red streaks and shook the sky. Finally she'd had enough.

"Stop," she said, "Stop it now. You're making me a nervous wreck." This was her refrain throughout our childhood: "You're getting on my nerves. You're making me a nervous wreck." My mother wished she could send us outside, and she looked out the window. Dark clouds were gathering on the horizon. A storm really was coming.

Another weekend, Daddy was home. The weather bureau had just issued a tornado warning. We knew something about tornadoes. Deep ravines tunneled through the twenty acres of woods behind our house. Daddy told us that these ditches were made when a tornado touched down years ago. We children sometimes dug odd pots and pans out of the walls of these ravines. We imagined little white houses like the one in *The Wizard of Oz* soaring up into the grasp of the dark, angry sky, and then being thrown down to splinter back onto the earth.

Unlike Dorothy, we didn't have a storm cellar, so we piled cushions and sleeping bags in our hallway and shut all the doors. My mother looked nervous, her hands were busy with her knitting. But even she sensed enough adventure in it all to manage a little smile. After all, she did marry my dad. My father was alive, electric, thriving. He snapped on the radio, listening intently. He told us to turn off our flashlights to save the batteries for when we really needed them. This was his element.

But Daddy listened to the radio for a different reason than my grandparents watched the TV forecast. He was not listening for the news that the storm was over; he was listening because he wanted to hear every detail of the storm. He didn't want our home to be destroyed, but he wanted the wind to rage, the air to burn, the clouds to shout. He needed the storm to come. To keep coming.

Daddy had popped a huge batch of popcorn and poured it into a brown grocery sack. As the storm intensified, we children played and munched on the popcorn. I watched Daddy. Like him, something in me was rejoicing in the storm. I loved the excitement, the new energy of adrenaline within me. I loved how the storm made time suddenly unhinge from all the frames of daily life. But more than that, I loved how we'd shut the doors, shut ourselves into that small space. We were close, as close as our family had ever been, will ever be. A tornado was spinning across Georgia, sucking up roofs and cows and lawn chairs, and digging ravines into the earth. But I felt strangely warm and safe and secure. I didn't want that storm to end.

Years later, on a clear, bright summer morning, I found myself in a courtroom for the first time in my life. I was twelve years old. I was scared and cold. My father's lawyer was Roy Barnes, who later became governor of Georgia. He was there, we were all there, to prove that Mommy was an unfit mother.

She was unfit because when I was seven years old she went to the doctor about her Raynaud's disease. He told her that she needed to loosen up, to talk about things. That she was holding too much in. She needed to drink a glass of wine now and then for her circulation.

My mother started to drink. She kept drinking. It was 1975, and all of her friends were getting jobs with divorces to match. Mommy decided that she wanted something more out of life. She went out and got a job as a secretary. Then she went out to parties at night. Always going, going. When she was at the house, she woke up late and vomited. Her eyes were puffy and her beautiful face was bloated. But she was not there much anymore. Neither was my father. They were always going out with friends. We didn't go to church anymore. "We're just doing our own thing," my parents said. I hated that phrase.

The house my mother kept spotless for fifteen years of her life filled with the smell of vodka and vomit and fear. Filled with the sound of screaming voices late into the night. The sound of pots and pans crashing down. The sound of children crying in the dark. Mommy was going, going.

Then she was gone.

One night my mother did come home and found me in my bedroom. She told me that she and Daddy were getting a divorce. She said it like it was some solemn news that would come as a surprise to me. Our family had been so broken for so long that this seemed almost comical to me. I just looked at her. "Aren't you going to cry?" she asked. "It's okay to cry." I just stared at her. *Didn't she know that I'd been crying all those years alone in the dark? That I couldn't cry anymore? That I couldn't feel anything?*

But on that sunny Saturday, I was at court to testify, if need be, against my mother. I was the one who'd been there that night when my parents were screaming on the back deck. I stood and stared at them through the screen door. My mother was drunk. She tripped and fell. She started yelling that my dad pushed her. She ran in and called the police. The police came. I was the witness.

Even as a child, I knew she was just saying all that because she wanted a good settlement. One of her boyfriends had probably told her that she deserved a portion of the land. I knew this because I'd heard her say that she was tired of being a mother. That she wanted something else. A different life. I knew that I was no longer what she wanted.

That day I looked at my mother sitting across the courtroom with her boyfriend. I did not make eye contact.

It turned out that I didn't have to take the stand. The court had enough evidence to pronounce the verdict on its own: Mommy was an unfit mother. Sole custody was given to my father. And he was there for us, ready to take care of us. He had mobilized for his children. He had become my hero. But what we didn't fully realize that day was that he was spiraling downward, downward into a dark, lonely place inside himself. That alcohol still had a hold on him. And as this storm ended, another one was starting on my horizon.

It took almost fifteen years for me to realize that I hated my mother so completely on that day because, at first, I'd loved her so much. And that she was the one who left me, because, at first, she was the one who'd been there so completely.

I heard the story several times throughout my life of the day my mother went into labor with me. The false labor had started back in January. "I had you thirty times over," she said. Her water broke around the fourth of March. "Finally this is it," she thought. "My fourth baby is coming today." But I didn't come. The doctor examined her. He was puzzled. He told her that the only thing he could figure was that my mother had two water sacs. That another water sac was still intact, and I was in it. She went home several pounds lighter, but I was not ready to be born.

On a breezy Saturday at the end of March, the contractions started again. "Honey, I think this may be the real thing," she told my father. But she'd been saying this for over a month now, and he'd already planned a hunting trip with his buddies. "Oh, don't worry," he said. "You stay here and make some sandwiches, and we'll be back for lunch to check on you." My mother spent the morning taking care of a six-year-old, a five-year-old, and a three-year-old. She made the sandwiches. Still, she felt the contractions growing stronger, surer, closer. She stood in the kitchen of her perfect house—thousands of miles from her birthplace in the Netherlands, hundreds of miles from her closest relative, a quarter mile from her closest neighbor. The contractions intensified. She began to wonder if she could drive herself and three small children to the hospital.

Finally, my dad and his buddies came back from the woods. My parents rushed to the hospital. My father wanted to stay with my mom during the delivery, but the hospital wouldn't let him. They took my mom to a room filled with about thirty other women in various stages of labor. Some were walking around. Some were moaning and writhing in pain. "I think the baby's coming," my mother told the nurse. "Oh, you've still got time," the nurse assured her. "Let's just try to use the potty." My mother tried to stand. She knew I was coming. I slipped from her womb and into her hands. The nurse scrambled to help, calling for a doctor.

Twenty-eight years later, I was pregnant with my first child. I'd been married for five years. I'd already earned a master's degree and had my first article published. These things were important to me. Any time previously in my marriage when I'd missed my period, I'd break out in a cold sweat. I wasn't ready to be a mother. I needed to accomplish some things first. I wasn't going to make the same mistake my mother did. I had it all figured out.

Then my biological clock started to kick in. Around that time, I found all my old dolls in the attic. Although I played with them often as a child, they still looked brand new. One was still wearing the little net over her hair, just like she did when I took her out of the box. I'd left it on her. It was important for me to keep my dolls in perfect condition. I never marked on them or cut their hair like my sister did. As I looked at the dolls, I remembered this part of me that always wanted to nurture. And I realized that I wanted to experience having a child with my husband. I felt ready. I began reading all the parenting books. "I can do this," I told myself.

The contractions started at 2:00 AM on a Saturday in October. They continued throughout the day. My water broke the next night, and the contractions stretched into another day. I checked into the hospital. The doctor examined me. I was still only dilated two centimeters. Some women dilate further than that without having the first sign of labor. The contractions began to grow painful. "Talk to me," I told my husband. "Don't stop talking."

I tried squatting and getting on all fours and walking. All the things I'd read about in the books. But the pain still increased, and it was all I could do to make it through each contraction. The nurse drew a little dot in the center of a piece of paper with increasingly larger concentric circles enclosing the dot. She told me to follow each circle with my eyes until I reached the dot. During each contraction, I followed the round shape of my pain to the central focus, slightly off center. But there was still no dilation. My baby wouldn't fit through my body. I was exhausted, and I started to vomit. "Honey," the nurse said. "I think it's time for you to take some pain medicine."

I took the medicine, then had an epidural. I felt better. But I was still vomiting, and my contractions never became regular. There was no rhythm to them. They were sporadic and chaotic. My body didn't know how to have this baby.

I spiked a temperature. We didn't want the fever to spread to the baby. I was prepped for emergency caesarean section.

My baby was born redheaded, wide-eyed, and crying. I saw him for about two minutes before he was whisked away from me to stabilize. My husband went with him. All the family saw the baby as he was wheeled through in his little clear plastic bassinet, and they went home, exhausted. I remained in the recovery room, my arms and legs still shaking uncontrollably from the epidural. I'd just given birth, and I found it strange to be so completely alone.

Suddenly, lying there, I realized that I couldn't breathe. I couldn't get my breath. A mild panic came over me. I told the nurse, "I feel like I can't get my breath." She said, "Oh, you're fine, just relax." I broke out in a cold sweat: *Why isn't she listening to me?* My lungs can't get enough oxygen. I felt like I couldn't move, but I needed desperately to sit up. I prayed with each breath that I was not dying. "I need to sit up," I finally told the nurse. "No honey," she said. "You just had major surgery. You need to lie back."

My baby who'd shared my body for nine months was somewhere, in another room, taking his first taste of air, and I was trembling, alone, trying to breathe. I stayed in a constant state of terror for almost four hours. I finally told the nurse again, "Please help me. I need oxygen. I can't breathe." She finally clued in. She went to get help. But just then they brought my son back to me. He was past the point of hunger, frantic and crying. I put him to the breast. But he couldn't latch on. But I was finally sitting up. My baby was in my arms, and, for the first time in hours, my lungs finally expanded. I could breathe again.

Later, after we took the baby home, my oldest sister called me. We talked about breastfeeding and the lack of sleep. Then she told me, "Well, I guess you realize that if it were a hundred years ago, you'd have died in childbirth." I hung up the phone and thought about what she said. I wondered, "Was I meant to be alive? Was nature trying to phase me out because my son wouldn't fit through me, because I wasn't fit to be a mother?"

I've read that what we consciously remember indicates something significant in our lives. A moment when everything makes sense. But I think it is sometimes the moments that don't make sense that catch on the barbs of our consciousness so that we can access them again later, turning them over and over like rocks in our brains until they grow smooth and round, and fit into place. Or perhaps there are other reasons we remember. I can recall a moment as a small child that I felt gelling into memory even as I was living it.

I was about five years old and I was in the VW bug with Mommy. It was raining and she'd made me wear the rain slicker that I hated, but I didn't really mind because I had her and the faint scent of her lipstick all to myself—my brother and sisters were at school. It was just the two of us snug in the tiny car, and the radio was playing and Mommy was singing in her lovely voice, *Sing, sing a song.* The dash dials were glowing in the dim day. *Sing out loud, Sing out strong.*

The rain was pelting down on the windshield, and the wipers were frantically swaying back and forth, back and forth, as we were traveling through the rainstorm. *Don't worry if it's not good enough for anyone else to hear, Just sing. . . .*

Perhaps there was a beauty in the voice and the rain and the wipers and the grayness and the glowing that I wanted to keep. But, for whatever reason, I somehow knew as I was experiencing it that the moment was seating itself into conscious memory. A moment when nothing was happening and everything was happening. Perhaps my subconscious knew that I would need a moment like this to keep in a pocket of my mind. This little memory that I could pull out and turn over in my mind like a well-worn stone, and say, yes, there was a time when I was happy with her.

My best friend, Lydia, told me recently that she doesn't like the rain, it depresses her. But I feel differently. A rainy day mutes something of the glaring reality of life for me. Somehow the rain washes all the layers of the modern expectations of motherhood away, and all that is required of me is to keep my children safe and dry. I know how to do this. My son and I make up the song, *Rain, rain, come and stay, the trees and flowers want to play.*

I love the rain. It is the sunny Thursday afternoon at three o'clock that I can't stand. The sunlight exposes me. I am sitting playing the shape game for the fifth time in a row, and my thoughts start to wriggle below the surface, struggling for life. Thwarted words start to scratch at my soul. I'm raising my children by choice. I'm determined to give them a good start on life. But, suddenly, I just want to have a moment to myself. I wonder how I'll make it through the stretching hours of Barney and feeding and cleaning up and bathing until my children are in bed asleep. I wonder how I'll hold on until those few moments when I don't have to be Mommy anymore.

My husband and I are now living in South Carolina. Michael is working on a PhD at the University of South Carolina. My little daughter is a few months old, and my son is about to turn four. The forecasters have just issued a severe weather warning. A hurricane is sending its spiraling arm of destruction all the way inland to Columbia. Michael calls; he is coming home early. Suddenly, time unhinges from its usual frames. An excitement rises like a bubble inside me. My family will soon be together.

I look out the window and watch the wind picking up, the tall trees in my backyard swirling like huge wooden spoons in the angry air. The sky grows unnaturally dark, casting an eerie glow onto the green leaves and grass. The first big drops of rain begin to splatter on the glossy leaves of the magnolia.

Michael comes home and greets our son. The baby is taking a nap. Michael says hello to me, but I'm still staring out the window. Suddenly, a yearning takes over. "I'm going for a walk," I say. "Are you crazy?" he asks. "You're going out in that?" But he knows I will go, and I do.

I add a light jacket and wide-brimmed hat to my summer garb and walk out into the rain. For a while the hat shields my glasses, but they soon become covered with raindrops—useless. I drop them into my pocket.

As I start down the sidewalk, I am a mother. A mother like my mother, not like my mother. I feel the cold, pelting rain, and I hear the rumble of distant thunder, and it is important for me to know that my children are safe and warm inside the house. If they were not safe and warm, then I could not be walking. I would still yearn to, need to, but I would put their needs first. But I walk on because I know Michael is with them, and they are safe and warm.

For months now, I have been nursing my baby for hours every day, feeding my baby from my body for hours every night. I have been filling my free moments with games and stories with my son so that he will feel loved, so that he won't resent his baby sister. And, now, before I can go back to my children, I just need to walk, to feel the motion of my muscles through the elements of this day.

As I walk on, I am the daughter of my father. The rain splatters down, trickling under my jacket, soaking into my shoes, but I don't mind; in fact, I'm glad. I hear the thunder growing louder, and I'm thriving, electric. I let the constant rain and the shouting thunder tune out all the words streaming, endlessly streaming, inside my brain. I walk until my body and my thoughts fall into rhythm with the rain. Some would say that I'm seeking death, but I know that I've come out to be alive, fully alive.

The rain begins to stream down my cheeks like cool, cleansing tears. It invigorates me. The water penetrates my hat and plasters my hair to my forehead. A car crawls by on the road beside me, its headlights glowing in the gathering gray. It slows even more when the driver sees me. The driver must be thinking, "What is that girl doing out in this? Is she lost?" But I don't turn toward the car, I just keep walking. The car drives on.

I'm not lost although I'm not walking anywhere except into the center of this storm. I must keep walking. Flesh and bone and sinew moving, moving through the thrashing wind and lashing rain. And I know that I'll keep walking until my tongue grows parched, until I open my mouth like a little bird to quench the raw thirst within me. I know that I'll keep walking until I arrive at that moment when I'm simply a child of this earth.

Nebraska
by Holly Day

when my mother first went crazy
she accused my father of stealing the ocean
and hiding it from her, just
to be cruel and mean. We were living
in Nebraska
at the time, and I can still remember the look
on his face
as my father tried to defend himself
from her useless accusations.

for two more years, we sat through
days when my mother wouldn't get up
or those that when she did, she'd spend entirely
in the tub. "The Atlantic
feels like this," she'd tell me, urging me
to dip my fingers into lukewarm water. "Soft.
And warm."

somehow she got better
all on her own, and in the meantime
I learned how to cook for both
my little sister and me.
And then one day
we woke up
and there was breakfast on the table
the laundry was done
and my mother was awake, out of bed,

ready to step out into the snow
and walk us to school.
it happened
just like that.

Eyes in the Back of Her Head
by Gayle Brandeis

They weren't sure their mother had a face.

When she read to them at bedtime, she sat on the edge of the bed, turned away. When they had nightmares, she lay on her side beside them, the back of her neck, the curve of her shoulder, blocking their view of the dark. When they drove in the minivan, they could only see the top of her forehead in the rearview mirror. When she stood at the stove, her hair swooped forward and shielded whatever glimpse they might have of her profile.

Her eyes are green, the oldest girl said. I remember seeing them when I was nursing.

Her eyes are brown, the youngest boy said. I remember seeing them when I was born.

Actually, she has one blue eye and one gray eye, the oldest girl said. I pried them open when she was sleeping.

They knew this wasn't true. She always locked her bedroom door at night.

She doesn't have a face, said the oldest boy. She's like a monster. If she turns around, all you see is a black hole.

The youngest girl didn't say anything. She turned away. She twisted her blanket around her thumb and sucked the satin acetate trim.

They contented themselves with their mother's back. They knew her back well. Her shoulder blades were expressive as eyes, widening and closing under her shirt. Her spine was a shifting string of beads, a teething ring flung open. The bit of extra skin that bulged around her bra was comforting as dough rising over a bowl. The tops of her hips fanned out like cheekbones. She had marvelous bone structure.

Maybe she can't look at us because she loves us too much, the oldest girl said.

Maybe she really has eyes in the back of her head, said the youngest boy. Maybe she's looking at us all the time.

You're fooling yourselves, said the oldest boy.

The youngest girl continued to suck on the blanket. The fabric began to shred between her teeth. She swallowed some shiny blue strands. She stroked the back of her head with her other hand. She could feel new hair growing underneath her curls, bristly and short, like a mascara brush, or eyelashes.

Gan
by Suzanne Kamata

My mother-in-law waited in her hospital room while my husband and I sat in the doctor's office. Our son, Kei, slept across my lap, his temple sweating against my forearm. I shifted his weight and tried to tune in to the doctor's words. There were many technical terms that I couldn't make out, but I understood *gan* (cancer) and *shutsu* (surgery). I watched Yusuke's face, gauging the seriousness of the disease in the tightness of his jaw. His eyes were dry. He nodded slowly and thoughtfully. He seemed to have hope.

But what if she died? What did Confucius say about orphans? Was a son then tied to his parents' graves? I knew that my mother-in-law believed her husband's spirit would get angry if she didn't put out green tea for him every morning, or light a cigarette and leave it smoldering at the family altar, like a stick of incense. Yusuke had always shrugged off these practices as superstitions, though he still knelt at the altar in the mornings and chanted a sutra.

I did none of these things. It was understood that I, as a foreigner, did not believe, and my heresy was politely ignored. I wondered if Okasan would pray to her dead husband when she found out that she had cancer. But after we bowed our way out of the doctor's office, Kei now draped over Yusuke's shoulder, my husband said, "Don't tell my mother about the cancer, okay? We'll just say that it was benign."

My jaw dropped. "Why?" If I knew my days were numbered, I'd hop on a plane bound for Tanzania. I'd visit all the museums I hadn't yet gotten to. I'd eat chocolate cake whenever I wanted and splurge on massages and manicures. Or, I might try to cure myself.

"If we tell her, she might lose hope. She must retain her vitality. She must be strong."

I didn't agree, but I nodded. "Okay. I won't say a word."

He got us settled in the car, then went back to check on his mother in her room.

~

A few days before the operation, we took her to the hospital and helped her settle in. Until the surgery, she was assigned to a ward with three other patients. They all stared at me, the foreigner, curiosity beating out politeness. I probably would have stared, too. There wasn't much to do in that room. A coin-operated TV sat on a table next to each bed. The window afforded a view of the parking lot. The other women had been in the hospital for weeks, and there was no one sitting at their bedsides.

My mother-in-law made a grand entrance. The only one with makeup and styled hair, she stood in the doorway and announced her name. And then she begged everyone's cooperation and tolerance: *"Yoroshiku onegai shimasu."*

"This is my son," she said gesturing to Yusuke.

He bowed and mumbled his own greeting.

She didn't bother to mention me.

I decided to cut her some slack. She was a sick woman, after all. And these other patients would find out soon enough who I was. I'd promised Yusuke that I'd take care of her, in the same way she had taken care of me when I was in the hospital before the birth of our son.

Okasan sat down on the edge of the bed, her spine straight. Her feet dangled a few inches from the floor. Her hands lay in her lap, cupped one within the other. She sighed.

"The food here is quite good," I said, wanting to reassure her somehow.

She snorted.

Ah, yes. I was the one who couldn't tell the difference between food cooked on a gas range and food cooked on an electric one, the woman who thought that Thai rice was just as tasty as the Japanese grain. What could I know about food?

A nurse came in then with a pair of pajamas. "Why don't you change into these, Yamashiro-san?"

My mother-in-law sat there for a long moment without acknowledging the nurse. I could tell she was going to be a difficult patient. Finally, the nurse laid the striped pajamas on the bed and strutted out.

The next morning, the day before the operation, I dropped Kei off at the neighbor's house with a pile of his favorite books and toys.

He started wailing as soon as I turned my back. His cries echoed in my head for the rest of the day. I could still hear them as I drove to the hospital, radio blasting, mind scrambling for conversational gambits to carry my mother-in-law and me through the next six hours.

I breezed into her room with a neatly wrapped parcel—pajamas from home, tangerines, and the long-handled tool she used to beat the stiffness out of her shoulders. I'd included a photo of Kei being silly. I figured the sight of a boy with pants on his head and tongue sticking out would add some much-needed levity to the situation.

She grunted when I handed over the bundle, but smiled when she found the picture. She immediately propped it up next to the TV.

I noticed that the lady in the next bed had an oxygen mask cupped over her face, whereas the day before she had been breathing on her own. It must be hard to keep up your spirits, I thought, when everyone around you was dwindling.

"That your little boy?" another patient asked, limping in with her IV pole.

"Yes," I said. I was sure that she'd already heard all about me.

"*Kawaii,*" she said. "Cute."

I tried to ignore her bald head. I made myself look straight into her eyes when I said, "Thank you."

When the woman had struggled back under the covers and flicked on her TV, Okasan finally spoke. "What's wrong with me? I want to know."

I froze. I thought we'd talk about the weather or how her orchids were faring. I had two or three anecdotes about her favorite grandson lined up. I wasn't prepared to talk about her diagnosis.

"You should talk to Yusuke," I said. "I didn't understand everything the doctor said."

She sighed. "I did talk to him. A small cyst, he said. Nothing to get excited about. But I know that he's lying."

I turned away so she wouldn't read the truth in my eyes. "I'll make you some tea."

I thought about fleeing. The door was just three feet away. If I made up some excuse—a fever for Kei, a long-distance phone call from my family—maybe I could make a graceful exit. But after I brewed the tea and handed Okasan her cup, she started to talk about something else.

As it turned out, the day went by more quickly than I expected. Visitors came with packets of money and boxes of cakes. I kept busy serving them tea and rounding up folding chairs. The ladies from Okasan's *ikebana* class and English conversation circle visited, and for half an hour Yusuke took care of the small talk.

By the time they'd all left, Okasan was exhausted and ready for a nap. She slipped into sleep, and I just sat there thumbing through magazines, trying to figure out which Japanese celebrity was bedding who.

After Okasan had been dressed in blue paper and loaded onto a gurney, after we'd pressed her hand and urged her to be strong, we went into a little room to wait. Other families waited with us. Some had been there for a while, to judge from the debris of meals. One woman was stretched out on the long vinyl sofa, her head pillowed by a bag of knitting. Her shoes and socks were off, revealing gnarls and corns. She snored softly. With time, I guessed, you could get used to that place, feel just as comfortable as you might in your own bedroom. Worry and grief crowded out shame. When someone you loved was on the table or hooked up to a respirator in the ICU, what you looked like to strangers didn't really matter.

So I didn't worry too much about the streaks of chocolate ice cream on Kei's t-shirt. Yusuke hadn't shaved in a couple of days, and his eyes were puffy from too much whiskey the night before, too little sleep.

I'd put on makeup and brushed my hair. My dress spilled smoothly over my hips. I thought that I looked good and that there was something obscene about it. Better if I'd smudged my mascara, wrinkled my clothes.

In the corner, a man was chain-smoking. A young woman fiddled with her cell phone, in spite of the sign prohibiting satellite calls. She belonged in some nightclub, a booth at Mister Donut, not in this purgatorial chamber.

Yusuke paced and sighed. Kei spent a few minutes studying our companions before he began raiding the bookshelf. Children came here often for last looks at grandparents, for their first lessons in mortality. The kids' books were well worn, thumbed through, some of the covers hanging like one-hinged doors.

Kei found a book about ships and settled on a sofa to "read" it aloud. I watched his rosebud mouth working out words, the thick lashes, the dimples in the backs of his hands. Like always, I got lost in his beauty. Sometimes it made me ache. I wanted to gather him up, the way children embrace teddy bears or favorite blankies. I even wanted to share him a little, knowing that his magic touch could change the atmosphere in that little room. He could make us forget about needles and knives. One little squeeze and all tremors would be gone.

The operation lasted for four hours. When, at last, the surgeon called our name, Yusuke stepped forward, and I pulled Kei onto my lap. He was half asleep by then, having run up and down the stairs more times than I could count. His belly was full of rice balls and bananas.

The surgeon smiled a little, and the creases in Yusuke's forehead softened. They bowed to each other, and then Yusuke turned to me. "They think they got it all," he said. "I'll go in and see her now."

I nodded. I started rocking Kei to sleep. I didn't want him to see his grandmother in a morphine haze, tubes trickling liquid into her veins. I wanted to keep his world perfect, free of sorrow and disease, for just a little while longer.

When I finally went to see her, I transferred Kei to his father's arms and went in alone.

She was small against the white sea of a bed. Her eyelids fluttered open. She whispered something. I leaned closer to hear it.

"*Gan, desu yo?*" Cancer, right?

I nodded, not quite sure if she could see me, or if she would even remember this later.

"But you'll be okay," I said. "The doctors got it all out."

Her eyes closed again, and she dove back into the twilight zone.

I put my hand on her forehead, the closest I'd ever come to giving her affection.

I wasn't sorry that I'd broken my vow not to tell. She had a right to know. Besides, she'd figured it out on her own. But when I saw the despondency in her eyes two days later, I wondered if she was going to put up a fight or if she had already given up.

She wouldn't eat, said the drugs made her queasy. The hospital gruel went cold and hard.

"C'mon, Yamashiro-san," the nurse said. "If you want us to take out the IV you'd better start eating."

She closed her eyes and set her jaw, mad at the world and one foot stepping toward the grave.

The doctor dropped by with good news. "Her blood count is good. The suture is healing nicely." But as soon as the doors had creaked shut, she'd hiss, "*Uso bakkari.*" Lies, all lies.

"Look," I said. "If you want to get better, you have to think positively."

"You don't care what happens to me," she replied. "You're hoping that I die. I know. I was a daughter-in-law once, too."

I brought in balls of rice wrapped around sour plums, green tea cakes, bits of fish—all her favorite things—but she wouldn't take a bite.

Finally, I brought in Kei and propped him on the edge of the bed with a spoon and some pudding.

"Obachan, say 'ahhh.'" Kei dipped the spoon into the cup and carefully launched it toward her lips.

She kept them pressed tight at first, but who could resist that little boy charm? She cracked a smile and then broke down for a taste.

Kei cooed and clapped. I pretended not to notice that she was giving in.

In the mornings, after Yusuke had left, I lingered over Kei. Sometimes I'd watch him for a full ten minutes before tickling him awake with feather strokes on his soles, soft kisses on his belly. He rolled into my arms, smiling, his eyes still shut.

He was big enough to ride a tricycle, big enough to wash his hands without my help, big enough to answer the phone, even. But I carried him like a baby to his place at the breakfast table. I watched as he woke to scrambled eggs and triangles of buttered toast.

His passion, just then, was dinosaurs. In between bites, he recited a litany of ancient beasts: mastodon, tyrannosaurus rex, brontosaurus, raptor. I asked him questions, just to keep him talking, just to stay a bit longer in the world that most interested him.

"Are brontosauruses carnivores or herbivores?"

"They eat grass," he said in his most professorial voice. "Herbivores."

"And how about raptors?"

"Meat."

One look at the clock told me I was running late. I'd miss my mother-in-law's breakfast time if I didn't get on the ball.

Kei was just going next door, to the neighbor's house, but I packed him a lunch and a bag of toys. I tucked a photo of myself in his pocket.

Mrs. Kitagawa wouldn't accept money for baby-sitting. She gushed about joy and honor every time I brought Kei over, but of course I paid her back. I'd already started tutoring her daughter, Maya, at a cut rate. I was parceling out my slang and colloquialisms at bargain-basement prices.

Kei could get dressed by himself, but I slid his pajama bottoms down his legs and pulled off his top, leaving Anpan Man inside out on the floor. My hands skimmed his back and belly, the shoulder bones jutting like angel wings. I breathed him deep before I tugged a t-shirt over his head, helped his hands find the armholes. He had an arm around my neck as he stepped into his pants. I'd seen him put on his shoes many times before, but as he sat in the entryway, I held his foot in my hand and guided it into a sneaker. Then the other one.

"Why do I have to go to Maya's house?" he asked, eyes dark, like it was a punishment.

"Because Obachan is in the hospital. You know."

"Why can't I go with you? You said I make her happy. I can feed her." He tugged on my arm. "I can help you."

Yes, every time he entered the ward, she softened. She tried harder. But it was not Kei's job to make her well. That was asking too much. He was only four years old.

"Obachan gets tired easily. She needs to rest, and there's nothing for you to do while she's sleeping."

He drooped. Kicked at the floor.

"Hey," I said, tilting his face up to mine. "I'll miss you. A lot."

I spent that day and the days that followed with Okasan, fetching drinks, bringing her boxes of tissues, and doing her laundry. I hummed along as she ran through her daily complaints, hovered while she took her medicine, and drew the curtains around her bed when she wanted to take a nap.

In the evenings, Yusuke took my place. We exchanged only a few phrases each day. That is, until one night when he burst into the room where I lay sleeping with Kei.

"Jill!"

I forced my eyes open and glanced at the illuminated numerals on the alarm clock. It was well after midnight. Visiting hours at the hospital ended at eight, but Yusuke often stayed later, especially when his mother couldn't sleep.

"Why did you tell my mother she has cancer?"

I saw his hands, curled in fists at his sides. I put a finger to my lips and nodded at our sleeping child, and then I joined him in the harsh hall light.

"I didn't tell her," I whispered. "She guessed it herself."

He shook his head. "You confirmed it. You could have told her that she was wrong."

"She's not a child," I said, my own voice rising. "She has a right to know."

He laughed—one short, sharp bark. "She thinks she's going to die. She's depressed. She's not even trying to get well."

"I'm sorry," I said.

"Sorry. Ha. A lot of good that does." He stormed down the stairs and out of the house. In the morning, he was still not there.

I brought Kei to the hospital that day for a few hours. I stood in the doorway for a moment until she noticed our presence.

"Kei-kun!" Just one look at him and pink was already flooding her cheeks. I became invisible.

"Go on," I whispered, urging him forward.

He stumbled toward her bed with a goofy grin, and she smoothed out a spot for him on the white sheets. "Obachan, do you feel better?"

I stepped out of sight, thinking I'd go get myself a cup of coffee. Halfway down the hall, I heard her laughter mingled with Kei's. I kept walking. She wouldn't be dying anytime soon.

Mama's Orange Robe
by Cathleen Daly

the 1970s wrapped my mother in a chic throbbing
neon-orange quilted robe with vertical magenta and
burgundy stripes
she may as well have been encased by the word groovy
it was a padded mama pillow, a psychedelic road map to
my small world
I thought she was the lady on the Yuban coffee can,
they sported the same dark bob
in my mind she was also Picasso's *Lady in Blue* sad and
curled hanging in the neighbor's hallway
it didn't phase me to see my mother's image plastered
on public artifacts
of course she was everywhere
the universe spun out in ragged milky trails from her,
the center my hub
Dad meanwhile sat in Thailand clumsily clacking
chopsticks making the waitresses giggle sending sis
and I two life-size dolls, little diplomats of
Distance and Abandonment
"where's your TV?" kids would ask first thing when
they came over and then inevitably "where's your dad?"
little four-year-old red-faced shrugger, I had no
answers
but I did have a life-size stuffed alligator in the
garage that we could sit on and pretend to ride to new
lands
having a split-in-half family in a world of neat
wholes baffled and embarrassed
but pride flooded my shy limbs if my mama ever graced

the red paved halls of my school
if her full-time job ever coughed her up long enough
to come visit, kids would eye her paisley minidresses, her black patent-leather
belts and matching
sandals
"she's pretty" "she's cool" whispers would ruffle the
still classroom air
once the neighborhood kids, sis, and I posed on our
new turquoise Volvo for a photo "say shit!" said mom
eyes wide, we burst into flames of laughter,
brighter even
than that neon robe

Blueberries for Mom
by Meagan Francis

Mom buckles me into the backseat of our 1979 station wagon, fastening the seat belt snugly. She is thirty-seven, young looking, pretty. She wears a belted sweater in a rusty shade of orange—just slightly outdated and out of season for a July morning in 1982.
We are going blueberry picking.

My mother died when my son, Isaac, was six weeks old. By that time her face was prematurely aged from years of drinking. Her hair, like her personality, tended to be unpredictable, frizzled, choppy. Though it was 1999, Mom still wore the circa 1979 orange-belted sweater, still drove old cars, and still earned a 1979 living wage. It was as though at some point Mom's connection to the outside world just stopped.

I sat nursing my new baby at the memorial service, listening numbly as the pastor and a few of her friends spoke. *Gee, isn't it nice that they're all saying such good things about Mom,* I thought to myself as I casually adjusted Isaac's latch on my nipple. Out of the corner of my eye I saw others—more distant relatives, acquaintances of Mom's—watching me. "How brave she is," I imagined them murmuring to each other. In truth, I just wanted to get home and get back to life.

When your mother is an alcoholic, you learn how to detach.

"We'll have to drive a little farther this year," Mom says, gripping the burnt-sienna steering wheel, squinting as she anticipates her turn. "They took down most of the woods to build more holes for the golf course."
I am only five, but the disdain in her voice at the words "golf course" carries with me to this day, a lesson in conservationism from my nonpolitical-minded mother.
I clutch my bucket with excitement as Mom pulls up to the edge of the dense northern Michigan woods.

The next day, we made the three-hour car trip to Cheboygan, where Mom's ashes were buried in the plot next to my would-have-been big brother, Patrick, who died suddenly, in 1970, at six weeks old—the same age as the fat baby I held, football-like, under my arm as I stood next to her grave. His death was when Mom's drinking began, so my older sister tells me.

It was a mild November day and I felt uncomfortable, like I wasn't doing the grieving-daughter thing quite right. Her death felt, to me, less like a loss and more like a release—a reprieve from that sinking feeling that somebody you love is going downhill, and there's nothing you can do but try to keep yourself from going down with them.

Later, on the car ride home, I glimpsed the death certificate and saw the cause of death: cirrhosis of the liver due to alcoholism. I felt a momentary surge of anger at the faceless coroner for his conclusion.

When your mother is an alcoholic, it's hard to get past the impulse to cover up.

"Look over here!" Mom says. "I found a patch!"

We pounce on the blueberries, dropping them into the buckets as we work our way, crouched low, around the plants. Wild blueberries don't plunk *into the bucket the way the ones at the grocery store do. They're small and firm, and they* plink.

They don't taste like grocery store blueberries, either. For every berry that goes in the bucket, one ends up in my mouth, tangysweet. "Remember to leave some for the gnomes," Mom says. "They don't need too many, though."

"Gnomes must have small bellies, right Mom?" I ask, carefully avoiding a few of the lowest, best-looking berries.

"Right, honey."

It wasn't until later, much later, when I was able to remember not just Mom last month but also the Mom I knew when I was five, eight, ten, that I began to grieve. Easier to cry for the loss of the mother who made Christmas ornaments with you every year than the mother who showed up drunk at your wedding and attempted to dance Latin-style with your new husband's crazy uncle. Her death made everybody's job easier. Now we could just remember Mom the way we all wished she'd always been.

I think it took me a long time to accept that Mom was an alcoholic because her usual behavior didn't fit with my childish definition of "drunk." I'd seen drunk in the glassy eyes of my boisterous uncle as he swung me dangerously over his head, laughing at my delighted squeals as the sober adults in the room nervously watched on, ready to spring up at a moment's notice to rescue a catapulting child from going through the front-room window. I'd seen drunk in the loud but good-natured political debates around the table at my aunt's house: die-hard liberals, right-wing conservatives, political scandals, and a couple bottles of good liquor. That was drunk, not Mom's bitter, angry irrationality that just happened to be combined with a sizable dose of Ernest and Julio.

And drinking wasn't the entirety of what made Mom difficult—it was simply the factor that could take her from slightly manic to something more, something harder to explain away. Sober Mom might nag me to do the dishes, but only drunk Mom would add, "You're just like your father, you think only of yourself, and you'll always be selfish." Sober Mom might sternly chastise my friend and me for trying to leave the house wearing too much makeup, but only drunk Mom would tell us we looked like a couple of two-bit floozies, her hands clenched, tears in her eyes: angry, but more than angry—threatened. Sober Mom welcomed debate, seemed to encourage my spirited side. Drunk, she seemed overwhelmed by the fact that I had opinions of my own, wounded by the force of my preteen will, and unable to cope.

On days like those, my best friend wouldn't commiserate, "Man, your mom's being a bitch," but would instead pretend—badly—that she didn't notice, perhaps imagining the conversation her parents would have over the dinner table when she told about what she'd seen: *It's sad, isn't it. I wonder if we can do anything?*

Sometimes when I've had a glass of wine and I lean in over my children to tuck them into bed and kiss them good night, I wonder if they smell the wine on my breath and if that memory will be forever etched in their memories, and if they'll one day associate me with that smell the way you associate pine needles with Christmas and melting candle wax with birthday cake. The smell of certain kinds of alcohol—particularly when covered up by a dose of mouthwash—jolts me into the past.

When your mother is an alcoholic, it can really take the fun out of drinking.

We're home. Mom is probably having a glass of wine, and we're sorting and cleaning the berries, then divvying them up into individual containers—some for freezing, some for snacking, some for baking. We've decided to make blueberry muffins today, blueberry pancakes tomorrow.

"What can I do?" I ask, pinching a blueberry from the empty Cool Whip container we'll use to freeze them in.

"You can get out a mixing bowl, the measuring cups, and a wooden spoon," says Mom. "Thanks for being a great helper."

I jump to the task, glowing.

My challenge becomes to determine which of my mother's behaviors were damaging (because, certainly, many were) and which were enriching. How can I separate the good from the bad? How can I take the person I am today and decide which parts Mom helped develop (so to emulate) and which parts she just messed up (so to avoid)?

It would be easier if it was as simple as "alcohol = always bad" and "no alcohol = always good." But it was my mother who, though most likely three-sheets-to-the-wind at the time, introduced me to Harry Chapin and the original Broadway recording of *Fiddler on the Roof*. It was my mother who, while accusing me of doing things that my older brother actually did (thereby causing me to question my own sanity) and handing out irrelevant punishments, also encouraged my writing, praised my singing voice, and cuddled with me on the couch while watching TV.

I have moments with my own children that scare me—moments of disproportionate rage, violent urges that come and go so quickly and sharply they leave me breathless. Sometimes my own (sober) voice seems to morph into the scary tone of drinking Mom—shaming, irrational, cruel, the sound that can make my children wither before my eyes. Other times, I hear the gentle, low humor of Mom on her good days: clever, quick-witted, *fun*. I'm not sure which I find more unsettling.

Mothering, for me, isn't just a matter of following what feels right. What feels right, I've been told by therapists, books, and armchair psychologists, is skewed—based on an upbringing filled with uncertainty, dishonesty, and blurred boundaries. I am not allowed to trust my feelings because they will mislead me. At first, I dealt with this uncertainty by mothering in ways that seemed socially acceptable—the hope being that using society at large as a mothering litmus test would keep me from screwing up. Yet my ever-present urge to rebel (thanks, Mom) against much of what is considered "good parenting" has led me to make up my own rules as I go. I'm not supposed to worry my kids with my problems, *that* much I know—but how much does a thoughtful parent hold back? What's healthy?

I find myself thinking about my parenting goals not in terms of "most wonderful," but of "least harmful"—when my kids look back on their childhood, I don't want them to remember a few really great moments amid a bunch of purposely forgotten black X-marks. My hope is not that the once-in-a-while good will be so outstanding that it blots out the bad, but that the bad will be infrequent enough that it fades away naturally. I wonder, sometimes, if I'm succeeding. I also wonder just how screwed up that kind of outlook is.

When your mother is an alcoholic, you learn to doubt yourself.

Mom and I have just finished the last of the golden brown muffins. We put our empty milk glasses and plates (mine licked clean of crumbs) into the sink, then head upstairs to bed.

Mom sits on the edge of my bed and reads me a chapter of Little House on the Prairie. *I can read it myself—she taught me how—but tonight, I'm only too happy to hear the steady, even tone of her voice as she reads the story of Laura and Ma baking sourdough biscuits.*

"Did you have fun today?" she asks when she's finished, tucking the covers carefully in around my shoulders. I nod yes, my eyelids heavy. I'm exhilarated by our venture through the woods, lulled into sleepiness by Mom's gentle movements. Mom drops a kiss on my forehead and I drift off to sleep.

I dream of Ma Ingalls in an orange belted sweater, holding a fat, happy gnome in her hand.

Word-Girl

by Mary Moore

You said me, mother, a word you warded,
a plaid-skirted word-girl, church-schooled.
You told me rosary beads of rules—
skip sidewalk cracks; throw salt shoulder-overward;

save pennies found; make luck. Worrier,
you shaped me as worries shaped your world.
The nine good angel-kinds, the stars that shined
through constellated window panes at night,

"Hail Marys," "Our Fathers," my Girl Scout
oath, my tables of allegiances—words
girded and guarded my world like household
gods. Words were all my plight. You shaped me

mother, like a word you loved and mouthed—
I, the bell of syllables, I, the smooth-sided labials. Words were all my troth.
So I rode the air like flying does, like sound.

No wonder falling woke me. I'd lie
spread-eagled, face up, under the wheel
of ceiling, its hub, the lightbulb's pear-
shaped egg—a whirligig of a girl

the bed had thrown. I was thud and bone,
a stone on the world's flat center. I heard
air's white noise, the just-missed cloud sigh after
birds pass through, the lisp of space. No wonder

the round-sided vowels could not buoy me.
I was a mote, but not of dust or earth.
You said me, mother, oath whose vowed to earth,
word you schooled in words. Now I say you.

Motherkind
by S. A. Miller

"I'll bet your mom visits a lot, living so close," my friend's mother says. Here for a week from across the county, she dotes on her daughter with kindness, good sense, and superior curtain-cleaning skills.

"Visits? Not so much," I answer in singsong. The next day a jar of homemade strawberry jam appears on my front steps with a label that reads, "For Susan from Lillian." I hardly know Lillian. I'm not sure if I knew her name before I saw it written there. But as I stand holding the jar on my front porch, I feel the heavy glass, like possibility. I finger the decorative rows of ripples and tap the round, silver lid. When I am sure no one is looking, I rub that jar like a cool hand across my cheek.

I store the jam, my ruby red secret, in the back of the fridge, meting out careful spoonfuls on my morning toast, savoring it as the delicacy it is. It tastes like someone's home. It tastes sweet, like fresh berries, only better. It tastes like mothering.

I am a motherless mother. As far as I can tell, there are many ways to earn this scourge of sadness, but death and emotional desertion that first come to mind.

My friend Thea, for example. We were on the playground a few years back in separate hormonal hazes, making the requisite small talk. Pushing our babies in black vinyl baby swings, we were literally trying to push the long day away. Thea didn't look at me when she said, almost casually, that just two years ago she still wasn't sure about having children, but her mother had told her she'd have a little girl someday. "I wish she lived long enough to know she was right." Thea's voice dropped to a whisper. I looked over and saw her face tighten. "My mother liked being right."

Or my friend Kathleen, who I held as her heart burst like a rain cloud pouring down sorrow for her mother who died before her daughter was born.

I think of Tennyson's "'Tis better to have loved and lost." And, goddammit, I wish like Kathleen that I had a mother to love before I lose her forever. I want my daughter to have a grandmother who thinks that little girl birthday parties should be frothy pink and utterly unmissable. I want a mother who'll play penny-ante with my son, the way my granny did until we both laughed so hard we peed our pants and had to flip the chair cushions before anyone saw.

My mother isn't dead. But she is the type of mother who fails you for much of your life and then goes on to fail your children. It hurts every day that she is around with her arm held up like a brace against yearning. It hurts like a wake that won't end. And then a jar of strawberry jam appears on the doorstep.

I want to explain my mother. I myself want to know the truth of her, but it feels like groping for my glasses in a pitch-black room.

I try to get oriented with the touchstones of my childhood. Nearly every day she battered me in some kind of depressive rage. She hit me more for crying. She called me a brat. As a girl, I would lock myself in my rainbow-colored room, throw myself on the bedspread she forbade me from sitting on, and smash together the delicate knickknacks that lined my bookshelves. Over the years, I sacrificed an entire collection of glass frogs to the purging of my hurt, though more than once I stood with a warty ceramic shard against my wrist and prayed for courage one way or the other.

I feel like I hold a few disparate clues to my mother. The first came many Christmases ago, in a boozy moment of connection, when she told me she didn't want to get married, but my father did. Yet when he died twenty years back, I never felt her liberation. The other clue: one-hundred-plus pairs of unworn white sweatpants stuffed into cabinets around her bedroom. When I add that to her Lady Macbeth imitation when a spot gets on the rug, her ballistic fury over spilled milk, and her need to discard everything old, including my father's war diaries and my beloved teddy, I make my armchair diagnosis of obsessive-compulsive disorder. So what does that mean? Love and emotions are too messy for her to control, so she simply doesn't deal in them? Maybe that's my longed-for explanation, but I'm entitled to despise its simplicity.

In seeking an explanation for her, I come up empty. She is not an abuse victim or an alcoholic. She is not, as I used to wish, a genius poet driven mad by suburban constraints. She is a skinny, pleasant church worker who constantly brags on the grandchildren she will never come to see.

At some point I started noticing the Lillians. They aren't all mothers, I imagine, but, in small ways, they mother. The woman in the grocery store who presses strong, old fingers with crepey skin into my arm and says, "Your little girl there. She's a gift from God." Or the Indonesian woman at the deli who comes around the counter to hand my son a thick slice of turkey pastrami. "Your favorite, honey," she says in a heavy, cheerful accent. I'll include the walker with the pastel jogging suits who joins our world almost daily with a smile and a few warm words as she passes our yard. And there's the frail librarian who has a tidy stack of ballet books set aside for my daughter because, she says, "We both love the ballet."

When friends who know my mother ask how I survived her, I tell them I had Florence growing up. She was an older woman, a mother of two grown boys, who lived two doors down from us. If thoughtful attention can save a lonely girl, that's what Florence did for me. Every Saturday we would sit together at her kitchen table and work out the crossword puzzle in the newspaper. She would fix me a cup of milky coffee and listen to all the pressing silliness that a young girl's world turns on. She loved my knock-knock jokes. She said I was smart. She never sent me away.

On Mother's Day, my mother and I exchange carefully selected cards with a few predictable words. Hers comes with a twenty-dollar bill and a note that says to buy something for the kids. I pocket the cash, treat it as compensation for the science experiment of abuse that was my childhood. A while back, battle-weary and broken, I had to give up the fight to have her. There's a tiny place in the corner of my soul that still hopes, and while hope is fine, it's also pretty damn draining.

And so I find a different place to put my love, love that I have only because someone, some mother or not, has given it to me. I write to Lillian, my most favorite pen pal ever, and thank her for the latest jar of strawberry jam that she now sends regularly along with newsy letters from Oregon. A little shy, I tell the librarian that my daughter and I would love to take her to the ballet one

Saturday afternoon, and her face actually changes shape when she smiles so large. I learn the name of the Indonesian woman at the deli: Halima. She tells me she has a daughter who lives with her sister and mom in Jakarta. She hasn't seen her in years because she needs a green card to bring her daughter over. "I talk to her every day, but I'm so afraid she thinks I forget her." She reaches easily for a framed photo and passes it across the counter. "I just want to make a better life for her." Then she cries so shamelessly that I am embarrassed.

When I return the photo, I hold Halima's fingers for a few seconds, and I tell her what I know is true. "Your daughter is beautiful," I say. "And she's lucky to have you."

Gray
by Sybil Lockhart

Dinner is over. My husband, Patrick, is on the phone. I'm trying to load the dishwasher while Zoë spins in circles holding her fairy wand and Cleo shuffles back and forth in Patrick's black loafers. It's the wind-up period before bedtime. I give them the five-minute warning.

My mother looks down at her lap, bending so far forward that I can see the hump of her back. Clasping her hands together, she looks up again with a plaintive, pained tightening of the skin around her eyes. Her mouth opens to speak:

"No. Never mind." She shakes her head, looks back down.

"What, Ma?"

"No, nothing. I'm just being stupid. Never mind me."

"Ma. Try not to use that word around the kids, okay? Plus, it's not true."

"Oh, I knew that. That was stupid. No, I mean—not stupid! Never mind. I'll just shut up now."

"Ma. What is it?"

But I know; I know it by heart, because it's the same every Friday night when she comes to stay. She wants the TV on right now, but the remote control confuses her. She needs the bed made up, but she doesn't understand how the thing unfolds. And she expects to be in bed by nine. If she doesn't get into bed by nine, she'll look up the stairs, wringing her hands and sighing loudly. She'll wonder out loud what's keeping me. Impatiently, she will flip through the channels, then fretfully pull at the couch, but stop herself and again glance up the stairs. If I tuck in the kids and walk back downstairs at 9:15, it may as well be 2:00 AM; the waiting and the uncertainty weigh on her that heavily.

When Ma doesn't do everything just so, something can slip through. It could be something small, like forgetting to brush her teeth. But it could be a stove burner left on, tall, hot flames licking out into the dark kitchen for hours as she sleeps. It could be the door left standing wide open with the black night yawning in. Or maybe her whole world will dissolve. The truth: It is dissolving, right there inside her head. Sticky mats of neurons slowly clot there, gradually obscuring patches of her own life from view. Some of her perceptions remain clear; others are very slowly melting into a murky blur. But she doesn't know what will go next. The schedule saves her. Clean and sure, it keeps her from wondering. Her list is intact, and she checks it off: 8:00 PM television, 9:00 PM bathroom, pills, read in bed. If nine o'clock comes and the bed is not made, something feels askew. She doesn't quite understand, but she feels out of control. Maybe she has missed something important. Maybe she's done something wrong. So she lives in a constant state of low-level worry that swells into a panic as the clock ticks past the hour.

Zoë zaps Cleo with her wand, eliciting a gleeful toddler shriek. She strikes again, but too hard, and Cleo bawls. Remorseful, Zoë picks her up and hauls her to the other side of the room, kissing her ferociously and yelling, "It's okay! It's okay!" I look feebly from Ma's anxious hands, wringing one another in her lap, to my two kids, now crying together in long, wavering wails. The distress Ma projects when her schedule is disrupted infects me immediately. As she begins to fret, so do I. This isn't right. I have to make it stop. I must get these kids into bed before they kill each other, but if I don't take care of Ma this instant, my own world may dissolve. And I hate her for it. I hate my mother for her helpless descent into the darkness.

As mother to five-year-old Zoë and one-year-old Cleo, I am so used to being able to fix things, to nourish. I kiss the boo-boos. I serve the food. I gave them my breast when they cried in the night. And I see them heal, grow, learn, flourish. But no matter how much I give to Ma, she only becomes smaller. My children rise up into the light, gathering knowledge, insight, and wisdom. As they play and think and create, becoming clearer and brighter, I can almost see the myriad intricate synaptic connections being sculpted, refined. Simultaneously, Ma's wiring runs amok; sticky protein oozes into her synapses, and the fibers that structure her neurons begin to crimp and tangle. Ever so slowly she loses comprehension of the world, and as she does, she loses pieces of the person she once was to me. That is how it works, that is how she incites my empathy and my rage in equal parts. I should be able to fix it. I can't.

My mother's name is Ruth. She began forgetting conversations we had after 5:00 PM a few years ago, but I attributed that to her deepening relationship with alcohol. When she began to forget big things, like the name of her newborn grandchild, or having loaned out $50,000, I insisted on a visit to the UC Davis Alzheimer's Disease Center. There, they diagnosed her with early-stage Alzheimer's disease, exacerbated by excessive consumption of alcohol. She was sixty-eight years old.

Throughout my childhood, Ma was warm and welcoming. She cared about animals, about teaching her first-graders, about the planet. She told me that the most important thing in life was love: finding someone to love, finding someone to love you. I know this to be true, and I say it to my children too. Ma believed in plain words. When the county jail down the road was rebuilt, the new sign said DETENTION CENTER. For three mornings after that sign went up, Ma walked the dogs down to the new building at 6:00 AM and tacked a banner reading JAIL over the new sign. She lettered her banner in the same beautiful calligraphy she used to make our Christmas cards and the leaflets she handed out at peace rallies in San Francisco.

In our family, Ma was the provider. She made most of the money—my dad was legally blind and received disability from the county—and she did all of the cooking. She taught us to read, and she took us for walks in the hills, where she shared her love of the outdoors. Friday nights, my parents' friends gathered for guitar playing, puns, political discussion, and drinks. While the kids ran wild, Ma served smoked oysters; she made the martinis. She was strong-bodied and had strong, simple principles: Don't make war. Love people. Don't lie. Take care of the world you live in. People should learn how to read. People need exercise, they need to eat meat, and they need sex.

I loved her desperately; I felt safe with her. But I couldn't be with her enough. I cried for her, and she didn't come. It was like this. The house we lived in was on a hill. It had an upstairs and a downstairs, but the two were not connected by an indoor stairway. When I was a baby, we all lived on the ground floor, which was the top floor. But before I had stopped wetting the bed, my sister, Alice, and I were moved to the two downstairs bedrooms. I remember the damp side stairs and the sweet smell of oleanders as we went down for bed. At first, Ma would come down to tuck us in. When she went back upstairs, even with my sister in the next room, I didn't want her to leave me down there. Many nights, I cried for her until I hiccupped myself to sleep. It just didn't feel right to be so far away from her. Daddy too, but Mommy more.

In winter and spring, when we rose before daylight and dashed through the rain to the warmth and safety of upstairs, it was impossible not to step on the snails. I felt the wet crunch as I ran up the slippery steps, and then there I was in the dining room, with wet hair and freshly dead, slimy snail innards all over my bare feet. I would frantically wipe the slime off on the burgundy shag rug, reaching for a tissue to get the last bits out from between my toes. There was always coffee brewing. The smell of coffee brewing meant I had escaped the nightmares and the monsters; it meant my parents still loved me. Today to me that smell still signifies the comfort of Mommy, of home.

I love passing on the snail-crunching lore of my childhood to five-year-old Zoë. She squirms, delighted and horrified to imagine it. But, she asks me, why didn't you have slippers on? Why didn't Aunt Alice and you get to sleep upstairs any more? What if you needed your parents in the night? And I understand that the desperate longing I felt those dark nights downstairs informs me now as a parent: This is what you don't do. You don't leave them not knowing where you are. You don't leave them scared and lonely on another floor of the house with the darkness and the rain and the slimy snails between you, when they are only six years old. Maybe this is why, when my turn arrives, as forty-year-old daughter-turned-mother, I just can't leave Ma downstairs, worried and waiting.

I ask Zoë, can she read a story to Cleo to cheer her up? Knowing that I've bought myself a maximum of one and a half minutes, I lead Ma to the futon. Together, we perform the ritual of arranging the five blankets and two pillows in exactly the same order as we do every Friday night. I tune the TV to the channel for her favorite program, *Providence*. I bring her the remote control, and carefully point out the "mute" and "off" buttons to her. Setting down her cup of Sleepytime tea, I kiss her soft cheek. I'm trying not to breathe in too much of her odd scent. My father died almost twenty years ago, and still it seems to me that her clothes smell faintly of his cigarettes, mingled with the odors of cooking oil and mildew. I tell her, "Tomorrow we'll go to Saul's for breakfast." Then I turn and herd the kids upstairs.

There, the air smells sweeter and the lights seem warmer. After I change Cleo's diaper, I pause to bury my nose in her soft, warm belly, eliciting shrieks of pleasure. I snuffle, breathing in the warm, sweet goodness of her skin. Patrick leans in the doorway with Zoë's toothbrush in hand, and tells us a joke. Wild and naked, Zoë bounces on the bed, and I turn to admire her lean stomach and legs. I heave a sigh of relief. We are a safe distance from Old; we are together, healthy, and sane.

In the morning, Ma is waiting anxiously in the kitchen, glancing pointedly at the coffeepot. She doesn't know how to work it. She does fine with her own machine at home. We tried to teach her. But she forgot the filter; she didn't think to look for the pot in the dishwasher; she couldn't remember how much coffee to put in, and didn't dare to guess. It's eight o'clock, and I know she's been sitting there since six, waiting for there to be coffee in that pot. "Oh, good," she says. "I guess now you'll make some coffee. I was starting to think I would never get any." I fight off irritation. "Just relax, Ma. I'm making it right now." Then softer, "It'll be done in three minutes. Let's heat up a mug for you while we wait."

The child-rearing books call this "managing her expectations." As long as I am careful not to become patronizing about it, much of what I've learned about parenting two- and three-year-olds transfers well when dealing with a seventy-two-year-old with dementia. It is a tricky disease, coming and going. There are whole weeks when she's bright and joking and normal-seeming. But fairly often she feels lost and bewildered, has trouble initiating conversation, and forgets what she's just been told. Sometimes she acts just like a tired kid.

Once, Zoë asked her to read a story. They sat cozily on the couch together, Zoë looking on as Ma read in her teacher-voice from a Winnie the Pooh book. I eavesdropped, hungry for this moment of apparent normality in my mom's role as a grandma.

Zoë kept jumping in eagerly: "Look, Tigger's tail is a SPRING!"

The first time Zoë interrupted, Ma nodded indulgently. The second time, she said, "Yes, okay, but let's continue with the story now." Zoë, irrepressible, kept it up.

"Gram! Watch me do the Tigger bounce!"

She was bouncing on the couch with one hand on Ma's back, jostling the book up and down, when suddenly Ma pulled back and threw the book on the floor.

"You're RUINING the story!"

"I am not!"

"You are too!"

"Am not!"

"I'm not reading to you ANYmore."

"I don't care, and don't throw books!"

As Zoë stomped angrily away, I sighed. Ma's outburst had startled me, and I was sad and angry to have to relinquish my ideal of her playing the perfect, patient, wise, old grandma for Zoë. I thought, my God, now Zoë knows: She'll never respect Ma again.

But Zoë isn't me. She wandered back into the room a moment later asking, "Wanna play LEGOs, Gram?" And this is the gift Zoë brings to my mom and me: She doesn't have any expectation of how a grandma should be, so she gladly accepts the two that she has. She's just happy to have another person in the house to play with. Ma doesn't usually bring presents any more, and she doesn't cook meatballs or do complicated art projects like her other grandma does, but Zoë doesn't mind that, only I do. Gram is just Gram, and Zoë likes her plenty.

When I watch Ma and Zoë bickering like peers, I feel embarrassed for Ma, but in some ways, Zoë is closer to her than I was to my grandmother. My grandparents lived only a couple of miles from the sea, and every summer from the time I was Zoë's age until I was twelve, Ma, Alice, and I traveled south to Laguna Beach to visit them. My grandpa was the fun one. Mornings, he chased us down the hall holding the orange juice pitcher over our heads, threatening to tip it. We squealed and giggled helplessly, scrambling to escape to the safety of Ma's arms, while Grandma looked on. After breakfast, we'd drop Grandma off at the hair salon or her Daughters of the American Revolution meeting, and drive straight to the main beach to see what color the lifeguard's flag was. Gramps and Ma would sit on a blanket catching up and reading, while we kids played in the waves for entire days. Evenings, there were stuffy car rides to boring restaurants with great-aunts and great-uncles who pinched my cheeks too hard and wore a lot of stinky perfume and aftershave.

The last time we made the trip to Laguna Beach I was twelve years old, and things had changed. My sister didn't come along that time. Gramps was dead, and Grandma was getting old. I was too young to go to the beach alone, and too old not to notice the stale stillness of the house. It smelled of puffed wheat and sour soil. The heavy drapes stayed closed all day. I tiptoed through the hushed rooms, recalling our voices. I slinked into my dead grandpa's private, no-frills bathroom, where I used to pre-shower after a day in the ocean so as not to get sand in Grandma's bathtub. Peeking across the dark hall I listened to the voices in Grandma's bathroom. The door was open a crack, and I caught a glimpse of Ma's flushed face as her strong, freckled arm reached for Grandma's thin, pale one. As Ma lowered her painfully down into the warm bath, Grandma gasped. Thin, faded skin flapped uselessly over her bones where muscles should have been. Grandma hated needing assistance from Ma or anyone else. Helpless, fragile, she cringed there in the water, and I heard her small cry of dismay, of shame.

It's midafternoon. The kids are napping, conked out in the car on the way back from returning Ma safely to her own house an hour away. I refold the futon. Ma has neatly folded the blankets and left them not next to the couch where they belong, but in a pile on the other side of the room, for reasons I can't fathom. On top of the pile are the thick flannel pajamas I keep here for her. As I lift them, I eye the crotch of the pants: The otherwise-smooth, baby-blue fabric is damp, yellow, and wrinkled there. I hold them up, sucking in my breath. A thing as simple as this. If these were Zoë's pajamas, I'd matter of factly plop them in the clothes hamper with a smile and a sigh. I'd reassure her that her bladder just had to grow and learn how, that this was perfectly normal. But that patch of urine-stained fabric sends me in such a different direction because it is my mother's. I feel I have a direct tap into her dismal future. She won't just get old and weak like Grandma did. Along with her strength and control of her bladder, she will also slowly lose her mind. I have been to visit the Alzheimer's wards of local nursing homes; I know about the group of silent, white-haired women in the lobby, slumped in their wheelchairs, sleeping or just staring. I take it further, envisioning a room with dim fluorescent lights, chrome bed, blinking machines, motionless hanging bags of liquid slowly dripping into tubes. In the bed lies a failing body; a life no longer lived but only suffered.

For the rest of the day, I am slightly irritable. Two AM finds me sobbing into my pillow beside my sleeping husband. I don't want to wake him. But I want someone to take care of me. I need someone to tell me everything's going to be okay. I tiptoe into the girls' room and breathe in the sweet-salty scent of their sweaty heads in great, needy gulps.

I wonder obsessively whether Ma ever felt that desperate need to smell me, to touch me. I've asked her, but it's too late. When I ask her questions about her mothering of me (Did you nurse me? Did you carry me in a sling?), the answers are always the same: "Oh, I suppose so. I must have, right?" She just doesn't remember.

There is one way in which I know she was different, though: Every Friday night without fail, for my whole life and many years before it, she got drunk. My father did, too. This was part of their life in college, and part of mine from birth, a fact I just accepted for most of my childhood. Their Friday night drinking was integral to our family social life. My parents' friends showed up around 5:00 PM, and a troop of kids romped about madly while the grownups talked and laughed and drank. Around seven, we'd all sit down for chicken and rice. After dinner the other families would drive merrily off into the night, and we would go to bed.

By the time I'd begun to develop breasts, though, the Friday night ritual had begun to change. The other families stopped showing up. The drinking began earlier in the evening and ended later. It began earlier in the week, too, and continued through the whole weekend. The year I started eighth grade, Ma just kept on drinking. After dinner, she'd have more beer. I would see her eyelids start to droop, her head to nod, and a helpless, desperate sadness would well up in me. So many times I tried to get her to go to bed before it happened. "Mommy," I pleaded, "just go to bed." I didn't know enough then to call it passing out. I couldn't put my finger on why I didn't want her to fall asleep at the table; it just wasn't how I wanted her to be.

Maybe the fact that this isn't the first time I have seen Ma diminished explains the unrelenting, self-righteous fury that sometimes boils up in me when she slumps wordless at my table or can't remember a conversation we had the previous evening. I think, maybe if she hadn't been drunk so often, her supply of brain cells would have lasted longer. The morning she was finally diagnosed, MDs in white lab coats with stethoscopes and clipboards told her plainly that alcohol exacerbated her dementia and she should cease all drinking immediately. Only then did she finally stop. Great, I thought. Now that it's too late. It's not fair, but in the deepest, hardest way, I blame her for the lost time.

The day of her checkup, Ma is wearing the same dirty, rumpled clothes she's worn the past four times I've seen her. She wears her greasy blue hat with the earflaps down. Her glasses, speckled with spots of food and flaked skin, cause her to squint, scrunching up her nose as she rushes headlong into the hospital room. She seems to expect the doctor to arrive any moment, and she hurries to undress even after I remind her that it's Kaiser, and they always keep her waiting a minimum of twenty minutes. She grunts, knees popping, as she bends to remove each shoe, and each loose, gray sock. "Dzok!" Cleo reports from her stroller. "Sheoo!" I spot an odd, curling, yellow knob of fungus on one of her toenails. "Contagious," the nurse-practitioner tells me, "and practically impossible to get rid of. They won't touch her at the nail parlor." Ma's fraying cargo pants fall to the floor in a crumpled pile, and she steps out, then gently folds them. I glance uneasily about, my eyes avoiding her body. I'm acutely aware of her white underpants. I remember the underpants she wore when I was ten: simple, worn, white cotton briefs that were obscene to me in their enormity. Haunted by the image of the pee-soaked pajamas, I dread the sight of them.

I try to remain casual. I have anticipated and avoided this moment. I fear the sight of her old and sagging breasts, her flaccid, spotted flesh. I've been watching the steady degradation of her personality: the loss of passion, of opinions, of esteem, of self-esteem, the loss of self. I'm afraid of seeing my old mom so vulnerable, so weak: naked. At the same time, I hold a morbid fascination for it, because it shocks, it unearths me, to experience this slow but monumental shift in her from laughing, competent, assertive woman to passive, ornery, humorless lump. Her body will give me confirmation of her mind's deterioration, I think, when I witness that fragile old skeleton drooping with the flesh of the infirm.

I can't resist. I look. And I look again, surprised. Her legs are full and alive. These legs have fleshy, muscled thighs and calves, shaped familiarly like my own. And something shifts inside me. She pulls at her bra: an unself-conscious act. Her fingers calmly follow a course set by many decades of habit. This too surprises me. Did I expect her to fumble, to blush at the intimacy of revealing herself to me? But she seems to give her nakedness before me about as much thought as Cleo does when I change her diaper.

And there. Out of her bra emerge two full round breasts. White. They are several sizes larger than mine, just as they always have been: big, earthy breasts. Why did I expect skinny, wrinkled tubular sacks hanging down to her bellybutton? There she stands, a still-attractive, shapely woman. She stoops only slightly. Without her clothes, and seen in this moment of unconscious activity, she is fully physical, generously feminine. Her gray hair falls sweetly to her shoulders as she slips into the blue gown. She climbs onto the doctor's table, tissue paper crackling under her, and leans back with a sigh. In that moment, I feel drawn to her with warm, complete affection. My mother has grace; she has a natural, innocent composure. Maybe her blurry indifference adds to this effect. But her animal body has an ease that her worried mind no longer possesses. Her yellow, chipped teeth, her graying hair, her muddied thoughts, cannot override the simple, beautiful fact of her womanhood.

Sometimes I forget that I'm aging, too. Last Thursday, the sun emerged and sent all of Berkeley into a heady preview of spring. Undergrads wearing shorts and tank tops sprawled on every lawn, soaking up the rare sunshine. I felt like the archetypal breeder, glowing and sexy and just bursting with juicy ripe ova. I wore a summer dress, feeling warm and sensual in the sweet breeze of this balmy afternoon. As I pushed the stroller lightly along the busy sidewalk, my body swayed lusciously of its own accord. Beautiful Cleo snoozed pinkly, a soft bundle of toddler plumpness.

I heard the jingle of keys behind me, and glanced back to see two students: slim, brown, with smooth skin and large dark eyes. Their identical black book bags were slung diagonally across their slim forms, causing perfect breasts clad in pastel knit to protrude just so.

"He's working for a big company now, doing telephone sales," said one.

"So he's a telemarketer?"

"Yeah! And I mean, this is, like, a career position, you know? I mean he works with, like, forty-year-olds; all his co-workers are, like, forty!"

"Weird."

"Good for me, though."

"Whaddayou mean?"

"I mean, like, so he sits next to some forty-year-old woman all day? What could be more safe?"

And just like that, I felt the weight of my thighs.

Friday I was standing in the high-ceilinged, airy gallery where the YWCA invites local artists to display their work. One painting looked suspiciously like another piece I had seen printed many times on posters and greeting cards. In the more famous work, red, brown, and gold fabrics drape lusciously the length of the narrow painting, framing the forms of two lovers; her eyes are closed, and he bends to kiss her pale cheek. The painting in the gallery appeared to be just one swath of that fabric, at close range. I glanced around the room, trying to guess whether each of these abstracts might have been copied from odd corners of paintings by that artist. And I searched my memory for his name. Came up empty. Not Kandinsky. K, K. A mild panic rose in me. Why can't I remember? I've always loved his work. I've owned prints of that kiss—that *Kiss.* For one long moment I struggled.

Klimt. Gustav Klimt. Mentally, I crouched, panting and sweating with the effort of retrieval. I felt the relief of having bridged a perilous gap. But I've always done this, I told myself. Tip of the tongue. It's a common phenomenon. This is normal. This is perfectly normal. This Doesn't Mean Anything.

Zoë is up from her nap. I am snuggled with her, watching *Pee-wee's Playhouse,* when I find the hair on the couch. Thick and springy as wire and about two inches long, it is a silvery blue-gray. I smile, thinking of my dad. When I was ten, my dad, the hairy and eccentric househusband, lost a hair from one of his bushy, wild black eyebrows. I came home from school that day to find said hair taped to a white three-by-five card he'd left by Ma's place at the table. The hair, thick, wiry, and glossy black, sprang upward in sloping coils, gently bouncing from its Scotch-tape tether. Next to the hair, penned in his neat calligraphic hand, was the question, "Can you guess where this hair came from?" "DADDY," I accused with a grin, fully comprehending the wicked intent of this puzzle, "it came from your eyebrow. And I know what you're trying to get her to guess." He laughed, lapping up my affectionate scolding.

I'm still smiling thoughtfully when it comes to me that no one here has bushy eyebrows, gray or otherwise. I realize suddenly that what I'm holding between my fingers is in fact my mother's pubic hair. Reflexively, I look to see if it has a root. There is something unappealing, something disgusting even, about a hair with the small fleshy bulb of a root still attached. There is no root. It is a handsome hair, shiny and shapely and silvery in the light from the window. I twirl it between my thumb and forefinger, thinking again of Ma's body. Then Zoë looks up.

"What's that?"

I drop it behind the couch, on some level unwilling to discuss Ma's pubes with my daughter.

"Nothing, just a hair I found on the pillow."

Zoë shrugs and goes back to her movie.

Why would I feel uncomfortable showing her the hair? It has nothing to do with hygiene. Revealing knowledge of Ma to Zoë scares me. It's as if she'll suddenly visualize the full horror of Ma's disease. And if she sees a piece of my mother in my hand, will she grasp that I, too, may fail in this way? In so many ways I am like Ma. I look and sound like her, I value so many of the things that she does, or did. I am a part of her. But I don't want Zoë to make that connection, because I am afraid of what Ma has become. I carry the legacy of my grandmother's shame. I don't want Zoë to see, by grasping how connected we all are, that I am, or ever will be, someone to be pitied. I want to be better than that; I want to be the Perfect Mama. I am not. I don't want my children to know that. Not yet.

Mitzraim
by Liz Abrams-Morley

> *Once we were all slaves in Mitzraim, slaves in our own Egypt.*
> — *From the* Haggadah, *every* Haggadah,
> *in every Passover seder tale*

My father's room is dark on a sunny day. *I'm confused*, he says, meaning he is not listening. *I can't hear you*, he says, meaning the shades are drawn, the blinds closed. Since he has kept more furniture than the scaled-down apartment will hold and has added a walker and then a wheelchair, I bruise my shin going from his file cabinet to the table and bruise the other going back again. He hasn't paid his taxes, his credit card bills.

Why not, Uncle Joe asks me, and I've come to find out, but I seem to be the only one in this apartment who is concerned.

"Why is your check balance so low?" I flip through the registry as my father flips through channels without focus, until he hears the familiar *Come on down!* Now his gaze is riveted on contestants as they fly to the front of the *Price Is Right* set and cast their bids on avocado appliances.

"Higher! Higher!" my father shouts at the TV.

"Dad? The checkbook?"

To my second inquiry about his banking he says only, *I'm confused*. The Greek chorus in the closet of my heart leers at me and dares me to keep light in my tone.

My heart is a tight space.

"Fuck!" I say as my shin hits the table leg. When my father's brother calls and calls again, we let the machine take messages.

"Call your brother," I tell my father. "He's worried."

"I know," he says.

Not yet October and already the garden goes fallow. The rain falls in biblical sheets. On the radio, a reporter's voice is even as he tells of a woman swept by a current under the wheels of a truck. She was crossing a city street.

Rush-hour in a crowded city. A woman with a briefcase, her umbrella blown inside out, useless.

Despite efforts of passersby the woman died, the reporter intones. His voice holds no tension. My jaw works closed.

"Why don't you call your brother back," I ask my father, "if you know he's worried?" The credit card company called Uncle Joe when they couldn't reach me.

"You do it," my father says, looking only at the fuzzy screen straight ahead of him. Bob Barker's handing the keys to a new Chevy to a large man in polyester.

The last time someone used the term power of attorney around my father, he walked away and wouldn't take our calls for a week but that was—what?— six months ago? Closer to a year?

"Dad?" I say.

"I'm confused," my father says, and my heart snaps shut.

I tell myself I am not swept away by a random rainstorm, that all life is precious, but the door to the apartment could be the bars of a cell and the windows looking out on the expanse of Heritage Acres might as well be glued to their own sills.

How can we all be slaves? the one elderly man in the Bible class I've joined asks, looking for answers. I, too, want answers. *How can we all be slaves in Egypt, when here in America we have so much?* and the rabbi says, *What if Mitzraim is not just a Hebrew word for Egypt?* He says, *What if it's a metaphor?*

We sit in a circle, the ark open, our Bibles open in our blue-jeaned laps, a collection of unreconstructed naysayers wanting to come to terms with faith on a gray Saturday afternoon.

Metaphor for what? one of us wonders aloud. We all wait.

What if Mitzraim is that place we are each slave to? the rabbi asks. *What if Mitzraim is any tight place we can't squeeze out of?*

The apartment smells like the rug in a kindergarten room, not the all-out smell of urine like in a nursing home hallway, not the antiseptic chill of a hospital room, but that faint waft of something unwashed, of something closed in too long.

"I brought your shampoo," I yell, as I poke my father awake from his afternoon nap. He lies on the hospital bed we have purchased to replace the queen-size bed he schlepped from the house in Jersey to the condo in South Philly and then from the walk-up condo to the one-floor apartment. Even after my mother is dead three years, he insists on taking their bed with him to the next, smaller apartment; but with this last relocation, there is simply no room for the expanse of platform bed. When the movers haul it away, he won't watch. At eighty years old he was still moving furniture himself, but this last decade, he has been an icicle under a heat lamp, the melting away of him so steady and constant I almost don't notice the loss most days.

"He'll scream at me," my sister-in-law says, when I ask her to be the one to bring him the hospital bed. It's less than half the width of the bed he loves and has aluminum bars poised to lift and hold him in when he gets too unsteady to rise by himself in the night. "I can't do it. He'll scream." So I am the one to present the new bed. When I do, I await the outburst, the knife edges of hate he could toss in a single sentence two apartments ago, maybe even one. But it's all worse than I imagine; he is docile.

"We had to get you a new bed, Dad. A single." I remember now how it was the day I told him.

"Okay."

I want to say he sighed. Did he sigh? Maybe not.

"I have your shampoo, Dad!" I yell now over the partially inclined bed. Even with the mattress angled, his breath trudges rather than slides to his lungs. He opens his eyes, the left one milky.

"Thanks," he says, and his smile is instant. "How should I pay you for that?"

"Try it," I tell him. "If you don't like it, give it back to me. It's the same kind Ben uses, or I'll use it on one of the kids. Eli maybe."

"Okay," he says. Another warming smile. "Okay. And who are you?"

"You look frantic," the physical therapist says. She finds me on my father's floor surrounded by his mail, his unpaid bills, his unopened get-well cards, all the charities thanking him for his many donations. "You look frantic," says Jen, twenty-something, pregnant. "You okay?"

"It's so fucked up," I say, gesturing to the piles of mail. "He gave all kinds of money to charities, but he doesn't pay his bills."

"I like his priorities," Jen laughs, and my father is suddenly, for a moment, someone who is not my father, and his rooms grow larger, admit light.

The sea parted, you see. We were all slaves, but the sea parted and some of us got across to the other side. We shook the fat drops of salty water off our hair and let the cold slide down our spines and looked up and found the sun close to the earth suddenly, and warming.

This is what I flash on when Jen laughs: I am a five-year-old, tossed in the diaphanous shafts of light cutting through the agitated waters of the Atlantic after a July storm, a wave tossing me under, around, over and over.

"You looked like a sock all alone in a high-water load in the washer. You were sure on the spin cycle down there," my father is saying as he reaches just one of his large, strong hands into the surf and pulls me up into air.

"I was scared," I said every time, every time the small pink balloons of my lungs were unable to catch and hold enough air for that first moment out from under. Every time, he just laughed.

"Don't be. I was right here," he'd say.

～

"What do you mean, who are you? I'm Anne. Your daughter."

He used to be so predictably mean at times; threat of belt, voice of the whip in the hand of an overzealous overseer. We were fed at the kitchen table early enough to be unseen and not heard each weeknight when he always got home promptly at six, after a ten-hour day on his feet. My brothers and I were happy to shut ourselves in our bedrooms as soon as the knob turned on the heavy front door, happy not to reappear downstairs until morning.

Then he got older and got predictably sweet, went to the grocery store, and made macaroni and cheese for my mother all through the brief, long months of her chemo treatments, because macaroni and cheese was the one thing she could hold down.

"I'm your daughter, Anne," I say now, loud, my face right in front of his so that he can read my lips if the hearing-aid batteries are low again. "I'm Anne," I say, "your one and only daughter," wishing now to be seen, to be claimed and duly noted.

"Okay," he says, as if to say, *if you say so*. And then he is asleep again.

I want to close my eyes and wake up in Oz. I want my father to close his eyes and wake up in a gone decade. Plant tomatoes in his garden, argue politics with my dead mother over dinner right after the *MacNeil-Lehrer Report*, both of them annoying and loud and pink-skinned and sitting upright. I want to shake my head over the way they are always on the same side and still manage to raise their voices late into nights when I choose to sleep over, knowing I can get into my car and drive home too fast on a fat highway come the morning after a cup of coffee and two quick hugs.

My mother's coffee is dark and rich. Good coffee. Why didn't I ever notice the good coffee or the way they argued so openly or the pleasure of being there knowing I could leave there?

When my father's phone rings, I pray it won't be Uncle Joe, and then think twice, and pray it will be Uncle Joe and not MBNA America. Then Uncle Joe is so mad, I'm thinking maybe better to deal with the bank.

"Who's been spending my big brother's money like water, I want to know," Uncle Joe asks me. "That nephew of mine got a new car not that long ago. You talked to him lately?"

"Frankie's not to blame, Uncle Joe."

Useless to remind him Frankie's car is three years old already. When you are in your eighties, I guess time compresses like a grilled cheese sandwich squashed down by a spatula while it's on the hot griddle. I picture Uncle Joe's memory like a frying Velveeta sandwich, all the logic oozing out from the sides.

"I think Dad's been spending it himself, Uncle Joe," I start to say, and I'm keeping my voice gentle, but he's not having any of it.

"Bullshit!" he says, just like my father used to say when I asked for help with math homework and proffered the wrong answer or spoke too tentatively when quizzed. Now my father mostly sleeps, and when he wakes, his eyes drift, dreamily, and his voice is hoarse.

"You find out who's spending your father's money, young lady," Uncle Joe says. "And I expect a report."

On the white Formica table, the thank-you notices make a tall, wobbling pile: the American Cancer Society, the Christopher Reeve Paralysis Foundation, a dozen agencies that claim to support the state of Israel, some touting politics my father would have abhorred when he was still reading the solicitations and still following the news.

Now the shrubs outside my father's tiny, unused kitchen are ornamented by fat wrens. They bend the slim branches with their slight weight. If they were red and green and gold, they could be Christmas balls, fat and frivolous and sweet on an anger-hangover morning. They lift and fly and I fly with them.

My heart.

I pry my heart open slowly as slowly my father opens his eyes from his nap. "We need to get a few checks written, Dad," I say, and he says, "You take care of it," meaning, *you take care of me.* The whole apartment exhales and refuses to draw a replacement breath.

When I was a child, three or four, my mother would take me to the library once a week and once a week I would pick out a book. Most weeks I picked the same book, *Peter Rabbit* tales in the smallest editions, scaled-down books I could hold in my three-year-old hands. The library building was an old house with small, irregularly shaped rooms, the children's room tucked at the top of steep stairs, under eaves. This was when tight spaces smelled of cinnamon and safety and what you could grasp with one hand was most desirable.

You take care of it, my father says before his eyes shut.

Now spring is a long time coming, the feast of Passover late this year, April before we will read of the parting of the sea and experience the liberation of our people as the waters made walls that held back disaster. Outside, a few flower pots still hold a fat dollop of snow and each dollop could be sweet whipped cream but it isn't. It's cold. On the table, a pile of "thank you for your donation" notes teeters tall as the pile of bills.

You take care of it, he says.

Outside his kitchen window, the wrens lift off.

Acts of Contrition
by Lisa Meaux

That night I watched Daddy walk across the yard toward my grandmother's back porch. I lost sight of him for a few seconds as he crossed under the massive cypress tree in our front yard and was absorbed by the black shadow it cast beneath a bright moon. It was the night that the grownups in my life cried, lied, and introduced me to unfamiliar emotions that I would perfect, perform, and perpetuate throughout my adult life.

We grew up in the country, right in the bend of Coulee Kinney, a small bayou that wandered off from the Vermilion River like a daydream. As was the custom of many Cajun families, my parents built our home behind Grandma's backyard, and the space between the two houses was our circus tent, our Tarzan's jungle, our Wild West corral. The fireflies on those humid summer nights were like shooting stars. We chased them and captured them, as they hovered too low for their own good, in mason jars with holes punched in the lids. Innocence allowed us to sleep with those magical jars next to our beds and tip them out into the damp grass the next morning while the fireflies were "still sleeping."

And right past our own big-as-the-world front yard, in the bedroom where we brushed her hair, my grandmother committed suicide. I don't know to this day if I really heard the shot, but some time after supper that night, a subtle awareness that things were out of sync slipped through the house. It was like a sea swell that quietly rolled in to cover the shore and then retreated, leaving my world subtly but irrevocably changed.

Mom was standing near the sofa in the den with the telephone to her ear, but she was speaking French to Daddy instead of talking on the phone. Daddy was fumbling through the clutter on the kitchen counter. He finally grabbed a set of keys and rushed out the den door to the driveway. That's when we ran, my sisters and brothers and I, to the living room picture window. That's when we saw Daddy swallowed up by the shadows of the cypress tree and emerge again in the moonlight to let himself into Grandma's back door. That's when we saw him carry out the long, wrapped-up bundle of my grandmother and lay her across the backseat of her old Dodge.

Mom was still on the phone, this time talking in a shrill voice into the receiver. Her face was a mask, a tight layer of panic distorting her familiar features. All five of us could make out most of the French words. Someone hadn't been feeling well. Daddy came back, but instead of coming into the house, he sat on the front porch and looked at his shoes.

My sisters and brothers and I might as well have been fireflies in a jar, and our loving, attentive parents forgot to punch the holes in our lid. Headlights came up the driveway, and strange men drove up and spoke quietly to Daddy under the carport. Father Theriot sat in Daddy's armchair saying a rosary with his eyes closed. My nanny and *parrain* came in sobbing. My mother was a banshee. It was way after bedtime, and we flitted around in the confusion and landed in the corner of our bedroom near the closet. Daddy finally found us there and told us that Grandma was sad and it made her too tired, so she just died. As I stood there no higher than my closet doorknob, I knew I had not been nice enough, had not spent the night with her often enough, had been too selfish to keep my grandmother from becoming so sad. I should have been able to save her.

Mom never told us the truth about that night, never acknowledged it as our baneful birthright. Our maternal legacy, like a water moccasin in the flood-soaked *coulée*, has been dark and silent. Sometimes lethal. For generations, the mothers in my family have been passing down the genetic disposition for depression and mental illness, and my own son will need big medicine for the rest of his life so that the landscape will stop telling him that ours is not the world to which he belongs. And of course I blamed myself and of course I added that to the tangle of muddy family roots that was planted along the banks of snake-ridden coastal waters the night my grandmother died.

My son has thanked me, throughout his recovery, for recognizing his struggle and facing it—for not making it a secret. I'm not my mother after all. But I understand her. My mother still keeps secrets. Big ones, and she doesn't know how to stop. She listens to me talk about genetic tendency and acceptance and therapy, and she says a novena. She blames my son's illness on my ex-husband, an abusive alcoholic who I thought needed saving.

We clean my grandmother's tomb on All Saints' Day, my mother, my sisters, and me. We paint it and top it with a plastic pot of yellow chrysanthemums, and then we make our signs of the cross and say our silent prayers. We never talk about how she died. Instead, we talk about kids and food and clothes and what's on sale at the mall.

My grandmother's home was sold and moved on a barge down the river to the southernmost part of the parish.

The cypress tree, over one hundred years old, reluctantly fell over during a hurricane in 2002.

I wish I could tell my mother that, in spite of what the church says, I believe that Grandma rests in peace.

Dad, In Red
by Sonya Huber

My son Jordan held the metal paint can above his head. That was my father, his ashes in the paint.

"You're never going to finish this," Jordan said. "I know it. You're never even going to start." He brought his arm down. He leaned with his shoulder into the doorjamb and twisted away to face the living room. I pulled off my jacket and threw it over a stool, dumped plastic bags on the floor near the fridge. I could feel my blood vessels constrict, half expecting him to throw the can against a wall. The Zoloft was supposed to help him with impulse control. Our squat house was covered with nicks and scuffs and patch jobs, which recorded Jordy's impulses over fourteen years. Last summer he experimented with homelessness for two weeks, after a fight about whether he could take my car on a road trip. He lived in the park with the punks. I drove and drove the streets of Minneapolis, thinking about where his body would be found. Then he reappeared like he had been away at camp.

I heard him flip himself over the back of the couch and land on the cushions.

"Jordy," I said. "No." Two caseworkers had quit, my supervisor slammed doors all day, and at the end of it nobody had an Advil tucked away in his or her desk drawers, anywhere.

I leaned back to look into the front room. Jordy's dark eyes and eyebrows were all that I could see above the back of the couch.

"You say you're gonna do it but you always wimp out. It's been seven months. We're gonna get haunted. And it will be all your fault." He raised himself up on his elbows over the couch back like a jack-in-the-box. "Do it, or I'll do it for you." That sounded like one of my clean-your-room threats coming back at me.

I slid the gallon of milk onto the metal rack and ripped open an envelope of instant noodle mix.

⌐

Seven months ago, I went to the lawyer's office to have the will read.

"It would honor me greatly if you would employ my remains in the creation of one or a series of painting." I could almost hear Dad in that sentence. The way he might say "honor" would make you think of something painful and ironic.

The men at the funeral home gave me a canister of ashes, and my friend Sarah mixed some of it in with red acrylic #42, but it wouldn't even all fit. A human leaves a lot behind, even cremated.

Maybe you've heard of my father, A. M. Franklin, photographer with a new book out every year in the eighties, black-and-white close-ups of everyday objects, transforming them into ghostly landscapes. A forest of pencil tips, stacks of magnifying glasses like blind eyes.

I tried to paint about three months ago, a late fall day off. The trees around Lake Calhoun and through Minneapolis turned yellow and orange and bright salmon-red. I wanted to put something on canvas and be done with it.

I put on my sneakers and grabbed my beeper and keys. The Department of Social Services made me carry the beeper so my supervisor could reach me whenever one of my forty-two cases, kids in trouble, ran into a snag.

I walked from our stucco shoe-box two blocks down Pleasant to Lyndale. We were supposed to have bad weather over the weekend, and all the vegans and hippies were stocking up at the Wedge Co-op on Lyndale when I crossed the parking lot full of old Volvos and VW vans.

News radio was on in the co-op, a story about a disease in Africa killing thousands of children. *Fine,* I thought. *If kids are dying in Africa, what am I complaining about?* One lousy painting.

The sun through the leaves and the beginning of a caffeine buzz made me see colors in my head, the beginning of an urge to sit and paint.

I pried off the circular lid and scooped up a bit of the grainy red paint. I added yellow, easing it into the color of warm brick. I wanted a black background and the orange color on top like flames in night. Working with the black, though, I thought of Dad, how relieved and pleased he would be to see me finishing one of his assignments. That soured it for me. It was the thing I hated about his work, too—doing it to get it done, twelve hours a day, to get the next book of photos to the publisher.

I scraped the reddish orange paint into the bathroom trash can. I waited for that red fire to go down from behind my eyes, and then I called Sarah.

"I threw some of that paint with Dad in it into the trash. It's with some Kleenex and hair from the shower drain."

Sarah sighed and then laughed her high, whistling laugh. "I'm sorry—it's not funny. I mean, it kind of is."

A flutter of panic rippled inside my chest. "What do I do with this— bury it?"

"Throw it in a Dumpster somewhere. Your dad was an artist. He would understand that you'd make mistakes. Hey, at least you're doing something meaningful," she said. "I'm over here writing copy for global warming fashions." The managers of the clothing company where she worked told the designers to focus completely on summer fashions for the long term. " 'But we won't call it global warming,' they'd said. 'We'll call it something cheerful like Endless Summer.'"

"You're not serious," I said.

"Do you want to trade? I'll make some god-awful painting with your dad, and you come over here and describe this sexy little miniskirt made out of mosquito netting."

Sarah kept talking with me until the layers of everyday bullshit started to fall off, like dirty papery skin of an onion, till it was down to the white wet heart. I flipped on my old paint-splattered radio to a classic rock station and sat there, almost by accident, listening to the Rolling Stones, that song that goes, "Send me dead flowers," which I always liked because young Mick sounded so cocky about putting roses on that woman's grave.

An hour later, after it had gotten completely dark and the wind started to hit the house and make it creak, I started to get into a groove. I turned the painting that was supposed to be all about flames into a mix of blues and yellows, like gas jets. An hour went by like a minute, staring into the canvas and working slowly. My head opened up.

I mixed some Dad with some yellow and was just sitting there, thinking about mixing up some more of that orange-red, when a small whirring made me sit back. There was a space of about seven seconds when I actually didn't know what it was. From deep within my purse, which hung over the banister of the stairs near the front door, sang my beeper. "*Nee-nee-nee-nee-nee-nee*," it wheedled. "Come to me."

I called in, and the woman at the switchboard told me with her clipped first few words that it was bad. "Teresa Czernowski's husband beat her up again. Broken eye socket. She's at the ER with her kid."

I dropped the brush, wiped off my hands, splashed water on my face, found shoes and a decent shirt, then a jacket, my purse, and the car keys. I wanted to smash something. Teresa's son needed to be moved from the emergency room, and if somebody who didn't know her went to do the paperwork, the son would end up in some overnight respite center, the kind of place that held on to kids and didn't let them go.

I scrawled a note for Jordy, who was out at a club. Not drinking underage, of course. Would, of course, be home by curfew, not covered with hickeys, and no used condoms stuffed in his pocket for me to find on laundry day. At least he used condoms.

Driving was an utter headache, and everyone in Minneapolis who was insane or on drugs seemed to be on Route 35W toward downtown, swerving and speeding up and slowing down with no warning, flashes of taillights in the rain. I began to hate my job with a pure rage.

I ran past the gray partitions, grabbed an incident report form, and then drove over to the hospital to try and find Teresa Czernowski in the ER, praying her husband hadn't shown up, hoping they had a cop with her.

I stopped a young floor nurse, who directed me to the area where they were treating Teresa behind a blue drape. Arthur Czernowski, five years old, wearing a striped t-shirt, was sitting in a blue plastic chair. When I walked up, he turned to look at me, his eyes like hot coals. And I started to cry—not a little, but full on, suddenly—and I ducked to my right, into a supply closet near the nurses' station so I could pull myself together.

That night, I came home so tired that my muscles ached like I'd played pickup basketball for hours. And I didn't touch paint again for weeks—the days just flew by. So, no, Jordy was right. That effort didn't really count.

Jordy ran upstairs, making *thunk-thunk-thunk* sounds as his tennis-shoe toes slammed all the way back against the risers. He ran back down and landed both-footed on the wood floor. He ran into the kitchen, laid a small board on our red wood table. The board was covered with gesso and prepped for a painting, one of about ten that I'd stacked upstairs.

He threw a brush down next to the board. With some wrestling he pried off the lid of the can of Dad with a butter knife. He twisted the plastic kitchen timer shaped like a green pepper. It ticked unevenly like a weaving drunk.

"Go!" he yelled. "Do it!" His eyes were so wide that I noticed the curvature, the shine of his eyeballs. It was strange that although Jordy and Dad were nothing alike and hadn't spent much time together, they both thought they could make me do something by sitting me down with a time limit and a task. I wondered if Jordy had learned this from me.

I stuck the paintbrush into the paint and touched the board, making one tiny red dot.

When I was sixteen or seventeen in the summer, Dad sat me down in front of a canvas with the paints he'd bought, and said I could leave when I'd finished something. My mistake had been to let him catch me drawing. "Every problem, Anna, can be solved with concentration," he used to say. It made me so angry because I could think of a huge list of problems to which that didn't apply. If I had had guts, I would've painted "fuck off" in wide black letters. Then. Now I see what he was trying to do.

"I can't paint like this, honey," I said to Jordan, "but it's nice of you to try." I made a few more motions with the brush on the board. A little red house, a tree, with traces of Dad, flecks in the red.

Jordan looked at me, fury tightening his lips, and I saw Dad in his face, in the sharp edges of his nose and chin.

The kitchen timer *pinged*, and we both held our breath for a second, startled. Then Jordan looked down and slowly stuck his finger deep into the paint. His eyebrows jumped in sudden excitement, and he drew out his finger slowly, thickly coated and bent into a hook shape. I held back the scolding on my tongue. This was art, I guessed, and he was trying to help. He smacked the full length of his finger onto the board like a fish, wiped down the center of the board, over the little red house, and left a mark like a murder scene.

When Jordy was six, and his hair was still coal-black and sticking up all over in a Mommy-done-bad haircut, he crept into the pantry off the kitchen in our old apartment, where I was painting, and looked around the edge of the canvas with serious eyes. I thought he was going to tell me war had broken out somewhere. Instead, with a voice as sure as a judge, he told me that he was going to be a clown when he grew up. I put down my coffee and swung sideways on my stool, barely missing my painting with my knees. The pantry shelves were lined with cans of beans and stale pasta and my paints. The pantry was the best place to paint because it had a door that could be shut and locked, and a window for ventilation.

"Honey, clowns don't make that much money, and it's probably hard, not as fun as it looks," I said. Obviously, I was qualified to give financial advice. I was a woman who sold a painting once every century and was paying the bills with catering jobs and a maxed-out credit card.

He squinted, lasering out a flash of hatred at me and at the world I represented. But his face stayed calm and grim, and his eyes flitted up to the left corner of the pantry ceiling, to a crack in the plaster. He was thinking a secret thought he would never tell me.

"Well, if it's so hard, then why does everyone want to be a clown?" he said sharply, and walked away, up to his room where he played until dinner, without any further questions.

At the time I saw it as six-year-old willfulness, and saw myself as being reasonable, trying to get him to adjust to the real world. He was six. I wanted him to hurry up and be a man. Oh, mean mommy. What kind of grinch, what kind of soul-crusher, would tell her little boy at six not to be a clown? Whenever I want to remind myself how awful I am, I replay this scene in my head. What other brutal things had I said that I didn't remember? Was that why he was so weird now, to get back at me?

"I just want you to paint again. You're such a bitch when you don't paint," he said mournfully. He looked closely at his red finger, inspecting it for black bits.

"Am I? Even more than normal, huh?" I asked. I tried to deliver that somewhere between sarcasm and sympathy. I had thought I was bitchier when I was painting—swearing when the phone rang, tripping down the stairs when we were late for hockey practice.

He scowled at me dismissively.

I opened the fridge, took out lettuce and a knobby cucumber, ran them under the faucet. "Jordan, don't you believe that I'll do this when I'm ready?"

Holding the open can, he scuffled across the Linoleum toward the sink in his ragged Chuck Taylors.

"We don't have any other relatives besides Granddad and weird Gramma Lewis in Saint Paul with her gross cocker spaniel. We're a dead end of the human race. You don't seem like you give a shit. This is such a cool, special, rad thing, and you don't even *care*." The fluorescent light in the kitchen made his hair shine like a beaver pelt.

He leaned against the edge of the sink, scooped up some of the Dad paint with his left hand, and dribbled it in small plops into the sink. When the swirl of water hit the paint blobs, they fanned out in diluted red. The black bits came clean and dark, dragging on the sink bottom and reluctantly making circles down to the drain.

"Jordan, stop," I said. I pushed the words out firm and sharp, but behind my voice was the high catch of panic. I had wanted to get rid of this paint, but to actually have it gone opened up a lifetime possibility of a big item on the to-do list never finished.

I reached into the sink for the can and he pulled it out of my reach. I hit the faucet to shut off the water. He looked up at me, his mouth twisted in sarcastically polite attention. I saw a resolute adult, the way the freckled skin around his squint seemed to hold his eyes hostage.

"No," he said. "I know Granddad would say enough is enough. Time's up. You snooze, you lose."

He dabbed a bit of red paint on his nose, looked at me seriously. I smelled burning and reached around behind him to turn off our burnt noodle casserole. This was how quickly a normal night could turn into war.

"Okay, okay," I said. I held out my hand for the half-empty can of paint. "You've made your point. I'll do it tonight." When he got manic like this, possessed with an idea, his fixation and intensity became scarier to me than whatever it was he wanted. I sometimes gave in. That's not recommended.

"No," he said. "It's always later, later, tomorrow, tomorrow. That's how people live and then you're dead."

He scooped a red handful out of the can and tossed it down into the open drain, flipped on the water and the switch to the disposal in two quick jabs.

I sucked in air. "Jordan, that was not yours. That was between me and my father and you were not supposed to just walk in and put your hands in that." My voice rose and rose like a whistle, and my joints seemed to get hot and liquefy. I'd given birth to someone who was throwing bits of his grandfather down the garbage disposal.

He squinted until I could barely see his eyes. He tossed the can on the floor. "Now you lose your shit. Great. You were supposed to do something, stop me. I was only trying to see what he would look like."

There were so many terrible things to be said right then, things about his granddad sitting in Maine with his hands in photographic emulsion when I gave birth. Fill in the blank. Sometimes you get into heaven based on whether you can keep your mouth shut. I looked at Jordan significantly and sighed.

Jordan knew the general tenor of what I had been about to say, somehow read it in my face. That happened sometimes between us, and it made the hair on my arms stand up.

"I know you thought he was an asshole. He probably was. But I bet *his* parents were assholes too," he said, his hand on the doorknob.

Here, he had the upper hand. After the way he left last summer, he knew that walking out of the house in a fury would make me melt. He slammed the door behind him.

I ran water into the skillet to soak off the burnt noodles. I slid down onto the pale yellow Linoleum and looked up at my dirty kitchen. One of my old blue paintings hung near the ceiling above the cabinets, covered with orange flecks of grease and dust. How did food get so high up?

I wanted to call someone, but I nursed a secret resentment against all of my friends who had living parents, and separate resentments against all of my friends who were either married or in good relationships. Sarah had a boyfriend but had sort of a shitty relationship with her mother and could be relied on to have an interesting work crisis that made me feel less like a loser. Plus, she wanted kids and was never able to have them. So we balanced each other out.

I got pregnant at twenty-five, after a few rounds of mediocre sex with Ryan, a carpet salesman from Portland, Maine, when I still lived near Dad. I think I had Jordy only because abortion seemed like something you did when a baby would get in the way of some grand life plan, which I did not have. Ryan and I did not last because Ryan was settled and dull even at twenty-four. I didn't think I loved him even immediately after sex. I moved back in with Dad while I was pregnant. Dad treated me as though pregnancy were a virus, a communicable disease that caused sloth and exhaustion. It made me wonder how he had treated Mom when she was pregnant with me.

When I think of my mother there is only a watery smile rendered in washed-out seventies Kodak print, the smell of a cinnamony perfume, long dishwater-blond hair like mine that she wore up in a loose bun, a woman with my smile who worked as a paralegal to support Dad while he was getting started as a photographer. I did not know her, not enough to carry a sense of her past, her death, and Dad refused to talk about her.

When I brought Jordy home, red-faced and squirmy, Dad held him and we had, I thought, some multigenerational moment when we looked each other in the eyes. "He'll be a screamer," said Dad dryly. "A time sink."

I picked at the curling edge of the Linoleum. That memory had been an anchor for my rage, the images of me packing the car, his impotent silence standing in the driveway, me feeling noble and slighted and alone. I had run my mind over that story so many times that I couldn't get the same buzz of hate out of it that I usually got. Maybe I had just worn it out.

It was only after the first half hour, after I'd calmed down and gotten up off the floor, that I started to feel really terrible. I washed the dishes, made a peanut butter and jelly sandwich. Then came the check-the-clock, check-the-door, edgy, itchy panic of imagining where Jordan could be at 10:00 PM. Then 10:08, 10:09. Each minute he was somewhere else.

When I called, Sarah listened and said, "Oh, Anna. Christ, and it's only Tuesday."

I brought up the paint in the sink for the third time. "I can't believe it's just washed down the drain. I had a wonderful weird job to do that I put off and now it's gone." I felt as though my rib cage was expanding to crack like knuckles. It felt empty. "He was an asshole with no redeeming qualities," I said. "Right?"

"Who, your father?"

"Yes," I said. "It was evil of him to make me paint with him, right?" I started to cry.

"Well, if you're so sad about it, mix up some more paint."

"I can't. There's about half-a-paintbrush worth in the can."

Sarah sighed and said, "Anna, a person leaves a lot of ash. There's a big urn of it still sitting next to that depressing painting in the front room."

I ran upstairs, clenching the cordless receiver between my shoulder and my sweaty ear. "Not like this is going to be any easier. Do you think that giving in to Jordy so often is screwing him up?" I dumped some of the ashes of Dad into a gesso can, turned the dirty mixture into an even lumpy white.

By midnight, Jordan had not come home. I made a deal with myself— I would not start to drive or call the police until 1:00 AM. I covered two large canvases and seven small pieces of scrap wood with the ashed gesso. I couldn't wait to cover him with delicate lines of orange, red, and blue, to paint what he was not and still do what he wanted, but backward. With him in the background, I could think.

VI.

Surviving Illness and Loss

Miscarriage of an English Teacher
by Megeen R. Mulholland

I
first person
would
conditional clause
would have
past perfect
would have had
past participle
you
second person

today, little one,
begun this New Year
with you moist in my arms,
the rise, swell, and down
of you captivating
your daddy and me until

we
~~embryonic breakdown~~ *personal pronoun*
would
~~unknown cause~~ *conditional clause*
would have
~~spontaneous termination~~ *past perfect tense*
would have breathed
~~postpartum~~ *past participle*
as deeply as
~~pacifier~~ *modifier*

we
personal ~~pronoun~~
would
conditional ~~clause~~
would have
~~past~~ *perfect*
would have watched
past ~~participle~~
you do—

beside ourselves
with sighs of
elation,
exhaustion,
euphoria,
everything
but this emptiness.

That
demonstrative, demonstrative, demonstrative pronoun
is
present tension
all
~~indefinite prognosis~~ indefinite pronoun
that remains now,

the New Year
capital, proper
already old,
yet one I know
will go

~~future chances~~ *future tense*
will be going
progressive future, imperative
must go
auxiliary ~~help~~ helping verb
on

Johnny
by Heidi Raykeil

John 1:5–9
5. The light shines in the darkness but the darkness cannot comprehend it. 6. There
came a person sent from God, whose name was John. 7. He came as a witness
to the Light, that through him, all of us might believe. 8. He was not the Light,
but was sent to bear witness to the light. 9. That is the true Light which lightens
everyone who comes into the world.

We got the call at 8:00 AM.

We had dared to take everyone's advice and go home to sleep. Now, after two weeks of telephone-phobia, it was finally the call we never really believed we'd get. It was my mother, or what was left of my mother. It was a puddle of a voice, lost between sobs.

"Honey," she choked, "it's . . ."

The sobs won. Another voice came on the line. It was the doctor—the one who never looked directly at me when he was talking. I could never tell if he wouldn't look at me because he thought medicine was men's stuff or too complicated for me, or because he was worried I would break down if he did. Sometimes, I felt as if he was afraid to look at me, as if he was physically trying to shield me from any extra weight his eyes might lay on me. To him, I must have looked like the last living leaf on a dying plant. Hanging on, but barely. He didn't want to be the one to finally blow me over.

The doctor tried to sound reassuring. What I remember most about him now is his voice. It was so gravelly, like it was in constant need of being cleared. Later, we found out his son sings in a band that plays on the radio. Sometimes now I'll be flipping stations and hear him. I stop and listen, and I hear that same voice. It brings me back. Except on his son it sounds cool and tortured and rock star. On the doctor, it just sounded like a death sentence. Before all this, I hated that band; I thought it was whiny and shallow. Now, I feel connected to it. I love imagining the doctor proudly gravelling on about his son, imagining them fighting when the boy was a teenager. I'm obsessed with the fact that in some tiny way I can know the doctor's son, and I wonder how much the doctor remembers about mine.

"He's pulled his respirator tube out. I really think he's trying to tell us something. I don't want to do any chest compressions. I don't want to give him any Adrenaline. Do you understand what I'm saying?"

Every cell in my body understood what the doctor with the gravelly voice was saying. I had understood it since last night, since I had given up, since I had actually said I wish it would just be over. I cursed myself now for those words. I felt sick. I understood. The doctor was going on and on about something, something about not rushing, not driving too fast. I didn't hear it. Somehow we made it to the hospital. I remember shouting, sobbing, leaving the car on the street because there was no parking. Now when I drive those streets, they're so crowded. I think, did I just mow people down? How on earth was there no traffic that day?

We ran down the hall we had walked down so often in the past twelve days. That damn hall with that damn hospital smell. The smell that made me too sick to hold my own baby when I came up in a wheelchair that first day. We ran over the pastel floor tiles, and the sound was deafening. In the sickly hush of that floor, we sounded like a herd of desperate elephants. All that noise, and we still seemed miles away. We ran past a man we had seen almost every day for the past twelve days. We saw his familiar sad gait, his dark eye bags. He was coming from a visit, perhaps going back to work. Back to the real world that went on, that knew nothing of babies that look more like small birds, or oxygen saturation levels, or bottle upon bottle of frozen breastmilk, the very definition of hope.

I knew the man's wife better than him. We had been tenuously hopeful together. Once I came in and found her crying in the family room. We talked about the absurdity of monthly bills and the innocent confusion of her older child. "Where's the baby in your tummy, Mommy?"

The man began to register us with the same compassionate acknowledgment we'd shared so often before. It's almost a look of relief, a look of understanding.

"I know," it seems to say, "'hello' is such a wasted word." The look is like a secret handshake between select members in a club no one should ever have to join.

I saw him see us run, saw him see the tears, the desperation. Our silent hello stopped there. There was an unspoken rule in the NICU: When parents are with their baby, you don't really acknowledge them. It's as if each of us knows that the seconds we have to actually hold the baby is too precious to waste on small talk. The same thing happened now. He knew we were already there with Johnny. He knew this was our moment alone.

When we came around the corner, my mother was standing there, looking smaller and weaker than I'd ever seen her. I felt like throwing up.

"It's a miracle," she said, "he waited for you."

My mother had been doing one of her early morning "vigils," as she called them, when the baby spit out his respirator. Later, she told me she'd had a premonition that he was going to die, and she wanted to spend as much time with him as she could. The rational and understanding part of me thinks now that she created these things to feel like she has some control, to feel like somehow she's involved or can fix unfixable things. But right then, I was well beyond understanding and rationality. I just felt territorial and annoyed—why would Johnny come to *her* in a dream when he was *my* child? Why would he have passed through her body instead of mine?

I looked past her and froze. For an instant, I barely recognized him. The child that I had carried with me for nine months, the most beautiful angel baby who made me weep the instant I met him, was gone. In his place, I saw a lifeless, dusky gray version of him.

Johnny was born full-term and was the biggest baby in the neonatal intensive care unit. Compared to his tiny, premature roommates, he looked like a giant and acted like an angel. When preemie babies cry they sound like little goats or creaky gates, and it can grate on nerves after a while. Johnny, born with severe brain damage, hardly ever made a peep. When he did, it was just these sweet little half-sucking noises. It made him all the more perfect.

The doctor said that most likely his brain had experienced some kind of "insult" in utero. That word summed up the guilt and responsibility I felt; I had insulted my own baby somehow. I hadn't done it by drinking or smoking or eating soft cheese or taking a bath that was a little too hot. I probably didn't do anything at all—someone had to be that one in a thousand. I'll never know. But what I do know is that I had failed the first and most primary task of motherhood: keeping your baby alive.

The nurse finished unhooking him from the monitors, the monitors that our own breath had come to depend on. The ones that sped up and slowed down so much you'd just have to look. The ones we had finally learned to live with. The ones he couldn't live without. She handed me the baby. Holding Johnny was like an instant sauna.

Over the past two weeks, my husband and I argued endlessly over who got to hold him. Finally, we settled on taking turns. Whoever's turn it was would take his or her shirt off and hold the baby, naked, except for all the tubes and wires, against the chest. The loser that day would have to settle for watching or reading, fighting jealousy the whole time.

When Johnny was whisked away right after birth, I couldn't see him for three hours. During that time, I felt like they had accidentally taken my heart out in surgery instead of a baby. Every part of my body ached for him. Yet, right before I got to see him, I freaked out. What if I wouldn't recognize him? What if I wouldn't love him?

I've heard about parents with sick babies who never come to visit, who can't bear to see their children like that, who just can't let themselves love something so fragile. For us, from the minute we met him, it was always Johnny leading the way. How could we not smile around him? How could we not beam with pride and dream and have hope while holding him? We were addicted to him from day one. When my husband first saw the baby, he told me how every transgression he had ever made in his life, every bit of pain he'd suffered, every hardship he'd survived, all were worth it, because it led him here, to me, to this perfect being we created. And it was true. Even then, knowing what we knew, knowing exactly why we were there, our feeling of wonder and gratefulness didn't change. Even knowing that we were never going to take him home, not ever, that he would never see the perfect nursery, never say "night-night" to his cow curtains, never meet the dog or use the stroller or wear his perfect little sneakers. Even knowing all that, the minute the nurse laid him in my arms, I was filled up with him. I was content.

We walked down the hall and the nurse ushered us into a private room. We sat in that room and whispered to him. We told him he was a good boy for waiting for us. We told him how much we loved him, how we would always love him. We told him about his room and his cow curtains and our dreams for him. And we told him it was okay, he had done his job just right.

I knew I was holding him too tight. I also knew it was too late to matter. It didn't matter anymore how I held his head, or if I supported his neck like it showed in *The Well Baby Book*. I handed my husband the baby, soaked with my sweat and tears. He grabbed Johnny, rocking back and forth, each rock too short and choppy and desperate to be soothing to anyone. I watched this man, the man I had promised happiness and health to—his heart destroyed. I watched him cry over the child he loved so much and could do nothing for. The son he was going to father as no father had done for him. He stopped rocking for a minute, his red, pleading eyes looking so confused. He put the baby's chest up to his ear, listening, desperately trying to comprehend what I already knew. I looked away.

We sat in that room a family, the three of us together, like we had always planned. We stripped Johnny's perfect little body of the last of the Band-Aids and wire tape sticking to him. He was covered in pinpricks, so many tests, so many needles, for what? Physician frustration. He was a medical mystery, and he bore the brunt of it, never even making a cry. He was such a good boy, such a brave boy. I took off my shirt and laid his naked body on my belly. If only I could put him back, where he was safe and alive. I would go on being pregnant for a lifetime if it meant he would be healthy and happy, turning somersaults and kicking the days away inside me.

The nurse came in and asked if we would like to bathe him. She seemed so calm. I wondered if this kind of thing happened a lot. My husband tried to make some half-joke about what a shitty job she had. We were insane. We were watching the life leave our baby, watching his body change, watching him leave. How could we not be?

"It's just his house," I said over and over again, trying to make sense of the stiff little legs, the porcelain white skin that used to be so bright. "It's not really him."

We bathed and dressed him in a cheap little christening gown the nurse had brought. It was their standard dead-baby outfit, I guess. Even though it seemed inconceivable, of course ours wasn't the first baby to ever die. Hospitals are prepared for these things. We stared at him in his little white gown and cap and decided he looked ridiculous. We never would have dressed him like that. The whole time he was alive the only clothes he wore were a hospital t-shirt and a Raiders hat we brought him. We undressed him and wrapped him in his blanket instead. Our families had arrived, and they were coming in the room one by one to say goodbye.

It seemed like we were in that room forever. I could no longer cry. There was just nothing left. I was so tired, exhausted. It must have been five or six hours since the call that morning. It was time. My husband called the nurse to take him away. As soon as she came in, I had second thoughts. I wanted to say, "We've changed our minds." Instead, I said nothing. After all, what would we do? Keep him in an ice chest in the living room? For half a second, I could actually picture it.

We held the baby together one last time. In the moment the nurse stood there waiting to take him away, I spent an eternity with Johnny. I held him to my breast and looked at him completely. I memorized his perfect face, his little hands and feet. I inhaled his smell. I had never felt anything so wholeheartedly real, so pure. The imagined lifetime of soccer games and birthday parties and romps with the dog disappeared. The fighting over cleaned rooms, the embarrassments, the late-night games of checkers, they all disappeared in that moment. The three of us had our own real lifetime together, one not tainted with hopes and expectations and letdowns. It just was.

The nurse laid a small, square hospital blanket on the bed. She placed Johnny in the middle and swaddled him right side over left, left over right, tuck bottom in. I had read about swaddling in one of my many baby books, books I would have to give away or burn now. Books that don't tell you things like, "Some babies die."

So what were we supposed to do? Where were we supposed to go? How could we possibly leave? Where would we possibly go, knowing we were leaving our baby there, wrapped like a sausage with the bar-code sticker slapped on top? *Best if used before* . . . . We left the room; we left the doctors and our families and the sad, helpless faces. We left our son, our first, our only baby. We left him there somewhere in a basement, in the morgue, locked up, barely just dead. We left him, and we left what we had known of our lives as we left the hospital that day.

What do people do when they leave their dead babies? When they can't stand to be in the same room with all those concerned, caring, devastated people? We went to breakfast. We sat across from each other looking like escapees from a mental hospital. When I found the waitress talking to me, I panicked for a minute. *Am I speaking English,* I thought? My mouth was moving but I couldn't imagine any other words coming out besides, "Our baby is dead." I must have really said, "Salad and a glass of wine," because that's what came. We sat there, food untouched, trying to make sense of a restaurant. Of the smiling waitress. Of the sunshine outside.

We sat across from each other, pale, half-dressed, frantic, puffy eyes staring back at each other and always giving the same answer. "It's over. He's dead," our eyes said. "Our baby is dead." My eyes shifted to the hospital ID bracelet on my wrist, the one that proved we belonged to someone, that let us visit whenever we wanted. All the writing had worn off except the very clear outline of the word "Mother." I looked across at my husband pondering his own wristband, and I knew he was trying to make sense of exactly the same thing. Just what the hell did that word mean now?

A month and a half after Johnny's death, our lives started taking on the appearance of normalcy. Somehow we made it through the memorial service, through a god-awful Christmas, and were now trying to make it back into the world. Family and friends showed hints of the helplessness they felt. They listened less and talked more, especially about things like acceptance and healing and moving on. They commented on how amazing we were through the whole thing, how miraculous Johnny was, how we were somehow bettered by the experience. But to me it seemed like a load of crap. Like it was just another way for people to make us feel better, to put what happened away in a tidy, neat little box so we could all go on, so we could stop hurting and they could stop hurting for us.

In truth we were frozen. It was late January but we were stuck in a never-ending December. I tried going out, getting on with life, but babies and pregnant women and curious neighbors lurked around each corner. I was terrified of running into the day-to-day people I knew while I was pregnant, back when I was human and normal and a part of their world. A world about a million light-years from where I was now.

I didn't know how to explain to them why I wasn't pregnant anymore but still didn't have a baby. Despite the birth/death announcement cards I had a friend leave on the neighbors' steps, there was no way to tell everyone, no way to show the world the black hole that had become my life.

The last three months of my pregnancy, I had been a walking billboard. My huge belly was a public marker of impending joy. Everyone had something to say, some excitement or advice or wonder to share. It should have gone from that to getting that same kind of attention for my baby. There should have been people standing over my stroller cooing or peering into my arms congratulating me on a job well done. Instead, I had nothing to show. When I was pregnant, everyone in the world could take one look at me and know what I was going through and how I got there. But now, I looked like a normal person; regular people had no idea what happened, no idea how beautiful he was, no idea how much I'd lost.

I thought it would be good to join the gym—it would keep me busy and the depression at bay. The first day I timed it perfectly to coincide with the prenatal water aerobic class. The locker room was boiling over with pregnant women. They stood in front of the giant mirrors, basking in their life-giving abilities; one rubbing the big belly I had newly grown to think of as disgusting; another one laughing, so delighted with her funny new shape, trying to tie a towel around her waist knowing full well it wouldn't fit anymore. They made me sick. They were so naive, so outrageously blissful.

From my hidden spot in the shower I watched them like prey, their bodies rolling around, navigating like slow-motion pinballs. I felt I had a secret that could destroy them. I fantasized about grabbing their cartoonish bodies and shaking them, screaming at these pregnant lemmings to wake up, to watch out, to show a little modesty for god's sake before it was too late.

I dressed openly, hoping someone would see the still-raw, fat, red slice across my abdomen, the result of an emergency C-section. I hoped they would wonder and ask about it. Then I could legitimately ruin their day without seeming to be as mean or spiteful as I felt. But in that room, filled with the high-pitched buzz of hope and expectation, no one noticed my body at all. They didn't notice the way my stomach hung loose with extra skin, the way the fat was gone, but so was the muscle, how there was nothing left for it to cling to. They didn't notice the way my breasts were loose and saggy, back to their normal size but hanging lower and all stretched out like forgotten water balloons, left in the sun to dry and shrivel.

No one noticed the bags under my eyes from not sleeping, the new wrinkles around the edges from crying hard all the time. They saw and knew nothing of the way I physically ached for my baby still. The way my arms were sore, heavy, and desperate. The way my whole being cried to hold him, to smell him, to absorb him.

Nobody knew how quickly I had lost my baby weight, how I could barely eat or take care of my body. They had no idea that I despised my body for its incompetence, that I couldn't forgive it for getting me into this mess. They didn't know how I never wanted to make love to my husband again, how I never wanted my body to feel good after all the pain it caused me.

In that horrible sweaty room, fighting back tears, I realized just how separate I was. Anger crept from that sense of isolation, and I raged at the world that dared to go on, leaving me behind with my losses. Beyond losing Johnny, I had lost my place in the world, lost the ever-important gift of rose-tinted glasses. From now on, like it or not, I would see God's world raw and exposed for what it is, unfair, random, dreamless. A world where some crackhead could do drugs and end up with a seemingly healthy baby, or where abusive mothers got to have three or four kids, while we couldn't have one.

I would never be the same, and I hated it. I hated the idea that my next child, if I ever had one, would only know this new me: the wounded me, the changed me. He or she would never know who I had been before, how I laughed and was silly and took things for granted and believed I understood a few things.

I hated that I spent Wednesday nights at a support group for people whose babies had died, instead of watching *Survivor* and rocking a fussy baby. I hated sitting around that gross brown table under those harsh hospital lights with other dumbstruck couples talking about our "losses." The first few meetings I just sat there, looking from face to tear-stained face, thinking, "Wait, I'm in the wrong place, I'm not supposed to be here. This is for people whose babies have *died*."

Later, I came to appreciate the support group as the one place where I felt almost normal. When I was there, the loneliness and isolation of my grief melted as I talked with others who were a part of the same strange world. We were like a morose cult with our own collective sense of humor, absurdity, and relativism. In that room I was no longer an alien but just another unbelievably sad shared story. The group was a place where I could put together the words "dead" and "baby" and not feel like a pariah unleashing a storm of unwanted sympathy. I could complain about the people who told me Johnny was in a better place now, I could rant about the nerve of a friend who had become pregnant, and I would hear stories that made me feel downright lucky.

It was a place where otherwise-defeated people lit up and proudly showed off photos of their babies that regular people would gasp at or turn away from. Pictures of babies with purply skeleton skin, no bigger than a hand, or bruised baby faces that haunted you with their perfection and overly still little bodies. "Isn't she beautiful?" the parents would plead. And she was beautiful, just as all our babies were. To us they were perfect. And for two hours every other Wednesday night I actually felt I belonged somewhere.

One such Wednesday, a woman shared a story about a man she knew who had lost his baby at birth. She explained how everyone thought he was dealing with it so well. How months later he had gone back to work, gone back to life. And then how finally one day the man got the courage up to go into the baby's room and start taking things apart. He took the tiny stocked-up clothes and laid them out neatly. He took apart the crib piece by piece, the changing table, broke down the unused jogging stroller and hanging mobiles. And then he went to the garage, grabbed a can of gasoline, and poured it over everything. And he lit a match and stood outside and watched the whole house burn.

We all laughed the nervous laughter of black humor when she told the story, and soon became silent as we drifted into our own sad worlds, perhaps all a little too comfortable with that image, a little too familiar with that feeling. That night I lay in bed imagining the man as he went on with his life. I imagined him and his wife at a party, or with friends, acting normal, doing normal things. But inside he's empty. Inside he's a burnt shell of a person. The frame is still intact, he can still speak, he can still move, but it's a front. Inside he is black and burnt and everything he knew, everything he counted on, is destroyed. Images of the future, his dreams, beliefs, are all charred and unrecognizable.

I wanted to burn, too. I hated my body for what it had done. I felt as though it had betrayed me, exposing me openly as a failure. I wanted to destroy it, to burn down this body that had destroyed my beautiful boy, that was useless and painful and hollow now.

A friend had told me about a tribe in South America where the women slash their upper arms to mark when a baby has died. That way, everyone in the tribe can see how many children a woman has lost. Western society, with all its medical glory, seems to have forgotten entirely that babies do still die. We don't even have a word for it. We have "widow" and "orphan" but we have no word to sum up what I had become. I wanted a name for my new status. I wanted a marker of what I'd lost.

I stood in the shower, cursing my husband for not using old-fashioned razor blades, jabbing my arm over and over with the dull, slippery face of his disposable razor. It slipped off my skin, drawing scarce blood here and there in a random pattern. I watched the blood crawl and mix with the water as it rolled down my body. I liked the way it looked, the way it stung and then dulled, resulting in something like a feeling of relief.

Coming out of the shower to admire my work, I was dismayed at how small and unimpressive my cuts were. At best, they would leave light scars that would fade with a tan, nothing like the bold badge of pain I'd imagined. Looking in the mirror I felt more embarrassed at my lack of cutting know-how than anything else. "I can't even do that right," I muttered, staring at the strange person looking back at me. In the foggy glass of the mirror I barely recognized myself. There I was, the same old body, the same features as childhood photos, the same resilient skin, but not one inch of me seemed familiar.

Later that week I went back home to Seattle to mark my twenty-eighth birthday. The trip was supposed to be the "show the new baby off/celebrate birthday" trip. Every year I tried to make it home for my birthday; I liked spending it with people who had known me my whole life. This birthday was supposed to be even more special, more perfect as I showed off my crowning achievement in life. "See, everyone, look how good I did. Look how beautiful he is. Look how happy he makes you."

The airport felt like a personal tarmac for anyone and everyone with a new baby. Toddlers used the cement-colored hallways as a takeoff runway, their short arms and legs working double-time to leave ransacked parents in the dust. Babies everywhere flew up into the air, then landed, giggling and safe into the sure arms of their parents. Off again they'd go, again, squealing with delight, a flawless combination of hopes and dreams tossed perfectly into round porcelain faces. I managed to find a chair with minimal child activity. When they finally called my flight for early boarding I almost went. "I should be boarding early," I wanted to say. "I should have a baby."

Being home was miserable. No one knew what to say or do and I spent most of the time in my room, crying in secret. It was hard to be around people who cared so much. I felt awkward and alien like a bull in a china shop—my over-size, unmanageable grief was the bull; the nervous, awkward "Let's just pretend things are okay" by family and friends was the china shop.

In an effort to escape all that, I went to visit an old friend. He wasn't someone I knew from childhood, he was someone I met while I was depressed teenager, so we already knew how to hang out and be depressed and not have it be awkward. In fact, he had been in the Bay Area Christmas Day, two weeks after Johnny died, and we had enjoyed striking against the merriment of Christmas together, sitting at the local dive bar, me and him and my husband and the baby's godfather drinking ourselves silly with the other bah-humbugs and old drunks. He listened and looked at pictures and kept his mouth shut and bought us shots of booze and never teared up or got uncomfortable. He was good at that.

He showed me around the new tattoo shop he had just opened. Years ago I had let him tattoo me in the grungy basement of a mutual friend's house. At the time, I felt a sense of inherent remorse the minute the tattoo gun touched my skin. It was as if I instantly knew I would never be the same, that this thing was a part of me forever. I was permanently marked with an ancient Greek inscription on my backside which, for all I know, could just as easily say, "If you can read this you're too close."

But sitting there in his shop, I was struck by how appropriate a tattoo was. Who cared if I didn't like how it turned out; I sure didn't care much for how my life had turned out, either. I was marked, changed, torn, whether I liked it or not.

We sat around looking through books of art and drawings, both determined not to leave until we created the perfect symbol for my son, the perfect way to remember him. I wanted something classic. My husband and I chose the name Johnny because it was a family name, but just as much because it sounded so cool and old style. When Johnny was first in the hospital they told us he'd probably just have moderate brain damage and suffer from seizures. We got through that by pretending he would start a punk rock band. He'd be up there on stage having a seizure, and all the kids would think it was so cool. It would become some new kind of dance craze. Only someone with a name like Johnny could pull that off.

I finally settled on the old mother-style, heart-and-banner tattoo with his name on it. We added some blue angel wings around the heart, his birth date on top, and the day he died on the bottom. We topped the whole thing off with tiny yellow forget-me-nots at each edge of the banner. It was perfect.

I decided to place it right above my heart on the left side of my chest. I sat in my ratty, old maternity bra, feeling the sting of the gun on my post-pregnancy breast. I loved the pain the needle caused as it burned Johnny's name into my flesh. It was nothing compared to the heartache I had felt over the past couple months; this pain was tangible, it made sense, it was finite.

Watching this man hunched over me with his medieval-looking tool, I got the feeling I was taking part in some kind of violent initiation ceremony; I had passed a test, gotten instruction from which there was no retreat. I was admitted to my new life and identity and would finally have the scar to prove it. I imagined nursing a new baby someday, looking down at the baby and seeing the tattoo and remembering Johnny. I loved the idea that I could never forget him, or forget the pain that came with that. I loved knowing that each and every day of my life to come this new inextricable, unalterable part of me would be there, like Johnny should have been.

"Who's Johnny?" someone asked me as my friend showed off his work around the shop. It was the first time I'd been asked that question, and I was unprepared. Later I would come to develop a whole new language, a whole new way of talking and being in the world. One that included the story of the baby I lost shortly after birth and the person I had become after that. But it was too fresh then, my new status still too raw. All I could utter was, "My dead baby."

That evening I went out with friends. I purposely wore a low-cut shirt that showed off the tattoo, still bright and shiny with blood and lotion. I wanted everyone in the world to see it. I didn't have a bouncing baby boy to show off, but at least I had a symbol, some marker of his life and my hurt. It was my equivalent of brag book and battle scar, all rolled into one. More than that, it was as if the permanence behind the sunburn sting of the tattoo pulled me from the shadows where I had been hovering in disbelief and loneliness, dropped anchor for me down into the real world, and locked me back into a body I could somehow start forgiving.

Namaste
by Rachel Iverson

tonight,
as every night,
i stand over you
 i place a cupped
hand on your chest to
feel your body fill with air
 reassured,
for now you are fine.
for now
 emotion burbles
in my head,
leaks into my ears
and out of my eyes
 i want everything for
you
 everything good
 marshmallows, a lemonade
stand, white sand, green corn
tamales, sidewalks and marine
layer mornings
 newsprint on your fingers,
bubble baths, earthworms in
black dirt, satellite t.v. and
and at least one big win
 grilled tomatoes, a dog with
yawning eyes, a place to hide,
hammocks in the summertime and
a moment like this

Hospital Quartet
by Phyllis Capello

Part I.
Everything Shifts to This Center

Nurse (great white form) pins him
(a wrestle-hold) strong black hands
hold fast his thin arms;
doctor searches small,
bruised wrist for best vein;
shining liquid slips in:
chemo will first poison,
then, perhaps, release;
I pat his little foot, watch,
as everything shifts to this center.
His strangled cry—silver-bright
needlepoint of human sound
in the white, throbbing room.

Part II.
I.V.

"Mama—hurts-a-me! burns-a-me!"
Cradle him, tell him stories:
"Remember, that time, on the beach,
your red shovel, and sister,
burying your feet?"

We have learned to rock
        upon this brink.

"Remember: you asked the name
for gull, then dashed into the sea?"

Hollow needles' steady pulse,
draw hope inside.
Drop by drop, I sit and watch,
each drop a jewel of light.

Part III.
Pediatrics

Nurses learn to live with it, but,
in their first year here,
the young ones
sob in the bathroom.

Through corridors of neither night
nor day, mothers rush, rumpled
and wild-haired, on endless missions:
Ice to the fever, blanket to the chill.
In the concentration of will
that holds back the avalanche
their teeth ring with dread.

Fathers slump, humbled and silent,
in bedside chairs, mark
(with barely rising eyelids) the passage
of white coats (tubes, tape, pills,
tears, fate, bills). Illness
has been their Delilah.

More vividly witnessed now—inner images:
uncertainty spiraling out toward infinity,
escaping their clenched fists.

Part IV.
Rounds

They prod his tiny scrotum,
his liver, his lungs,
speak ciphers, side effects, reckonings, drugs,
cell counts and secondary infections.
Parades of calamity roll off their prideful tongues.

Then, examinations done,
they wave (in sickening, mock frivolity)
lollipops, before the cowering child.
They volley (like imbeciles on holiday)
an inflated rubber glove;
I measure the distance between jobs and sons.

My boy, whose black eyes swim in a sea of pallor,
who shrinks (like time gone backward)
whose curls fall out, who wakes without his lashes.

Dear Friend
by Vicki Forman

I want to tell you why: I cried in your office; bought myself an expensive purse; don't talk about the details of my life; smile a lot; give short, simple answers. It's not because I have a son without eyes. It's because you think someday he will: wear glasses, do puzzles, sit in a kindergarten, learn to read.

You told me a story, friend, of the boy born with water on the brain, who needs glasses, who walked when he was two (so late!), who talked finally at four (so late!), whom no one expected much of, but who now does fifty-piece puzzles.

"From the inside out," you said. "He starts in the middle, he examines each piece, he turns it this way and that. He makes a decision, he's a savant."

I looked at you, dear friend, and wondered, *What am I supposed to gain from this?* You love me, this I know, so perhaps you were thinking, *I want my sunny pictures, doesn't she?*

You told me another story then, of the girl who could not see, or talk ("She was a preemie too," you said), who lay about the rug of the classroom and made sounds and gestures no one could understand. Of the teacher who could not teach; of the students who could not reach her. "Her parents must not fight for everything she needs," you said.

And what I thought, but did not say: *With a child like that, there is no fighting. There is only living.*

My son, you took: Topamax (seizures); Inderal (heart); Vigabatrin (seizures); Phenobarbitol (seizures); Demerol (pain); Ativan (pain); Lasix, Albuterol, Decadron (lungs). I took: Seconal (sleep); Ambien (sleep); Prozac, Wellbutrin, Celexa (depression); Ativan (sleep); Topamax (kicks).

"I gave him Ativan to help him sleep," the nurse said. "I gave him Phenobarbitol so he won't remember. I gave him his breathing treatment, he saturates so much better after the Albuterol, I gave him Tylenol."

"Tylenol?" I asked. *A child with scars across his body, a tube down his throat to help him breathe, one eye (at first) then no eyes (at last) and you gave him Tylenol?* "Does Tylenol really apply?"

"Should I give him more Ativan? Morphine maybe?"

"Morphine sounds good," I said.

I have brought you: into life; home from the hospital; to the heart doctor who said you would not live; to the eye doctor who would not look at me; to the neurologist who said you may look normal but could easily one day shrivel up into the cripple of the worst sort. "Like this," he said, pretending to be Quasimodo.

Back to the hospital then. Into surgery rooms, CT scan rooms, MRI rooms, more hospital rooms, and home again. You are the same boy but different now: diagnosis, medicine. The parts that don't work: your eyes; your heart; your stomach; your mouth; your brain; your lungs.

The parts that do: your smile, your laugh.

I brought you home, took you to see your grandparents *(she will be traveling with a disabled child; she will need help)*, and to the grave where your sister is buried. I took you to soccer games, Brownie troop meetings, the park (on oxygen, a tank hoisted across my shoulder), more doctors' offices. I took you to schools where I teach, to meet colleagues, to hear questions, "Will he ever see? Walk?"

Will he ever toss a ball, do a puzzle, turn the pages in a book?

I bring you to school like a roasted pig, hoisted above me for all to see. "Look, here's Evan! Hi Evan! Good morning Evan!" I place you on the floor, beside a basket of toys. "Look Evan, here are your toys." I put your hand on the basket, I move you to a toy. You pull back, you shake your head, you bend over into your pose, the one that says, "Nope, not now, no toys for me. Right now I want to stand upside down with my head on the ground, the feel of my hair on the rug." I step back. I try not to make too much of this basket, these toys. *Haven't I brought you here for a reason? Aren't you supposed to be here, to learn, to play?*

My dear friend, can you picture the boy on the floor, laughing at his own joke? "Look at me," he says. "I can't see, I can't talk, I can't do puzzles. Maybe I never will. But I crack myself up, make jokes no one else understands. I know yoga poses: downward dog, bear, child's pose, the lotus position, virasana."

"Science is so amazing," you say. "They can fix the parts that do not work, there are advances every day. Why just yesterday—"

"Yesterday is not today," I say. Yesterday is not the day I brought my son to school where he is meant to dress himself, feed himself, walk to the playground, find the swing, climb the structure, sit on a chair without sliding off, hold a spoon, put food into his mouth. Chew, swallow, drink. Know his friends' names.

Yesterday is of no use.

The boy with the glasses and the watery brain. My son.

Sometimes you don't like something your whole life but you're still meant to be here on Earth. That is the beauty, the struggle, the true puzzle: fifty pieces and more, upside down, inside out, right side in.

Down Will Come Baby
by Rebecca Kaminsky

I trudged down Ocean View Drive, just off College Avenue, on the way home from Market Hall with some groceries. I wore Simon in his baby sling. My head was down, as usual, as I focused on getting us to the apartment. I was able to get home by recognizing the gardens, my eyes rarely lifting. We lived on the top floor of a pale blue craftsman at the end of a block of bungalows and two-story craftsman houses, painted in varying shades of pastel colors. Walking with my head down, I knew which lots were studded with purple and orange lantana, which were growing wild with sour grass. Almost home, I just wanted to sink into the couch, turn on the TV, and nurse Simon. Talking to the ingratiating clerk at the store had simply taken too much out of me.

Ever since the accident, I felt as though I was disappearing. I spent time alone and mostly stayed at home, taking Simon on a walk each day only to get food or run necessary errands. It was hard to participate in conversations. I hid behind Simon. Everyone fussed over him with his beautiful blond hair and fat red cheeks. All the store clerks knew him by name.

He had recovered, just like the doctors said he would, thriving as if nothing had happened. But his robust physicality and happy nature did nothing to quell my devastation. I had failed him, that was that. Letting others fuss over him and fading into the background was easy, but more than that, it was what I deserved.

The time between Simon's birth and the accident seems like a blur now.

It took me the first four weeks of my new son's life to get comfortable enough to breastfeed in public. When I finally felt like I could nurse without feeling self-conscious, Jack and I decided to celebrate—we'd have dinner out with the baby. We'd even dress up, meaning we'd wear clothes without spit-up on them. I was excited to discover that I already fit back into my prepregnancy jeans, and I decided a nice dinner out was reason enough to pair them with my favorite blue platform-heel sandals. It looked great. I looked great. My satiny blouse (also pre-baby) clung to my new post-baby figure; my breasts were so much bigger than before. I brushed my hair, deciding to let my long brown curls hang loose. I felt sexy. Looking in the mirror, I felt a little charge of the past, my old pre-baby self snapping back into place for just a moment.

We got all our baby gear together and went outside. I led the way, carrying Simon. Jack followed with the diaper bag and stroller. The narrow paved walkway around the building was unlit, and the bushes were overgrown and crowding the path.

As I edged along, being careful not to let the stray branches scratch the baby, I thought about whether I wanted lamb or chicken curry. I couldn't wait to get to Ajanta, our favorite Indian restaurant. I had just nursed Simon and, with any luck, he would sleep through the first part of our meal. I imagined dipping a samosa into tangy coriander chutney. My stomach rumbled.

I didn't see the crack in the pavement. The toe of my platform sandal got stuck. I jolted forward, tripped, and felt myself falling. My life suddenly went into horrifying, movie slow motion. I felt Simon pitching out of my arms with the uncontrollable force of my body weight—right onto the cement.

As I struggled to get my bearings, I looked up and saw Simon, a tiny bundle of blankets in a heap on the driveway next to the curb, like a lump of tattered clothes forgotten by a homeless person. My knees were shaking. My own forehead was scraped and bruised from the fall, but I wouldn't see that until much later. I felt only numbness in my body as I focused in on Simon. *Oh my God*, I thought. *Oh my God! Don't Die Don't Die Don't Die!*

His eyes were open. He was breathing—I could see the rise and fall of his chest—but he wasn't crying, just totally stunned and silent. There was a white mark, edged in red, on his forehead. The beginning of an angry, fat goose egg. That image would plague me far into the future.

My gaze shifted away from the sidewalk and I spotted a good friend heading toward us about a block away. Simon weighed hotly against me in the sling, and

I was thirsty. My friend was in between me and the refuge of my apartment. And I looked like crap. I couldn't bear the thought of making small talk—of having to mouth the usual new-mom automatic response of, "Oh, I'm fine, a little sleep deprived, but he's so beautiful! Being a mom is worth all the hard work!" God, I hated hearing new moms say that, because I knew it was fake. I fantasized about shouting at them: "TELL THE TRUTH! Sometimes it just sucks! Sometimes you just want your old life back! And then you cry because you love your baby so much and you know you can't have both."

My hair was in a messy ponytail and I could practically feel the bags under my eyes. I wore the only thing not in the growing pile of dirty laundry by our bed, a maternity dress. It was comfortable, but it must have looked like a burlap sack.

On the street, my friend was getting closer. I crossed to the other side, hoping he hadn't seen us.

"Becca, hey, Becca!" I heard him calling.

Shit. I looked down at my dress. There were spit-up stains, and my legs weren't shaved.

Before the accident, food was one of my chief pleasures in life. After the accident, eating seemed like a bother. After the accident, I ate only when necessary, when Simon was awake and happy—or better yet, when he was asleep and I wouldn't be interrupted with him needing me if he suddenly became fussy or hungry. I lost weight steadily. My hunger felt kind of good, clean.

But I slept at every opportunity. As soon as Jack came home I went to sleep, and awoke only to nurse Simon back down after his nighttime awakenings. I told myself that this was normal, that it would end, and I'd spend more time with Jack as soon as I "caught up" and became more rested. My secret was that I'd fallen in love with sleeping, become addicted to it. It was the only time I felt free, undistracted. I could think whatever I wanted, let my mind wander. I dreamt of college, of my activist past, of old loves, of feeling sexy and powerful. Upon awakening I greedily counted the amount of hours I had slept, when Simon awoke, and how long it took him to get back to sleep. Two hours here, three hours there . . . four whole hours of sleep at one time!

Everyone told me how great (meaning thin) I looked so soon after having a baby. I didn't contradict them, because I knew they couldn't see me. After all, I was invisible. I barely weighed a hundred pounds—borderline for my five-foot-tall body. My hair was falling out, the springy curls I gained during pregnancy darkening my pillow in large clumps.

The friend I spotted crossed the street. As he got closer he said with a half-sweet, half-mocking smile, "Did you just cross the street to avoid me?" My face went red with shame. Simon beamed up at him from the sling.

"Wow," he said, "you look great! And he's so cute! How is life as a mom?"

"Oh, I'm fine, a little sleep deprived, but he's so beautiful! Being a mom is worth all the hard work!"

Then I walked home.

Jack's first reaction after the fall was to bring Simon inside the house—he would be fine, just a big bump. But Simon's silence was too weird, too chilling.

"Something is very wrong," I said to Jack. "We have to take him to the emergency room. Now."

Jack took Simon and began strapping him into his car seat. I remember thinking if Simon were an adult we wouldn't move him for fear of back injuries or concussion. What if the seat belt straps crushed or further injured him? Still, if there is one mantra you hear as a new parent, it is *always use the car seat.* So instinct took over: Jack strapped him in.

I went around to the other side of the car, but even moving those few steps away from my baby son felt like too great a separation. I sat in the backseat with him, my arms reaching around the car seat in an awkward embrace, as he remained eerily silent all the way to the ER. I think I must have been crying and saying things like, "I can't believe this is happening," because I remember Jack's comforting voice: "Sweetie, Simon needs us. We can't lose it now. It's going to be okay."

Would it ever be okay again? It felt like someone had punched me. Just that afternoon I had been praying that he be quiet or asleep during our dinner, for just one night of peace. And now this. What exactly had I been praying for? How could I have wished for silence over a healthy newborn cry?

For most new mothers there is a moment when it hits you: the fact of your complete and utter responsibility—and the vulnerability that comes with it. This was mine.

I pressed the buzzer of my therapist's building, a small Victorian in downtown Berkeley. I hadn't been to see her in four years. I felt like a wind-up toy just before its key is released. I needed to tell her the worst before I lost my nerve.

Right after we sat down, I said, "I'm just going to say this without thinking. I need to do it." I clenched my hands together and lowered my head to let my hair cover my face. I had to force the words out. I explained quickly how my emotions had overtaken me, how I had been banging the wall in frustration, biting myself on the hand if Simon wouldn't sleep or if Jack and I would argue. I ended with, "Sometimes there are bruises, bite marks on my hand. But not so much that you'd notice . . ." I couldn't look at her.

I breathed in. Slowly I raised my eyes. She was still there. She told me about the many women who had previously graced her office, compatriots whose existence I hadn't dared to imagine. Some tore out strands of their hair. Some locked themselves in the bathroom and ranted and screamed into a pillow. Some cut themselves. She told me, "We can find another way. You can get through this." I exhaled.

I had expected her to think badly of me, to treat me like a crazy person. Instead she saw everything and didn't flinch. My world slowly got bigger. The whole story came out. The accident, the months I spent barely leaving the apartment, the harsh judgment I imagined from other mothers, from her. She told me when women feel guilty over conflicting feelings concerning their children, they often lash out at themselves. They do this rather than lash out at their children, or their partners, or the society that pressures them to be perfect. Self-inflicted pain is a release, a way to demonstrate inner pain on the body.

In the next weeks and months we trained a flashlight on the darkest part of me. I forced myself to find a baby sitter in order to be able to go to therapy alone. That in itself was a huge step. I was able to walk deliciously unencumbered to her office, noticing trees and storefronts on the way. My line of vision changed. I looked up when I walked.

Still, I hated myself for the accident. For wanting a break and deciding to take Simon out and have fun. For hoping he'd fall asleep. For dressing up that night. For Simon's skull fracture. For letting him fall out of *my hands*. And for all the weeks after, for letting the sadness and anger take over. Wasn't I stronger than this?

After one session, I went home and pulled the blue platform sandals from the bag where they'd sat in back of my closet since the accident. I traced the height of the heel with my finger, examined the soles for scrapes, skid marks, evidence of the fall. I touched the shimmery blue sandal straps and remembered that night, getting dressed for our first night out with Simon. How I had wanted him to sleep so I could enjoy time with Jack.

That was an okay thing to want.

Feeling sexy and wanting to go out that night wasn't bad.

All my memories of that night had been steeped in superstition—my depression combined with sayings from my childhood like "bite your tongue" or *kayn ein hora*, the Yiddish expression meaning "to ward off the evil eye." It struck me that all of that superstition centered around being punished for reveling in happiness, showing off joy or pride, or around warnings such as "Be careful what you wish for."

Slowly, I began to see I didn't need to live my life like that. My experience could be different. I could relax, walk tall. Literally. I had hidden the sexy shoes away as if they had jinxed me. But no magical power had said, "I'll show her, I'll make her evil wish come true!"

I put the shoes on. Wanting to have my own self wasn't bad.

I was not God.

It. Was. An. Accident.

VII.

Healing the Past to Live in the Present

Answers
by Lisa Suhair Majaj
(for Nadia)

What I carry with me?
Secrets. Peppermints. The smell of rain.

What I remember?
Specks of ash on a warm baked egg.

What I know?
How many songs till bedtime.

What I forget?
The exact color of my grandmother's eyes.

What I left behind?
Light on the river the morning you were born.

What I learned yesterday?
How to dance a jig barefoot, with bunions.

Where I'm going tomorrow?
With you, to a meadow of daffodils blooming like days.

Fragile Season
by Cindy La Ferle

Spring is just a few weeks away, yet the barren landscape outside my office window looks more like the moon than southeast Michigan. Piles of brittle, gray snow flank the curb, and the sidewalk shimmers with black ice. Only die-hard neighbors stick to their evening jogging routines. Spring is just a mirage.

On the liturgical calendar, it is the Lenten season. According to T. S. Eliot's poem "Ash Wednesday," it is the time between "dying and birth."

It is not the ideal time to face a changing identity, pending menopause, a stalled career, or a recently emptied nest. It is the time of year when, despite my better judgment, my cheerful disposition is easily frayed. Lately my writing life seems like a long wait in line at the post office.

And it's not that I'm seriously blocked. Just lonely. For the past five months, my only child has been happily settled in his cramped dormitory room at a university in another state. I'm still adjusting to the hollow echo of his oddly clean and empty bedroom, looking for remnants of my old self—my mothering self—in the bits and pieces he left behind.

Empty nesting, I'm convinced, is harder on mothers who work at home—mothers who stare into a computer monitor until the garden thaws in mid-April and children migrate home from college.

Heeding the advice of a friend who happens to be a local pastor, I've learned that community service is the best antidote for what we Midwesterners describe as acute cabin fever.

"You need to leave your comfort zone. Use your gifts in the community," urged the pastor. In other words, do unto others and get over yourself. Which is how I ended up working an afternoon shift at a warming shelter for the homeless.

Answering a need during the cruel winter months, a small church in my neighborhood opens its kitchen and dining room to approximately fifty homeless men and women at a time. Job counselors and social workers volunteer their expertise to those who struggle with substance abuse or unemployment (or both).

Churchgoers are recruited to serve meals, scrub sticky tables, pour pots of black coffee, and perform simple clerical tasks for the understaffed warming center.

The visiting homeless are required to wear name tags. Before starting my first shift, I was advised to call each person by name and to refer to the group as "guests."

I have worked with the homeless in other circumstances. But I am always a bit shy at first. These people—the guests—have formed their own community, complete with its own set of rules and rhythms. I am an outsider in their midst; a white journalist from Planet Suburbia. I feel inept and alien when confronted by so much horrific need, yet I have come to serve and, in a small way, to mother.

My first assignment was to ladle out steaming heaps of ham and potatoes to each of the hungry guests who had lined up at the serving table.

That day, there were close to fifty, mostly men. Most were eager to talk and visibly grateful for a free meal. I was taken aback, initially, at the way each guest wanted me to spoon his portion onto a plate and hand it to him. Not a single person would take the plates I had already filled and set on the table in the interest of moving the line quickly.

Nearby, in a cluttered corner that served as makeshift office space for the center, another volunteer was keeping company with a guest whose name tag read "Marian." Aloof and unkempt, Marian flashed angry, intelligent brown eyes and wore a burgundy wool cap over her brow. Playing a game of Scrabble on the office computer, she didn't mix with the other guests, nor did she want to converse with my fellow volunteer. Her body language wasn't hard to translate: *Keep out. Don't touch. My heart is not open for business or charity.* She didn't look up when we asked if she wanted a hot lunch. Fixed on the computer screen, she mumbled something about a candy bar she had eaten earlier, and declined our offer.

One by one, all the guests except Marian were served, and I was told by the center organizer that it was time to clear the tables for dessert. I began my assignment quickly, grateful once again for the focus required of even the simplest domestic routines.

Then, suddenly, a voice.

"Excuse me, excuse me?"

I barely heard her over the metallic clatter of roasting pans and serving utensils. It was Marian, the Scrabble player. Without turning from the screen, Marian repeated her question, more audibly this time, to anyone within earshot: "How do you spell 'fragile'?"

Slowly, carefully, my fellow volunteer voiced the letters aloud and repeated them: F-R-A-G-I-L-E.

Fragile.

Returning to the kitchen with an armload of dishes, I reconsidered the word and what it meant. I recalled how carelessly I'd been using the adjective to define or describe the strange terrain of my new empty nest. And how, in a single instant, its meaning, its very etymology, had changed forever.

Why My Garden
by Ericka Lutz

The night train stops at dawn with a heave and a sigh. The sound of a whistle, a small bustle outside the compartment window. I look at my watch. Almost 5:00 AM; we're still an hour from Kraków. All night, the train rocked gently from Prague, yet I slept uneasily. Woken at the Czech-Polish border by pounding on the door—Passport Control. I slide off the top bunk, careful not to wake my sleeping little girl in the middle bunk, my husband on the bottom, and I carefully raise the blackout blind. It sticks and the catch pinches my finger but I finally raise it enough to see out. A white sign hangs outside, framed perfectly by the train window. BRZEZINKA. The name sounds familiar but it takes me a moment to remember—it's the Polish word for Birkenau, the largest of the three Auschwitz concentration camps.

Auschwitz! The word is ashes, sirens, and stomping boots, my baby ripped from me and trampled, vomit and diarrhea and starvation, choking for breath. It's fear. I shut the blind; I'm not ready to be here yet. This morning we'll continue on the train to Kraków. Tomorrow I'll come back alone to Auschwitz. Tomorrow is why I, an unobservant American Jew, just before my fortieth birthday, am on this train. I am a Jew, and this is my destination.

The train whistles, lurches, and pulls out of Brzezinka and into the Polish countryside, heading for Kraków through the green, foggy fields at dawn. Bill and Annie still sleep in their bunks, but I reopen the blind to watch the passing countryside with the strongest sense memory I've ever experienced. This is the first time I've been to Poland, but I bear an Ellis Island–butchered Polish name and this place touches something deep in me. Instead of feeling the horror of Auschwitz so close, these fields, these misty colors, release a deep, ancestral memory and I feel home.

I've rarely considered myself a spiritual seeker. Except, perhaps, now on this journey to Auschwitz, the place I fear the most. Auschwitz may seem an unlikely site to seek meaning. Unless you're a Jew.

I was raised as a countercultural, Jewish-Atheist, red-diaper grandbaby in San Francisco and Marin County in the '60s and '70s. My father was a member of the "lost generation," bar mitzvahed by a nonobservant merchant family, who rebelled against all things traditional. My mother was a dancer. Her family, revolutionaries in Russia, socialists in Nebraska, and Tolstoyan vegetarians in upstate New York, communists and labor leaders in the '30s, believed in one world/one people and hated the rigidity of the old Jewish traditions to the extent that they celebrated Christmas with Christmas trees, caroling, and advent calendars. Our family never talked about religion except to scoff at those who practiced. We never addressed why people seek a deeper understanding of life. Religion was the refuge of little minds, the opiate of the masses; churches were political forces up to no good. We did not trust, we distrusted. And yet we were Jewish.

By the time I boarded this train to Kraków, I was a typical Bay Area nonreligious, Jewish, pseudoskeptic; a double Libra with my Venus in Scorpio who didn't believe in astrology. I kept a nineteenth-century Thai Buddha on my mantelpiece and tried to emulate his serenity. Decembers were Hanukkah candles, latkes, and Christmas trees. On the Harmonic Convergence, Bill and I drove up to Mount Tamalpais to greet the dawn; not to converge, but merely to witness the crystal-blessing, flute-playing scene. I didn't believe in God, unless you define God as physics. Sometimes, however, writing at dawn, I'd watched the auras of my houseplants glow. The one time I took mushrooms I was deeply aware of the universe's layers of consciousness, and of myself as a small part of the whole. I believed in meaningful coincidence, serendipity, that we are not what we seem, yet I'd rarely been to church, except as an anthropological experience in other countries, and I'd been to temple only twice, when invited with friends.

The train rolls through the countryside, the towns, the industrial outskirts, and into the city. We gather our luggage and disembark. A new country for us; unlike in Budapest and Prague, nothing is in English and we don't speak a word of Polish. We're in bad temper and nervous, just seventy kilometers from Auschwitz.

Auschwitz was the biggest of the World War II Nazi death camps. It was actually three camps: Auschwitz I, which held mostly political prisoners; Auschwitz II–Birkenau, a huge concentration and extermination camp where over a million Jews, Gypsies, and political prisoners were gassed and cremated; and Auschwitz III–Monowitz, a chemical factory. The Auschwitz-Birkenau State Museum, open to the public, comprises Auschwitz I, an educational museum and memorial shrine, and Birkenau, three kilometers away, which was burned and bombed by the retreating Germans and has been left as it was. Auschwitz-Monowitz is closed except by special arrangement. Tomorrow, I'll visit both Auschwitz I and Birkenau.

I haven't always been ready to come here. When Annie was a baby, Bill and I took her to Europe and found ourselves one afternoon in a mad, driving dash across Germany to catch an airplane out of Amsterdam. Rain, crying baby, hungry, low on gas, we pulled off the autobahn to gather our wits, came to the exit, and saw a sign pointing left: Dachau. "Get back on! Get back on the autobahn!" I yelled, and Bill did a quick U-turn and drove us as far and as fast as he could.

This time, I want to be here. I will go by myself—Bill will go alone the day after. The reason for this is pragmatic: One of us needs to stay with our now-seven-year-old daughter; and it's emotional—an experience this extreme is best not filtered through another's reactions. It's a journey we each need to take alone.

Auschwitz is the last stage in a journey we began in Budapest ten days ago. We spent a week teaching in Budapest and then traveled to Prague. Our plans to come here tinted the rest of the journey; I'd been in Budapest and Prague before but this time I saw everything through a Holocaust lens, as if World War II had just ended.

In the Budapest synagogue, the ghosts of the Jews who had sat in the benches rose around me; I felt them. I walked through the branches of a metal weeping willow memorial tree, each leaf engraved with the name of a Holocaust victim, and the fingers of the dead reached out to catch my hair. In the Budapest flea market, on a wooden table amidst the cultural detritus, I stumbled on a three-inch-high lead soldier wearing a Nazi uniform and armband, his arm raised in a "Heil Hitler" salute. In Prague: Bill's last name on the Pinkas Synagogue wall; a military antiquities store window filled with Nazi nostalgia. On our last night in Prague, I dreamed about Auschwitz. In the dream, it was just another Holocaust display. I awoke distraught. All my life I'd read books, seen pictures and movies, names on walls and sculptural trees. At Auschwitz I'd really be there. Where it happened.

How am I a Jew? It's confusing when your ethnicity bears the name of a religion. A few years ago I tried to become more Jewish. I started with the traditions that my family had left behind. I read about Shabbat, a time for reflection once a week, an evening to light candles and be together, a peaceful break from a busy life. For a working mother who woke up in the middle of the night to finish the day's tasks, this idea of an island of stillness soothed like water on a thirsty throat.

At a store selling Jewish books and supplies, I shopped for a pair of brass candlesticks. My heart pounded every time I entered the store (imposter!) but I persevered, finally working up the courage to actually purchase them, along with a supply of white, stubby candles. I lit the Shabbat candles three or four times. I explained it to my two-year-old daughter as a little party, a time to celebrate the week. These were the words I used; they came from one of the books I read. Bill went along with me, bemused and slightly indulgent.

And I felt like a phony, a faker. Because I wasn't *really* Jewish. Because I didn't know what I was doing, reciting words in a different language, waving my hands superstitiously over the flames and then covering my eyes. Because I didn't believe in God. Because I couldn't support an oppressive religion, and all of them were. Because I didn't really want to be Jewish, a victim, a hated, big-nosed, hairy, nasal, whining, smart-mouthed neurotic. Because, really, I'd always wanted to be normal-looking, not dark and exotic and Jewish-looking. Because what, in my confused state, was I teaching my daughter? The candlesticks dulled, and I didn't shine them.

After getting Polish *zlotys* from an ATM, staring at maps in the station, and almost getting ripped off by a cab driver, we head off for the center of Kraków on foot, our backpacks heavy on our backs. We find the Hotel Saski, a small hotel near the square, and we walk from there to Kazimierz, the Jewish ghetto. I know this place from the movies: *Schindler's List, Jakob the Liar*. It's a mess, still a ghetto. Boarded-up windows, trash in the streets. Next to an impoverished synagogue, a cemetery of stones torn up during the war, every tooth violently yanked from a mouth, reset, now, in arbitrary rows. A Jewish bookstore. A few restaurants and stores catering to the Israeli tourist market.

The man in the bookstore speaks some English. A sign on the window advertises tours to Auschwitz I and Birkenau. "You don't need a tour," he tells us. "You take the bus, not the train." He looks like my cousin. He writes down the schedule for us. The bus leaves at 9:30 AM. It arrives at Aushwitz I in Oswiciem (the Polish word for Auschwitz—it's a town, too) at 10:45 AM. The minibus from Auschwitz I to Birkenau leaves at 1:30 PM. It takes five minutes to get there. At 3:05, the minibus goes back to Auschwitz I, and at 3:30, the bus goes back to Kraków. Don't miss the bus and get stuck at Auschwitz. In gratitude, we buy a book from him. *Auschwitz: Nazi Death Camp.*

The rest of the day we sightsee. The center of Kraków is beautiful. Nuns and priests in black habits everywhere, the famous Wawel Castle on the hill next to the cathedral, the old town square bordered by shops and outdoor cafés. We hire a horse cart, we climb the tower. From the top, we see beyond the ring of the quaint old city limits into the new part of town. Huge industrial complexes, Soviet housing blocks, a nuclear power plant along the river. Until a few years ago, this city was one of the most polluted in Europe. I stare out at the horizon. It's there, seventy kilometers away.

In the morning, I leave Bill and Annie at the Hotel Saski and walk to the bus stop. In Auschwitz, in my imagination, the trees are always bare, lashed with wind and blinding rain and sleet. The skies are always gray, the people always gray with hunger and weariness. Shreds of clothing hang loosely, the sky shrieks, the babies die, the mothers weep. It's a dark place and there's no daylight.

In contrast, the Polish countryside radiates in a spring far greener than the wet green winters of Northern California, my home. Young colts frolic in the fields, birds sing, the ground pushes up fertility, farmers till the land, small castles dot the rolling hills. Lush forests. And every once in a while, a road sign. OŚWICIĘM. I cannot breathe. I am going to a funeral.

We pass small towns and old farmhouses. That barn was there then, did Jews hide inside? What happened on this land? A young farmer, covered with dirt and straw, and stinking of booze, stumbles on the bus and sits behind me. I welcome his stench; it matches my internal reality better than the clean, spring air. I photograph and take notes frantically. The acceleration of the bus whines like air-raid sirens. We parallel the train track now. Almost there. We pass car dealerships and small hotels. We've arrived.

The moment I step off the bus, my feet and legs lose all feeling. Disembodied, I float through the wooded outskirts where the guards lived into the Auschwitz-Birkenau State Museum parking lot, where the buses belch diesel fumes. School buses. There's a large new building here housing the museum shop. The cafeteria. A theater where they show an informational movie (in English, twice every day). The ticket booth. I skip the movie, pass through the glass doors, into the grounds of Auschwitz I in line with a number of teenagers. A sign tells us to respect the sanctity of this place.

I want a Jewish star to wear. If there is anywhere on earth I want to wear a Jewish star it is here.

ARBEIT MACHT FREI. Above the arched metal gate, the words "Work will make you free." I pass beneath them and cross the railway tracks. I walk away from the crowds heading toward the crematorium and down the railroad track because I need to be alone. I'm here, and like a grown child visiting a childhood home, it's smaller than in my nightmares; and like a nightmare made real, too solid, the buildings are too building-like, the trees too much like trees. Birds sing.

Many of the barracks have been made into museum displays. Several house the general exhibition: Extermination; Material Evidence of Crimes; the "Death" Block. And eight have been set aside as separate exhibitions: U.S.S.R., Poland, Czechoslovakia, Yugoslavia/Austria, Hungary, France/Belgium, Italy/Holland, the Jews. Alone, I walk into the Jewish barrack where nothing is left as it was, the building as impersonal as any museum. TV monitors show black-and-white loops of Jews herded into ghettos. A large blowup photo of Anne Frank smiles down at me from the wall, a large blowup photo of piles of dead bodies in a mass grave. Like my nightmare in Prague: the same images as in any Holocaust museum. Alone, I follow the prescribed path through the exhibition. Near the end, an homage to seven Jews in the Polish Resistance movement. What! As if the Polish Resistance didn't sell out, turn in, sabotage, kill the Jewish Resistance in Poland.

The final room is a dark chapel lit by a single candle in the center of the floor. I press a button on the wall and a kantor's voice sings the kaddish, the Hebrew song for the dead. Near the candle, sunk into the floor, a single gravestone with a Star of David on it, cracked in half, glassed over. The candle flickers. Six million people dead, and this is what we get? A single grave, a religious song, a candle?

I walk quickly from the room back into the light, out of the barracks and into the yard.

Now I rejoin the crowds, tour the museum exhibits, cozy up to the tour groups, hear about the killing techniques, systematic starvation, torture. The experiments: irradiation, castration, twin studies, injections with contaminated blood. I see the gallery-long cases of hair, shoes, suitcases, combs and brushes, piles of wire-rimmed eyeglasses. The cans of Zyklon B gas pellets. I walk past the Wall of Death, through the assembly square, bright in noon sun. School kids giggle anxiously and tourists rest against the walls, pull away from the tour groups, numb. A high school girl stands to the side of a building, her face white and running with tears.

I'm devastated by the horrors I see but confused, too. It still doesn't feel real, a movie set. Auschwitz is too small to be Auschwitz. The evil is silent. And yet it's here. And yet it's not. And I notice more: no pictures of Jewish inmates, only Poles. The famous Wall of Death where they executed ten thousand people, all political prisoners: none Jewish. They wouldn't waste a bullet on a Jew.

I'm stunned, a tourist in a tourist attraction with a political agenda; this is not really Auschwitz anymore. The focus is wrong. The Auschwitz-Birkenau State Museum, established in 1947 by the Soviet liberators, is a monument to the Polish victims of World War II and, oh yes, all the other victims of National Socialism, too. Even now, they don't acknowledge that 90 percent of the people who died at Auschwitz were Jewish. They say "many." They say "the majority." It's dishonest, a final disrespect. Betrayed, I walk out the gate and stand at the bus stop, waiting for part two. Birkenau.

Waiting for the minibus to Birkenau, I wonder what made me think that this locus of evil, Auschwitz, where the cruelest and most cynical acts against humanity occurred, would give me clarity about how and why it happened. The How seems understandable. Perhaps. The devaluing, the systematic approach, the slow, lazy slide into evil. The only Why that seems reasonable is unbearable and too easy—it's because human beings do things like this. It's in our nature. We have so little reverence for life; the human race is a race of horrors, humans are not capable of humanity.

Is this what I'm passing on to my child? Annie is not here with me today, won't be here with Bill tomorrow, but we've dragged her through so much these ten days—synagogues and cemeteries and ghettos. We've taught her about Auschwitz, the worst in us, before she knows about the ways people save and nurture each other, the thrill of accomplishment, the power of resistance. Have we done this thoughtlessly or as a warning?

It's a short ride to Birkenau.

In Birkenau, left as it was, there's less room for political revision. A few tourists step off the minibus with me and we walk through the open Gate of

Death and immediately dissipate in the immensity of this complex. It's huge. Huge! I walk an hour and a half, swiftly, the last ten minutes at a dead run. Walking the full perimeter of Birkenau would take twice that time.

Acres of ruins. Rows and rows of shadows of barrack foundations covered in waving green grasses, the crumbles of brick chimneys like tall gravestones behind rusted barbed-wire electric fences, the ceramic circuitry still crisp and white. Everywhere, everywhere, green grass. I walk and walk west down the railway tracks where day and night cattle cars crammed with Jews pulled through the Gates of Hell. It takes me fifteen minutes at a rapid pace past the women's barracks to the Selektion platform. Here the barking, snarling dogs, patrolling soldiers. Here the trains coughed their loads of Jews: Some were pointed left to the camp toward extermination through work; most were pointed right to the crematoria to immediate death. The gas and ovens working day and night. Killing.

Yet I can't see or feel this. Birkenau is silent, the silence of nothing, the emptiness of a long railroad track to the diminishing point of infinity. There are no ghosts here. At Tikal, the Mayan jungle ruins in Guatemala, I stood near the killing stones beneath the pyramid; I laid my hands on the stones and I heard the screams and smelled the blood. But those people belonged there, believed in their sacrifice. No people belonged here. The dead dissipated with the smoke, the few who lived through it departed, leaving nothing behind.

The air is warm and clear, the sky blue. At the collapsed rubble of Crematoria III, I turn north, past the baths, through the woods, past the long foundation outlines of "Canada," where the deads' belongings were sorted into huge piles of shoes, eyeglasses, luggage, clothing, combs, catalogued and sent in the now-empty cattle cars back to Germany to pile up in huge warehouses. A small pile of spoons rusts beneath chicken wire. I flush a wild grouse; it flies away low and brown.

I pass a stand of trees. In these forests, Jews sometimes stood all night waiting for room in the gas chambers, knowing they were going to die. I come to the meadows where piles of corpses burned in the open air when the numbers overloaded the crematoria. A still, natural pool in the meadow.

There, four black, granite, nameless tombstones. The grass and trees glow with exuberance as if sprouting from the essence of life itself. Today, after almost sixty springs at Auschwitz, frogs, lilies, flowering reeds, the sky deep blue, the sun bright and yellow, the meadow lush and in bloom.

This is no locus of evil. Only humans create evil. Dead is dead. Ground renews.

There's a resignation in this, a lightening.

Past the ash fields, the path goes east through Sektor III skirting the men's camp, gypsy camp, "family" camp, SS headquarters, quarantine area. As I round the guard tower at the final corner I stop next to the fence. Some who made it past Selektion into the camps chose death by suicide—running toward freedom into the electric wires. I pick up a few shards of the white ceramic knobs used to bear the wires, a few pieces of long-ago burnt metal. I look at my watch. I'll miss the minibus. I run the rest of the way.

Until I visited Auschwitz-Birkenau, I'd always measured myself against the survivors of the Holocaust. Would I have had the internal tenacity and grit, the inner goodness to survive? Yet only 23 percent of the 1.1 million Jews deported to Auschwitz ever made it past Selektion. The rest were gassed and burnt immediately. By the time the Russians liberated Auschwitz in 1945, only seven thousand prisoners remained.

I understand now: If I were born a few decades earlier in Europe, I wouldn't be able to choose or reject my Judaism, test my mettle, question my beliefs. If I didn't look right, at exactly that second on the Selektion platform, if I was too young, too old, too sick, disabled, if I didn't fill a quota, if I was like 77 percent of the Jews who arrived at Auschwitz, I'd be dead immediately. I wouldn't be a human being, just a problem, part of a day's work, kilos of ambulatory meat to be destroyed. If I made it into the camp, I'd be exterminated through starvation, disease, murder. I'd be dead.

Post-Auschwitz, the whole world was Auschwitz for a while. We spent a week in Paris, the famous city of light, and all the buildings looked like bone. I walked the streets in a blind panic, afraid to stop walking, exhausted, and sick. A week of rain and visiting cemeteries. The catacombs, six million dead bodies, the bones and skulls stacked in macabre piles. Père Lachaise Cemetery. I toured the cemetery alone. I walked unprepared into a row of memorials for the deportees to Bergen-Belsen. Dachau. Mauthausen-Gusen. Majdanek, Buchenwald. Auschwitz. Gaunt sculptures, gray faces of agony. An outstretched, gaunt arm.

Who is this woman, sobbing in the rain, and placing pebbles on the memorial stones of people dead almost sixty years?

For me, Auschwitz was a wake-up call. We live on an injured planet. Here, in Northern California, the oaks die of a *Phytophthora* marched in on human feet, miles of funereal forest, thousands of hundred-year-old trees gray and skeletal, their branches like the arms of concentration camp victims reaching for the sky. The whales suicide on the beaches, governments shout and topple, war screams in the Middle East, and is my friend Ayala safe there? I cannot hold my daughter close enough: A nuclear cloud can reach us in days.

There is no haven. The world turns gray and Auschwitz. I cannot, ultimately, trust human beings. We have great reserves of good in us but are tainted by our ability to do evil. While the universe strives for balance and equilibrium, human beings are the bullies of the playground. Nature has great power to heal our wounds; it's what it does, growing over the gashes, reusing the ashes. But how far before it's too late? I am not optimistic.

There isn't enough time. It's important to pay attention to life in all its complexity, to choose to defeat the inhumanities and intolerances within myself. I think of Birkenau itself, vast and green, thick with life. Almost sixty years ago, six million people were slaughtered. In another sixty years, give or take, I'll be dead, too, my body returning its nutrients to the ground. This gives me hope. Nature replenishes.

When I came back from Auschwitz, I wore a Star of David earring for a few months as a statement of my cultural identity, until the Palestinian Intifada began again and people saw the symbol as political support of Israel. Since then, I've turned forty and forty-one. I've started a writer's community. I've planted a garden; vegetables and flowers and bulbs, vines and roses. I dig, weed, move stones. I mother my daughter, revel in her love and zest for life, and try to consciously teach her about the goodness in people. I focus in on my marriage. I still have the Buddha on my mantel, the seder at Passover, the Christmas tree in December. A Christian symbol does not make me Christian any more than wearing or not wearing a Jewish star will help me if the jackboots stomp for me in the night.

My father recently posted a quote by Bernard Malamud in his house: "If you ever forget you are a Jew, a Gentile will remind you." After Auschwitz, I know my being a Jew has nothing to do with my choice of religion or my spirituality or my politics. My ethnicity does not wash off in this world. I will never again apologize for not being Jewish enough. Just so, I will not use my ethnicity to apologize for cruelty, horror, oppression.

I don't know if I've faced down my terror of Auschwitz. I'm still on my path. I know that I have it in me to be evil so I strive to be honest and kind. I seek equilibrium, struggle to notice detail, appreciate what I have, walk in the woods every day. I wonder about life's fragility and tenacity. I wonder for myself, and I wonder for all those women who looked like me, who thought and felt like me, who were ripped from their homes, shoved onto trains, and died at Auschwitz. I wonder for all who are ripped from their homes, for those buried under the collapsing walls of home.

I keep my fragments of the ruins of Birkenau in a plastic bag in my top bureau drawer. Sometimes my fingers find them accidentally as I rummage for keys or an old receipt. If I open the bag, I can touch the pieces, the white knobs that carried the imprisoning electricity, the metal fragments the ashy color of Auschwitz. Stumbling on evil is not always a bad thing. Perhaps I'll plant them in my garden.

The River

by Amy Hudock

They took my shoelaces first. Better to not have temptations, I guess; but I wanted to tell the hospital attendants who flocked around me that strangulation had never been my thing, so they might as well let the gaping hole in my shoes stay sealed. But I stayed quiet. Talking took too much effort. Then I changed into shapeless sweatpants and sweatshirt. When I'd packed to come, I hadn't known what to bring. After all, how was I to know what the insane wear? I sat down with a kind-faced nurse who took my information. She filled in all the little spaces with writing. Sign here, please. Then I was in. Through the security post with its codes and keys. Past the nurses' desk where curious looks followed me. Into a hospital. The place smelled like a hospital. I hadn't thought of this as a place for the sick, only for the mad.

A physical. Blood-taking. Then drugs. Lots of drugs. They put me in a small cell-like room. There were no bars on the window, but I imagine the frame was filled with safety glass. Breaking it would do no good. Like the windows they put in windshields, it would fracture in a big spider pattern, but the pieces of glass would not separate. I sat on my bed and looked out the window. The books I had brought to read sat unopened. Couldn't read. Couldn't really think. Couldn't really feel. The medication was like those S-shaped Styrofoam fillers that come in boxes from mail-order catalogs, but instead of protecting a new CD or book, they came between my flesh and the knifepoint. Muffled, I could still feel its movement but not its bite. So I just sat and stared out the window at the hills that rose above the Ohio River and imagined the river I couldn't see.

Physical wounds are easy to understand. Soul wounds are not. I was fighting the impulse to cut myself, or in some other way try to make that pain tangible, explainable, manageable, understandable, visible. I heard a friend's voice in my head: "She is just doing it for attention." But I knew that it was not about the attention. I just wanted the pain to stop, and I just didn't see any other options. But mostly, I was tired of not being known, of keeping the pain inside and hidden, of living a lie. Death seemed more honest. Clean. Open.

I sat in my quiet room, drugs keeping me still as effectively as restraints. But inside, the need to live battled with the desire to die. Killing myself was not as simple as I originally thought. The physical act was not the hard part. After suffering so much pain in the soul, it would be a relief to feel it in the body. The hardest part would be the choice to give up the good as well as the bad in living. Even as I longed to leave life, I remembered swimming breaststroke, my head just above the warm water, as I watched green terns walk on the river's edge. Moving like a turtle, I swam close without disturbing them. Just a few feet away. They accepted me as one of them, and I swam alongside them for nearly an hour. Connected to them, to the water, to the movement of my body, I sensed the universal other in us, the spark of what some people call the divine. Peace. Remembering this moment made it hard to choose to never have another one like it.

In my first days on suicide watch, I noticed that they tried to remove temptations. The showerheads were recessed so no noose could hang from them. The dinner trays had broad, thick, rounded corners. Salt and pepper came in cushy packages, apple juice in plastic containers. They gave me plastic spoons to eat my soft, mushy food. Most doors were locked, and I had to call the keeper of the keys to get a towel, to go to the bathroom, to get my toiletries, to get into my own locker.

They thought they made sure there were no sharp edges in the outside environment to match the ones inside me. However, I did see some dangers they overlooked. A framed picture of a small village along a curve in a river hung on the wall in the waiting area. The glass had been replaced with Plexiglas but the metal frame came to four quite sharp points. Curtains that could easily be twisted into a death scarf adorned the windows behind my head. A fake potted plant hung from a plant holder long enough to break a windpipe. Electric sockets sat there, uncovered. If I wanted to kill myself, even in there, I could.

But I didn't. I felt protected by the walls. Womb-like, the hospital gave me food, air, space to live. My psychiatrist, who diagnosed me without ever meeting me, went on a long weekend holiday and left no instructions for me other than the drugs, so I didn't have any therapy and wasn't required to go to group meetings. I was left to myself most of the day. In the evening, visitors came, good friends, who brought me homemade soup, pasta heavy with garlic, and other offerings from the world of the living. Then I slept. Days of sleep. I slowed the frantic pace of my life to a crawl. I felt the spaces in between activities. The pleasure in doing nothing. I lay in my bed in a fetal position, hearing the beating of my heart. Like a baby deciding to come into the world, I learned to breathe again. And for right then, breathing in and out and not stopping was enough.

There was something seductive about being in a psych ward. I could act in any way I wanted. Most of the people on my floor, the fourth floor, suicide watch, were old, very old. Most sat and stared. The younger ones moved around, talked, walked—but rarely did they meet each other's eyes. And often they spoke to no one visible. Given this, strangeness was expected on my floor, which allowed some of the patients to be seduced into exposing the real. I knew that I could have run up and down the hall, arms flailing and mouth stretched in a screaming "O"—and few people would even look up. Kinda weird. But the good southern girl that I was kept her clothes on, her voice modulated, her social face intact. Even in here. But the potential for something else waited just outside my peripheral vision.

My roommate was a woman in her late forties/early fifties whose husband was quite cruel to her. Bess told me of the nasty comments, the lack of attention, the jealous outrages, the fights, the blows. I asked her why he wasn't in here rather than her. "He's the crazy one," I said. She seemed surprised. "I am here," Bess said, "because I have to learn to accept him and love him for what he is." She continued, "I am in the Christian counseling program." That explained a lot. When she started to try to convert me, and when her counselors came in and tried to convert me, I tried to be polite. But soon I got angry. They were like vultures, preying on the weak. Finally, I told them that I was a Buddhist (thinking of the religion that might shock them the most). They moved her out of my room, away from my contamination, and I went on staring out the window, considering whether I should continue living—especially in a place where those so-called Christians were believed to be the normal ones.

Because I didn't actually try to kill myself, the staff started believing and then saying: "You're looking better." The doctor on call moved me off suicide watch and onto a regular ward, two floors down. I gained three roommates then. All were getting shock treatments. One because she heard voices. One because she believed she had a painful tumor no one could find. And one for some problem I could never understand. We talked to each other quietly that night while lying in bed. Electricity still sizzling in their brains, the discourse swung fragmented, loose, free, like a Kandinsky painting.

Two of the women talked of learning the right words, the right tone of voice, the right gestures to make it stop. Just to make the electric shock stop. They were like rats, given electric shock when they stepped on the wrong pad. The other woman was different. She believed she deserved the punishment. When both pads are electrified, the rats learn just to sit still. The doctors call it "learned helplessness." She sat still, like those rats, accepting the pain. I wondered, "Is this healing?"

After they fell asleep, I lay there, afraid. What if they try to do that to me? I was here on a voluntary basis. But what if it became involuntary? What if I didn't get better? Would they try that classical conditioning crap on me, too? Me, a rat in an experiment. In my cold terror, I became more interested in getting better.

Such defeat in that room, that ward. Many of these people would never leave. Sue, the quiet teenager who sat in the back of rooms trying to disappear, had been there for years. Janet, hair frizzy because of the numerous electric-shock treatments, lived precariously outside but came back every few months. And Kate, the stunningly beautiful woman whose body communicated the pain of her soul in impulses that told her brain "tumor" rather than "sadness." Even Bess, who was not allowed to talk to me now, whose husband beat her, and who kept trying to believe it was her fault though her body told her otherwise. But even as I wondered about their lives, I knew mine would be different. I stood on the inside for now, but I knew much of me was still on the outside.

As a lawyer, I had trained my mind to work independent of my body, my heart. I could analyze, consider, think through problems even as the rest of me wanted to die. The mind kept going despite it all, and while sometimes I hated how unstoppable it was, my analytical distance kept me from being one of them.

A friend brought me a tape of *The X Files* episodes to watch. When most everyone else was at Group, I took it to the patients' lounge and plugged it into the VCR. I watched a full episode, then started a second one when other patients started coming in and quietly sitting on the floor. Soon the room was full of attentive watchers, too attentive. I looked around the room as the bizarre unfolded on the screen and thought, *There is at least one person who believes this is the truth.* When I got up to leave, the boys down the hall asked to borrow the tape. The TV room became even more packed, full of silent stares.

At the other end of the hall from the TV room, a room with tables and chairs for the patients just wanting to sit together without the TV had one window, close to street level, that opened up to the outside world. The window was blocked by heavy curtains so no one could see in, and so those inside wouldn't have to look out at all those people going about their everyday lives. I couldn't help it. I peeled back a small corner of the barrier to watch those people, already so far away from me and my experience, walk past on their way to the bank or to get coffee. "What do they have that I don't?" I wondered. Then I looked around me at the other patients, feeling my difference from them, too. I belonged to no one. Singular.

A nurse came into the room, and I dropped the curtain. The nurses had been kind to me, but most people just left me alone, perhaps sensing that I didn't really belong here either. So I was surprised when she asked me to follow her into a private room. Her face was grim. She pulled up a chair, sitting down so her face was level with mine, and uncomfortably close. We sat in silence. "Is there any chance you might be pregnant?" she asked. I looked at her in quiet horror, my mind spinning away from my grip. I had been told I couldn't have children. That I shouldn't have children. When I didn't reply, she took my hand in hers, and said, "Dana, your blood work came back from the lab with, well, a strange result. We'd like to retest you."

Then, I knew.

Back in my room, I curled up in my bed, my mind fumbling with an idea too large for my shaking hands. My doctor had told me women with bipolar disorder shouldn't have children. "They'll be bipolar, too," she said. And it seemed true. Studies suggested the children of bipolar parents were at high risk of having the same disorder; some experts even suggested sterilizing bipolar patients so they couldn't reproduce. But was the risk of producing another bipolar person enough of a reason to not have a child? I mean, really, was having bipolar disorder so awful that I wished I never had been born? Yes, it had been hard. Immeasurably hard. But did I wish I had never taken breath? Was my illness the only thing about me that could define my life? And, most important, could I justify my own existence enough to make another person who might be like me? I stroked my still-flat belly, imaging its fullness.

I rolled over toward the wall as another thought bothered me. Was life worth offering to a child, bipolar or not? With all the chaos of the world, with all the despair, with all the pain, would life bring my child enough beauty and happiness to make it worth it? All children come into the world heading toward death. Was what happened between birth and death enough of a reason to be born at all? I wasn't sure if I was committed enough to life to make life.

But most of all, I worried. I couldn't care for myself. How could I care for a child?

Weeks before I had come to the hospital, my mood swings had begun to cycle rapidly from high, to low, to the empty middle. At first, bright, sharp, manias, hard as crystal shards, made me powerful, creative, tireless. I felt invincible. I spent days on the best high I had ever known or heard about. In my job as a public defender, I tried to save the world, over and over again. I worked until I collapsed, exhausted. I committed to too many social engagements, too many clients, too much emotional wear and tear. I became sexual, highly sexual, and sought the human touch to ground me, help me find my body.

It must have been when I was in one of those states that I got pregnant, by a handsome, dark-haired visiting poet I met at the reception after his reading. His poetry was full of pain, clear and direct, like I would have written if I still could write poetry. I found myself nodding throughout his reading, seeing myself caught in his stanzas.

At the reception, I had to wait in line to talk to him. As I complimented him on the rawness of his work, he moved close to me and whispered in my ear, "You understand, no?" We left the reception for a bar, and he taught me to play pool, standing behind me to help me shoot. As he was holding my arm to guide it, I saw a long scar on the inside of his wrist. I touched it, feeling its hard ridge. He jumped and pulled away.

After a few games, we sat down. He raised his glass to me, gesturing to the other people in the bar, "As only the sane can do." I didn't laugh. Neither did he. He pulled back his sleeve to let me look at the scar again. I knew what it was. We spent the night making it not matter.

He left the next morning, but I would have ruined it anyway. I was impatient with others who seemed to move so slowly, whose thoughts I could finish. I was snappy, imperial, a queen among peasants. I was hardly relationship material.

Then, I paid for the crystalline beauty of the mania. I fell into a deep, dark depression filled with slow water that dragged on me. It took me hours to wash the dishes, sweep the floor, do a load of laundry. I sat in the bay window that looked out of my house on to the street, watching the rain fall on the pavement and the car lights reflect on the mirror the road had become. I was empty, closed, cold, flat. When I finally got up to eat, I looked at the clock. I had been sitting there for over five hours. I didn't know. I had lost time. And I had missed an important meeting with a client.

Later, I moved into the middle ground—normal—but the repercussions of the mood swings, the residual traumas of my life, and the pain of living beyond them paralyzed my soul. I wrote pages of dull legal briefs, and rarely felt inspired to write anything else. No poetry came from me. My journal pages remained empty. My body kept on with my work, my life. Soulless. I longed to end the hypocrisy of continuing life as if I wasn't wounded. The final insult of the world was that no one else, besides a dark stranger who could only stay a night, looked deeply enough to see the hurt I could not ignore. I spent whole days looking out through pain-ridden eyes noticing no one notice. *How can they not see?* I would think. I was tired of not being known. I wanted to externalize the pain, mark myself like an ancient warrior. So, I ended up here, in a place where that part of me that I had tried to hide from others for so long could be seen. Now, the normalcy was the hidden part.

Could I be "normal" enough for a child?

One of my roommates, a sixth-grade teacher with red, frizzy hair who periodically returned to shock therapy whenever the voices got too loud, came into the room and laid a light hand on my shoulder. She knew better than to ask "What is it?"—no one around here asked that. Instead, she sat next to me in quiet sympathy. I folded in around myself, holding my stomach as if it had the answers.

I heard the bolt clank shut behind me as I walked through the lobby toward the exit. That is the last time, I thought. That is the last time I will ever hear that awful clank. I carried with me all that I had brought into the hospital stuffed in a gym bag in one hand. With the other, I reached for the outer door. Through the heavy glass, I saw the sunlight, the sidewalk, the people walking to get their morning coffee, and the exterior door became too heavy to open. In freeze-frame, I began to push my feet into the carpet like a Clydesdale moving a heavy wagon. Inch by inch, it gave. Suddenly, the door fell open, and I was on the sidewalk, too. Among all the other people. Dazed in the sun. I realized I could still smell the hospital stink on my clothes, in my hair, and on my skin. The release papers in my hand. I signed myself in. I could sign myself out.

I started walking, just walking. I knew I should go to the halfway house that was meant to ease my transition back into the world. Help me with my new, baby-friendly, all-natural, experimental omega-3 oil treatment. Set me up for further introductory meetings with my neo-hippie, New Age psychiatrist who believed that I could have a baby and maintain my mood balance—all at the same time. But I passed the friendly-looking building by. My legs just kept moving.

Though I still couldn't see it, I knew it was there. I sped up when I saw the gray concrete of the massive flood wall. I walked between the gates, looking way up the painted numbers that indicated how deep flood waters had grown in the past. The markers went to the very top. What had the citizens of the city thought when they could see waves at this remarkable height towering over their homes? Did they feel small and helpless at the threat of thundering water they could not control? Why did they continue to live with that threat? Why not build elsewhere? The walls were full of chips, scratches, chunks missing or cracked. I reached out to touch one deep groove made by some floating debris. The concrete felt cold, hard, and strong. Regardless of how many times the water had pushed against them and then receded, the walls were still here, guardians of a city built on a floodplain and ever subject to the ebb and flow of larger forces.

I continued through the gate, down the steps, and toward the water. My feet echoed hollow steps as I crossed the planks of the wharf. The banks were largely empty, even on this sunny day. But it was early. Later, children would come to Rollerblade on the paved riverside trails. Office workers would walk over from the business district with their lunches, sitting on the grass in small groups. And couples would walk hand in hand, looking out at the movement of barges, tug boats, and tankers on the water highway before them. But now,

I only saw a few homeless guys hanging out at the edge of the park, nearly out of sight.

I didn't hesitate. I slipped off my shoes and stood with my toes wrapped around the edge, and held my arms out wide. I made a nice, clean dive into the water swirling rapidly below. No splash. My diving coach would have been proud. I stayed down in the colder current as long as I could, looking up at the light filtering through the upper layer of water, which made a translucent pale green I have never seen anywhere else but from underwater. I once could hold my breath for nearly five minutes. Not anymore. I followed my bubbles up to the air, breaking the surface with a gasp.

I started with breaststroke, the most quiet and peaceful of the strokes. Turtlelike, I kept my head above water so that I could see what I passed as I hugged the shoreline. I poked along, barely rippling the water with my movement, letting the current do most of the work. A family of ducks swam close by, the little golden ducklings paddling frantically to keep up with their mother. They hardly noticed me.

After a while, I began to tire, so I rolled over to float on my back, the sun on my face warming my skin. As I relaxed into the water's movement, I felt the hospital stink wash off of me, cleansing me. I thought about the little water creature within me, floating in her own private river. She and I floated along, and I felt bigger than just me. I felt our twoness as well as our oneness—the essential contradiction of creating life. As I expanded the concept of myself to include her, I also included the river, the ocean that was this river's goal, and all that the ocean surrounded. As we touched water, it also touched shores, boats, islands, and continents on the other side of the world. We became part of it all, my former boundaries that had defined me now indistinct and permeable and variable. I gave into the ambiguity of myself and of our future, and simply allowed myself to drift. A deep knot untied at the center of my being, its ends, too, floating free.

I righted myself, clean and open, and turned toward shore. *Time to build*, I thought, *even if it has to be on the floodplain.*

The Plant
by Andrea J. Buchanan

Piano teacher with one room to rent, Steinway B to share for practicing, Sunset District.
It couldn't have been more perfect if I had written out my ideal scenario
and tacked it to the conservatory's "Housing to Share" rental notice board. I
would be starting graduate studies in piano performance at the San Francisco
Conservatory of Music in a month, and I still didn't have a place to live. I
jotted down the number and called, hoping to be able to have my graduate
housing problem solved then and there.

The piano teacher with one room to rent invited me over right away,
and we sat and talked over coffee. She was nice, she seemed easygoing, she
understood what life was like as a pianist, and—more important even than the
size of the room she had to rent—her Steinway was in perfect condition. She
politely excused herself to the kitchen while I tried a few phrases of Ravel, a
bit of Beethoven, too shy to play out anything whole. But I could tell it was
perfect: the piano, the room, the house, all of it. By the time we had spoken
for an hour, and she seemed close to handing over a key right there, it seemed
time to tell her the truth about me. So I told her I was sick, that there wasn't
any diagnosis any doctor had given me that didn't make me sound crazy—
Epstein-Barr virus, fibromyalgia, parvovirus, chronic fatigue syndrome. She
took it well; she sat there smiling. She asked me questions about what it felt
like, and when I was done talking she just nodded her head. She said, This
must be hard for you. She was compassionate, one of those Bay Area mindful-
meditation people who really does believe in good vibrations.

When I moved in, she had the room where I would live for the next year
or so fixed up nicely. Would I mind that her earthquake-preparedness kit was
stashed in my closet, would I still have enough room? My sweaters and wrinkly
shirts dangled sparsely over her bottled water, a brick wall of PowerBars. In
front of the window that nearly took up one whole wall of the room was a
table with a small potted plant on it. This is your welcome-to-your-new-home
present, she said, and a way for you to gauge how kind to yourself you are. I

was taken aback. The responsibility of the plant daunted me, and I was afraid it showed. But if my new housemate was offended, she did a good job of hiding it in a tranquil smile.

The plant is a metaphor for your health, she said. When you water the plant in the morning, that should remind you to make sure you nourish yourself, too. When you see your plant drooping, it should make you check in, so to speak—ask yourself if you've been neglecting yourself, or, on the other hand, if you've been pushing yourself too hard. Taking care of this plant will help you learn to take care of yourself.

What kind of plant is it? I asked. An African violet, she told me. You couldn't have started me out with something more self-sufficient? I asked. A cactus? She laughed. This one's pretty sturdy. It'll be fine, she said. Just take care of it and take care of yourself. The two of you will thrive.

This was before I had children, in fact long before I ever imagined myself in a relationship, let alone married with kids, and the pain in my body was not the stress of sleep deprivation or the daily toll of caring for two energetic, relentless human beings. This was vague, amorphous pain, the grand and tragic pain of heartache and romantic literature, pain that never got better but also never got worse. It was pain that throbbed sometimes and ached others, pain that felt like shin splints, like muscle separating from bone, pain that didn't respond to Advil or Naprosyn or Prozac or Zoloft. The pain divided me into two parts, my mind and my body, and each seemed at war with the other. My new housemate left me alone to unpack, and I sat on my new bed and stared at the plant and silently apologized to it in advance.

The plant thrived at first, despite my inexpert care. The first week I mostly glared at it, sitting in its orange clay pot, my smug master. What could this plant teach me about dealing with pain? This plant was in for a rude surprise. I was not like my supercompetent housemate, I was not prepared for earthquakes or disaster. I had arrived in San Francisco with barely enough money to merit a checking account, I was waiting on student loans, I was signing up for credit cards and using them without thought for how I might pay the bills later. I was tired. I was sick. I was in pain, and my pain thwarted the doctors I saw, thwarted my desire to be active and sleepless and energetic. I laid in bed that first week and blamed the plant for just sitting there, serenely blooming, brazenly waiting to be cared for by someone and trusting somehow that I would be the person to fulfill that role.

The next week I tried to make peace with the plant. When I took my round of antiviral medication in the mornings, I'd channel my housemate's chipper demeanor and say, "Time to take your medicine, too!" as I poured a mixture of water and plant food into the pot. The plant seemed unmoved, it sat there in the morning sunlight at the window looking much the way it had the week before. I remembered doing an "experiment" for a science fair in grade school, taking two houseplants and playing music for them, and seeing which one thrived more. We didn't have much of a selection, so for one I think I played an old Earth, Wind & Fire record, and for the other the soundtrack to *The Wizard of Oz*. Of course, because I was quite strict about the protocol for musical exposure but less so about the actual watering, both the plants died. My third-grade scientific conclusion: Plants are not music fans. Perhaps to make up for my less than rigorous foray into plant science back then, I left my clock radio on, tuned to the classical station, whenever I would leave the room. It was a small gesture, but it seemed the least I could do.

My graduate school classes finally started, and I began trying to increase my stamina, practicing piano for longer intervals, resting less throughout the day. I had an old high school friend in the East Bay, and I went there often to visit. I was busy with my classes, with my repertoire, with coping with my pain and trying to have a normal life, and I forgot about the tentative truce the plant and I had made. Sometimes I would return to my room after a long weekend with friends and be surprised to see the plant still standing tall in its pot. Guiltily, I would water it—flood it, really, to overcompensate for the several days of inattention. Gradually I noticed it shriveling some. I felt bad about this.

My housemate was always solicitous about my health. She often offered to do the heavier cleaning, despite our attempts to divide things more or less fairly. She enjoyed cooking and many times invited me to have whatever she was preparing, sparing me the chore of making food. We would sit and eat at her table and talk about all kinds of things—her piano-teaching, my repertoire, stories of music politics and tense moments from her own musically competitive youth. We talked about earthquakes and natural disasters, about recycling and conserving water, about politics and organic produce and health food stores. One night during a dinner she had put together, she asked me if I'd ever tried hypnosis for my pain. I hadn't. She had had troubles with carpal tunnel syndrome, and of all the things she'd tried—acupuncture, Rolfing, Western medicine, Chinese herbs—hypnosis was the one practice that had actually made a difference.

What was it about it that helped? I asked. She considered this and then said, Have you ever thought about inviting your pain into your body? I said no. She nodded. Pain is a signal that something is wrong, she said. We resist it, we fight it, we get tense around it, and eventually that makes the pain even worse. What hypnosis did was help me invite that pain, really consider its purpose in my body and in my life. And when I did that, she said, I was able to work with it and gradually start to heal.

I hadn't thought about my pain like that. I had spent two years, by that point, actively resisting it, forcing myself to be "normal," putting a happy face on for those around me so that they would not sense the enormous burden of having to take me into consideration, so that they would not flee for fear my pain would contaminate them, infect them, make them aware of their own pain. I don't know, I said. I don't think I could do that. She nodded, wrapping her hands around her coffee mug. Pain is a frightening thing.

When we said our good nights and retired to our rooms, I averted my gaze so that I would not have to look at my plant. I turned on the TV, watched falsely jolly late-night shows that irritated me with their studio audience laughter. Finally I turned off the box and laid on my bed. What would it be like if I invited the pain into my body? What would happen if I really let myself feel it, accept it? I closed my eyes and tried to relax. I ached all over. My calves, my thighs, my arms, my chest. My bones hurt. I tried to resist the urge to tense up and panic as I took note of each thing that ached or throbbed, and I laid there and took a deep breath and for the first time let myself feel.

I was overwhelmed. What I felt was so raw, so searing, so powerful, I felt as though I was drowning in it, I was losing the small space I desperately clung to that was immune to pain, that had no pity for it. It felt infinite. I began to panic as my body was flooded with the pain signals I had for years been working to suppress, and I opened my eyes and sat up, sobbing. I cried for nearly a half hour, wrenching, exhausting sobs that seemed to overtake me; each time I tried to calm down, I found myself crying again, against my will. Inviting my pain was too painful, my pain was too intense to merely contemplate. Better to block it out, disrespect it. How else was I supposed to make it through each day? I looked up to the darkened window and saw my plant, half-brown, the soil cracked like a desert landscape. Despite it all, it was still blooming.

I'd like to say this story has a happy ending, that I was able to revive my plant, that we nursed each other back to health, but that's not what happened. I failed my plant, it died a brown, crumbly death, and my housemate wordlessly removed it from my room one day while I was at a master class. I returned to find the table empty, an Indian-print scarf covering the spot where the plant used to be.

A year later, I lived in the East Bay, I saw a physician who specialized in chronic fatigue syndrome named—no joke—Dr. Rest. I took herbal remedies, I boiled pots of twigs and bark, I drank chlorophyll, and these things reminded me about my plant and what it was supposed to teach me. In the end, I gradually regained my health. My old housemate might say that my pain was invited in for contemplation over a period of months in which I took some time off, learned to set limits for myself, tried to learn how to respect the messages my body was sending me. Unlike my poor plant, which had no choice in who might care for it, which so tragically was doomed to a dysfunctional relationship with someone like me who didn't understand the basics, I learned to seek out people who might nourish me. I stopped looking for water and sunlight from people who didn't know how to provide that, and instead sought out support and compassion the way my plant valiantly tried to grow toward the light through my housemate's lacy curtains. Eventually my pain ebbed to the point where I realized it had been so long since I had thought about being in pain, it must have stopped completely. And it had.

My pain now is transient and, when it comes, finite. My pain now is the pain of laboring to birth a six-pound baby, then, three and a half years later, a seven-and-a-half-pound baby. It is the pain of stepping on the sharp corner of a LEGO, or of watching my daughter fall on the playground. The pain of an aching back from stooping to whisk a twenty-seven-pound toddler from a bowl of cat food, or of a bone-tired week of sleepless nights soothing a teething baby. And the living things I have in my care these days are more insistent than plants; they are loud and occasionally obnoxious, sometimes demanding and exhausting, and always, always loving. There is no illusion that my care for them mirrors my care for myself, or even encourages me to remember myself at all; that is not their purpose in my life. The intensity of the care my children need blinds me to nearly everything else, and if anything, what I give to them I give to the exclusion of anything I might desire for myself. It is good this way. When a thing requires immediacy and depends so much upon my response, there is no possibility of neglect.

This is not to say I have improved as a caretaker of living things in general, or that my ineptitude with plants is a thing of the past. To the contrary, in the years between that first plant and now, I have murdered a miniature bonsai tree, a houseplant my mother-in-law forced upon us, a giant palm some well-meaning friend gave us as a housewarming gift. I am not proud of these things. But six months ago, some doctor friends asked us to baby-sit their houseplants for them while they traveled for one of their residency rotations. I warned them of my history with plants, but they didn't believe a month of plant-sitting with a serial killer would scar their plants for life. Our friends returned to find their plants limp but, unbelievably, still alive, and I took that as a personal victory, a small step toward horticultural competence.

Still, when my four-year-old daughter offered up a plastic green cup full of dirt for me to balance on the hood of our stroller at preschool pick-up time last November, I was reluctant. Do we have to take this home? I asked her. What is it? I asked the teachers. Yes! My daughter shouted. It's just a pumpkin seed, one of the teachers told me. Then she whispered, so that my daughter wouldn't hear, It's probably not going to actually grow, though. None of them have sprouted so far, so we just wanted them out of the classroom. I agreed to take the cup of dirt home, and I put it on the computer desk next to all the other detritus collected from my daughter's cubby.

It sat amidst the piles of preschool watercolors and pipe-cleaner crafts projects that also didn't have a place in our apartment for two months until one day my daughter rescued it. Mommy! She shouted. My plant! Your what? I asked, and then I saw it. Oh, the cup of dirt. Let's water it! she yelled, running to the sink. Okay, I told her reluctantly, but I don't think there's really anything in there anymore, sweetie. We watered the dirt and found a place for the cup on a sunny windowsill, and then we both forgot about it.

Then, suddenly, one morning it was there: a small green bud on the end of a fuzzy green stem just barely protruding from the dirt. My plant! Emi cried. Mommy, look at my plant! It's growing! I could hardly believe it. We watered it some more, and checked on it daily, and eventually another bud sprouted up from the dirt. It has a friend, Mommy! Emi said. My plant has TWO plants in it!

Last week she told her preschool teachers about her plant, and they looked at each other like we were crazy. You're sure it's really growing? they asked. I nodded. It's tall, I said. The two sprouts are sticking out of the cup now. The teachers seemed surprised. It's a pumpkin seed, right? I asked. Don't we have to move it out of that cup? I imagine it can't keep growing in there forever. I don't know, said one of the teachers. No one else's pumpkin seed ever actually grew. Mine was the only one? Emi asked. It looks that way, said her teacher. You must be a special plant person to have it grow like that for you!

Eventually, we will have to move it from its plastic cup to a bigger home, though living as we do in an apartment building, that will be no small feat. And more than that, a part of me fears that thinking about a move for this plant is a bit premature. With my track record, after all, there is no reason for these pumpkin sprouts to survive, and I don't want to disappoint my daughter by encouraging her enthusiasm for something that might not pan out. But standing there, watching her dance with excitement as she rushes to the windowsill to check on her plant, seeing her carefully hold it under a stream of water, making sure to saturate the clumps of soil surrounding her sprouts, I feel something. And this time, when I invite that feeling in to consider its purpose, it doesn't frighten me with its intensity. Instead, I find myself feeling cautiously optimistic, with a strange and surprising confidence that it's safe to trust whatever might happen next.

It feels a little bit like hope.

Contributors

Liz Abrams-Morley is the author of the poetry collection *Learning to Calculate the Half Life* and the chapbooks *What Winter Reveals* and *Memory Waltz*. Her poetry and fiction have been read on NPR and NPR-affiliate KUSP. She is a founding partner of Around the Block Writers Collaborative, online at www .writearoundtheblock.org. She lives in Pennsylvania and serves as an artist-in-residence in schools throughout the state.

Kimberly Greene Angle lives in Gallipolis, OH, with her husband and two children. Her work has appeared in *CrossRoads: A Southern Culture Annual*, the *Chattahoochee Review*, *South Carolina Wildlife*, the *Flannery O'Connor Bulletin*, and *Skirt!*, among other publications. Her first novel, *Hummingbird*, will be published by Farrar, Straus and Giroux in fall 2007.

Barbara Card Atkinson's work has appeared in *Salon*, the *Christian Science Monitor*, *Skirt!*, and numerous now-defunct multimedia websites. She lives in Santa Barbara, CA, with her husband and two children.

Marguerite Guzman Bouvard is a mother and grandmother. She has published several books on women and human rights, including *Revolutionizing Motherhood: The Mothers of the Plaza de Mayo*. She is a resident scholar with the Women's Studies Research Center at Brandeis University and a member of the American Society for Research on Mothering.

Gayle Brandeis is the author of *Fruitflesh: Seeds of Inspiration for Women Who Write* and *The Book of Dead Birds: A Novel*, which won Barbara Kingsolver's Bellwether Prize for Fiction in Support of a Literature of Social Change. She is writer-in-residence for the Mission Inn Foundation's Family Voices Project and is on the faculty of the UCLA Extension Writers' Program. She lives in Riverside, CA, with her husband and two children.

Andrea J. Buchanan is managing editor of *Literary Mama*, author of *Mother Shock: Loving Every (Other) Minute of It*, and editor of the Seal Press anthologies *It's a Boy* and *It's a Girl*. Her work has been featured in the *Christian Science Monitor*; *Parents* and *Nick Jr. Family* magazines; and in the collections *Breeder*, *The Imperfect Mom: Candid Confessions of Mothers Living in the Real World*, and *About What Was Lost*. You can visit her on the web at www.andibuchanan.com.

Amy Burditt is a voracious reader, fledgling writer, and freelance photography producer who lives in Oakland, CA, with her husband and son. *Literary Mama* marks her first publication.

Writer, musician, and performer **Phyllis Capello** lives in Brooklyn, NY. She is a New York Foundation for the Arts fellow in fiction and a prizewinner in the Allen Ginsberg Poetry Awards. Her work has appeared in the Italian feminist journal *Legendaria*, *Families: A Journal of Representation*, *Kolkata*, *The Milk of Almonds*, and *Literature: Reading, Reacting, Writing* a college textbook. She teaches poetry and music and entertains hospitalized children in the Big Apple Circus Clown Care Unit. She has a grown daughter and son.

KerryAnn Cochrane is a writer, freelance translator, and mother of two who lives in Montreal. She is a member of the Caravan Collective, a group of seven Montreal-based writers.

Nicole Cooley is the author of two books of poetry, *Resurrection* and *The Afflicted Girls*, and a novel, *Judy Garland, Ginger Love*. She lives in New Jersey with her husband and two young daughters.

Barbara Crooker lives in Fogelsville, PA, with her three children. Her poems have appeared in publications including the *Christian Science Monitor*, *Poetry International*, the *Atlanta Review*, and *Boomer Girls*. She is a six-time Pushcart Prize nominee and the author of ten chapbooks of poetry, including the award-winning *Ordinary Life*. More of her work can be read at www.barbaracrooker.com.

Linda Lee Crosfield's poetry and prose appears in *The Fed Anthology: Brand New Fiction and Poetry from the Federation of BC Writers, Room of One's Own, Word Works, Horsefly, Words Journal*, the *Nelson Quarterly*, and *Turning Points*. She lives in Castlegar, British Columbia.

Cathleen Daly writes poetry and experimental theater. Her poems have appeared in *Slow Trains Literary Journal, Poetry Super Highway*, and *Seeker Magazine*. She has a chapbook titled *Ode to the Unhinged*, and the last play she wrote, *How to be a Secret Agent Girl*, won Best of the San Francisco Fringe Festival.

Holly Day lives in Minneapolis, MN, with her two children, Astrid and Wolfegang, and her husband, Sherman. She currently works as a freelance entertainment reporter and teaches writing workshops at the Loft/Open Book Collective in downtown Minneapolis.

Peggy Duffy's short stories and essays have appeared in numerous print and online publications, including the *Washington Post*, the *Chronicle of Higher Education, Main Street Rag, Brevity, Octavo, Drexel Online Journal, SmokeLong Quarterly, So to Speak*, and *Whole Terrain*. She has an MFA from George Mason University and is the mother of two adult daughters and one teenage son.

Lizbeth Finn-Arnold is a mother, freelance writer, and independent filmmaker who lives and works in suburban New Jersey. Her work has appeared in *Independent Film & Video Monthly, Brain,Child, ePregnancy, Welcome Home*, and *Nurturing* magazine. She publishes monthly webzine the *Philosophical Mother*, and records an almost-daily account of motherhood on her blog at http://travelswithlizbeth.typepad.com.

Vicki Forman teaches creative writing at the University of Southern California. Her work has been nominated for a Pushcart Prize and has appeared in *Philosophical Mother, Santa Monica Review, Writer to Writer,* and *Faultline.* She lives in Southern California with her husband and two children. Her work can be found on the web at www.vickiforman.com.

Meagan Francis is a writer and mother living in Michigan. Her work has appeared in *Brain,Child, Salon, Organic Style, Skirt!,* and *ePregnancy,* among other publications. She writes a parenting humor column that currently runs in the *Lansing State Journal*'s *NOISE* and *LINK.*

Ona Gritz is the author of two children's books, *Starfish Summer* and *Tangerines and Tea.* Her poetry has appeared in many publications, including *Ekphrasis, Moment, Poetry East* and *Heresies,* and online in *Literary Mama* and *Plum Ruby Review.* Ona lives in Hoboken, NJ, with her son, Ethan.

Joanne Hartman lives with her husband and daughter in Northern California. Joanne's work has appeared in local parenting publications; her alumni magazine, *J Weekly;* and the anthology *The Knitter's Gift.* She is *Literary Mama*'s profiles editor and can be reached at profiles@literarymama.com.

Peggy Hong is the author of a poetry collection, several poetry chapbooks, and a fine art letterpress book, *Hoofbeats.* Her poetry has appeared in *Spoon River Poetry Review, Rhino, Bamboo Ridge,* and *Mothering* magazine, among other publications. She lives in Milwaukee, WI, with her husband and three children and teaches at Alverno College and Woodland Pattern Book Center. She is a regular columnist for *Literary Mama.*

Sonya Huber's writing has been published in *Fourth Genre, Passages North, Buffalo Carp, America, Main Street Rag,* and in many anthologies. She is an economic justice and labor activist, and she lives with her son and her husband in Columbus, OH.

Amy Hudock, PhD, is *Literary Mama*'s editor in chief. She is a coeditor of the book *American Women Prose Writers, 1820–1870* and a volume in the *Dictionary of Literary Biography* series, and the author of scholarly essays on nineteenth-century American women writers. Her nonscholarly writing about motherhood has appeared in *ePregnancy*, *Pregnancy and Baby*, the *Philosophical Mother*, and local parenting magazines. She is currently working on a critical book exploring the mother's voice in literature.

Rachel Iverson is the poetry editor and a regular columnist for *Literary Mama*. Her poems and prose have appeared in *Illume, a Journal of Universal Ideas*, the *MFC Forum Magazine*, *edifice WRECKED*, *Books and Babies*, *Onthebus*, and the *Philosophical Mother*. She is the author of two chapbooks of poetry and is a member of the Los Angeles Poets and Writers Collective. She is currently at work on a novel and a collection of essays. You can read some of her previously published work at www.racheliverson.com.

Suzanne Kamata lives with her husband and bicultural twins in Shikoku, Japan. She is the editor of *The Broken Bridge: Fiction from Expatriates in Literary Japan* and the author of numerous essays and stories. Her work has appeared in *Brain,Child*, *Utne*, *Philosophical Mother*, *Calyx*, and the anthologies *It's a Boy* and *It's a Girl*, among other publications.

Rebecca Kaminsky lives in Berkeley, CA, with her spouse and two sons. Her work has appeared in the locally best-selling anthology *Wednesday Writers: 10 Years of Writing Women's Lives*. Rebecca also writes a column, "Down Will Come Baby," for *Literary Mama*.

garrie keyman lives in Lititz, PA, where she writes online columns for www.LititzPA.com (Lititz With a Twist) and www.TyrannosaurusPress.com (the Illuminata webzine's *KeyCOMMentary*). Her work has appeared in many online and print publications, and in the poetry anthologies *Cosmic Brownies* and *Reach of Song*.

Cindy La Ferle is a nationally published essayist and author of *Writing Home*. Her essays and columns have been published in the *Christian Science Monitor*, *Detroit Free Press, Cleveland Plain Dealer, Better Homes & Gardens, Reader's Digest*, and many other publications. She lives in Royal Oak, MI, with her family.

Jennifer Lauck is the author of the *New York Times* best-selling memoirs *Blackbird* and *Still Waters*. Her new book, *Show Me the Way*, has just been released in paperback. Read more about her at www.JenniferLauck.com.

Sybil Lockhart is reviews editor at *Literary Mama*. Her writing has appeared in Brandeis University's *Artemis* magazine, the *Journal of Neuroscience*, the *Journal of Neurobiology*, the Bay Area's *Neighborhood Parents Network Newsletter*, and *Ladybug*. She also writes a column, "Mama in the Middle," for *Literary Mama*. Sybil lives in Berkeley, CA, with her husband and two daughters.

Laura A. Lopez lives in Moline, IL, with her husband and two daughters. Her work has appeared in *Clamor* magazine, *Voces Weekly*, and Augustana College's literary magazine, *Saga*.

Ericka Lutz is the fiction editor for *Literary Mama*. She is a recent fiction fellowship recipient at the Virginia Center for the Creative Arts, and is the author of seven nonfiction books, including *On the Go with Baby* and *The Complete Idiot's Guide to Stepparenting*. Her fiction and creative nonfiction has appeared in numerous books, anthologies, and journals, including *Scrivener Creative Review*, *Green Mountains Review, Kaleidoscope, Sideshow, France, A Love Story, Child of Mine, Toddler*, and the *Big Ugly Review*. Ericka teaches writing at UC Berkeley and through UC Berkeley Extension. More of her work can be found online at www.erickalutz.com.

Lisa Suhair Majaj is a Palestinian American writer, scholar, and mother. She has coedited three collections of critical essays: *Going Global: The Transnational Reception of Third World Women Writers; Etel Adnan: Critical Essays on the Arab-American*

Writer and Artist; and *Intersections: Gender, Nation, and Community in Arab Women's Novels.* Her poetry and creative nonfiction have appeared in many journals and anthologies. She lives in Cyprus with her husband and two children.

Lisa McMann is a mother of two whose writing has appeared in *Pindeldyboz,* the *Glut, Monkeybicycle, Sexy Stranger, Gator Springs Gazette,* and *Snow Monkey.*

Lisa Meaux is the mother of two adult sons. She teaches and lives in southern Louisiana. "Acts of Contrition" is her first publication.

S. A. Miller embraces mothering her own children.

Mary Moore's poetry has appeared in the *Sow's Ear Poetry Review, Perihelion, Mockingbird, Nimrod, Poetry, Field, New Letters, Negative Capability,* and *Prairie Schooner,* and in the anthology *I've Always Meant to Tell You: Letters to Our Mothers.* She is the author of a book of poetry, *The Book of Snow,* and a scholarly book, *Desiring Voices: Women Sonneteers and Petrarchism.* She teaches Renaissance literature, poetry, and writing at Marshall University in Huntington, WV.

Megeen R. Mulholland teaches English at Hudson Valley Community College, where she edits the student literary magazine *Threads.* Her work has been published in literary journals and anthologies including *Women Writers, EastWesterly Review, Phoebe, Earth's Daughters,* and the *Seattle Review,* and in the book *Roots and Flowers.*

Jennifer D. Munro is at work on a book about fertility issues, entitled *Not Suitable for Children.* Her essays have appeared in *They Lied! True Tales of Pregnancy, Childbirth and Breastfeeding; Secrets & Confidences: The Complicated Truth About Women's Friendships; The Knitter's Gift; Under the Sun; Room of One's Own; Calyx; Iris;* and *Kalliope.* Her fiction has appeared pseudonymously in *Best American Erotica 2004, Best Women's Erotica 2003, Ripe Fruit, Shameless, The Mammoth Book of Best New Erotica Volume 3,* and other publications.

Sarah Pinto is a mother and a postdoctoral fellow in the Department of Social Medicine at Harvard Medical School. She is currently conducting research on postpartum depression. Her essays and articles on topics related to motherhood, birth, and traditional midwifery have been published in journals and collections in the United States and India.

Heidi Raykeil (a.k.a the Naughty Mommy) is senior columns editor at *Literary Mama*. "Johnny" is an excerpt from a memoir she is writing about her son's brief but miraculous life. Heidi and her husband have since gone on to have a beautiful baby girl. Her first book, *Confessions of a Naughty Mommy: How I Found My Lost Libido*, will be published in 2006. She can be contacted at hraykeil@comcast.net.

Lori Romero is author of a chapbook, *Wall to Wall*, published by Finishing Line Press. Her poetry and short stories have been published in numerous journals and anthologies, including *Branches Quarterly* and *Plum Biscuit*.

Lisa Rubisch is a TV commercial director and partner of Bob Industries, helming spots for Ikea, Polaroid, Puma, Nike, and many other companies. She lives in New York City with her husband, Ian Kerner, and their two-year-old son. Lisa's writing was recently published in her husband's book, *Be Honest— You're Not That into Him Either*.

Rachel Sarah is *Literary Mama*'s senior columns editor. Her dating memoir, *Single Mom Seeking*, will be published in fall 2006 by Seal Press. She can be reached at www.rachelsarah.com.

Cassie Premo Steele, PhD, is an award-winning poet and writer living in Columbia, SC. She is author of two books and hundreds of poems and essays on healing women's bodies and spirits.

Deesha Philyaw Thomas holds a BA in economics from Yale University and a master's degree in education. Her work has been published in various online literary journals, and she is currently working on a novel. A native of Jacksonville, FL, she currently lives in Pittsburgh with her two daughters. Deesha writes a bimonthly column for *Literary Mama* and can be contacted at deesha.thomas@verizon.net.

Gabriela Anaya Valdepeña is a poet and teacher living in San Diego. She is the author of a book of poetry, *Exaggerated Gender Signals*, and the mother of a sixteen-year-old girl.

Karen Vernon is a writer, a public health researcher, and the mother of two girls. "The Gift" is Karen's first nonacademic publication.

Jennifer Eyre White is a former engineer and current mother of three. She writes a regular column for *Literary Mama* and can be reached at jennifer_eyre@ yahoo.com.

*A*cknowledgments

We would like to thank our tireless, selfless editors and copyeditors (past and present) for the incredible amount of time they have devoted to literarymama .com in the midst of children, jobs, lives, and other responsibilities. Thank you, thank you, thank you to Barbara Atkinson, M. H. Davis, Dawn Friedman, Katie Granju, Caroline Grant, Libby Gruner, Joanne Catz Hartman, Rachel Iverson, Rebecca Kaminsky, Amy Kessel, Jen Lawrence, Sybil Lockhart, Ericka Lutz, Jennifer Margulis, Laura Mazer, Eve Pearlman, Sophia Raday, Heidi Raykeil, Kristina Riggle, Lisa Moskowitz Sadikman, Rachel Sarah. Without you literary mamas, there would be no *Literary Mama*. Thanks, too, to the members of the Berkeley "Writing about Motherhood" group, for their encouragement and support.

Thanks to Jill Rothenberg, our patient editor, and to Laura Gross, our wonderful agent. Thanks to Danielle Rosenblatt, Andi's excellent intern, for her help in the initial work of assembling this manuscript.

Thanks to our families for being supportive of this venture back when it was just a crazy idea, and for continuing to support us as it evolved into the lowest-paying full-time job we've ever had.

Thanks to our children, who not only provide us with inspiration and consistently fresh material, but who have transformed us from writers into mothers who write: literary mamas in the truest sense.

Thanks to our dedicated readers, and, finally, to the writing mothers who continue to tell their stories and submit their work to the site. Thank you all.

Selected Titles from Seal Press

For more than twenty-five years, Seal Press has published groundbreaking books. By women. For women. Visit our website at www.sealpress.com.

It's a Boy: Women Writers on Raising Sons edited by Andrea J. Buchanan. $14.95, 1-58005-145-6. This is Seal's edgy take on what it's really like to raise boys from toddlers to teens and beyond.

Inconsolable: How I Threw My Mental Health out with the Diapers by Marrit Ingman. $14.95, 1-58005-140-5. Ingman recounts the painful and difficult moments after the birth of her child with a mix of humor and anguish that reflects the transformative process of becoming a parent.

Above Us Only Sky: Essays by Marion Winik. $14.95, 1-58005-144-8. A witty and engaging book from an NPR commentator, this collection delivers Winik's trademark combination of searing honesty, unfailing wit, and down-to-earth wisdom.

Confessions of a Naughty Mommy: How I Found My Lost Libido by Heidi Raykeil. $14.95, 1-58005-157-X. The Naughty Mommy shares her bedroom woes and woo-hoos with other mamas who are rediscovering their sex lives after baby.

The Truth behind the Mommy Wars: Who Decides What Makes a Good Mother? by Miriam Peskowitz. $15.95, 1-58005-129-4. This moving and convincing treatise explores the new-century collision between work and mothering.

The Risks of Sunbathing Topless: And Other Funny Stories from the Road edited by Kate Chynoweth. $15.95, 1-58005-141-3. These wry, amusing, and insightful stories capture the comical essence of bad travel, and the uniquely female experience on the road.